From Idea to Launch at Internet Speed:

How to Identify and Develop Profitable Opportunities

From Idea to Launch at Internet Speed:

How to Identify and Develop Profitable Opportunities

Catherine Kitcho

Pele Publications
1833 Limetree Lane
Mountain View, California 94040

Visit our website at: http://www.pelepubs.com

Printed in the United States of America

Library of Congress Cataloging-in-Publication Data

Kitcho, Catherine.
From idea to launch at Internet speed: how to identify and develop profitable opportunities / Catherine Kitcho. – 1st ed.
p. cm.
Includes bibliographical references and index.
ISBN: 1-929936-00-1
Library of Congress Control Number: 2001087701
1. New products – Management. 2. Marketing.
I. Title.

For David,

who knows the challenges of living with
a chronic entrepreneur,
and puts up with me anyway.

From Idea to Launch at Internet Speed:
How to Identify and Develop Profitable Opportunities

Table of Contents

Part Two: Strategy and Planning

Part Three: Launching New Products and Services

Part Four: Momentum

Acknowledgments

This book was brought to you by a virtual network of dedicated people. I had the privilege of working with a team of business experts who provided the best editing any author could hope for. Thank you for your competence, Ken Sonenclar, Paul Riskin, Violet Leff, and Nina Price. An extra measure of thanks goes to David Bernstein, who spent many long and frustrating hours of his spare time to perform his editing magic. Your careful attention to detail, and your generosity of time will forever be appreciated.

Carrie Zeidman once again did a brilliant job of cover design and layout. Thank you for your patience to go through all the many iterations this project required.

Kevin J. Kennedy took valuable time from his busy schedule to write a thoughtful and targeted foreword. Thank you for working from what had to be a rather unattractive manuscript!

Twenty executives provided valuable source material and input for this book. I thank all of the following people for making the time to be interviewed and reviewing your quoted material (and for meeting all the deadlines.) These twenty executives include:

Rob Abel, Vice-President of Strategy and Business Development, Eduprise
Joe Becker, President and CEO, Dolphin Ventures
Kathy DeMartini, President and CEO, MediaSnap
Brooks Fisher, Chief Marketing Officer, Intuit Corporation
Jose Geronimo, Banner Ad Program Manager, Cisco Systems
Carole Gum, Director of Corporate Marketing, Vertical Networks
Cynthia Holladay, Marketing Executive at large
Maribeth Lazich, Principal, Market Keen
Ciree J. Loftus, Software Development Manager, Luminate
Tony Lustig, CEO, Red Oak Software
Karen Mackey, Software Development Expert at large
Fred Nikolac, Product Line General Manager, Acuson
Mike Oitzman, Product Manager, Remedy Corporation
David Platshon, CEO, Fatbox
Steven Puthuff, Chairman and Founder, Sybersay
Randy Shattuck, Founder and CEO, The Shattuck Group
Narry Singh, Vice-President of Global Trading, Rapt. Inc.
David Stoner, Principal Consultant, DNV
Bob Yee, Marketing Manager, Cisco Systems
Bob Zeidman, CEO and Founder, The Chalkboard Network

Janis Lamar and Luther Smith of TRW provided thorough and thoughtful review of content related to the TRW-ESL new ventures program. Thanks for being so responsive and mindful of my production schedule.

Many business professionals reviewed the various stages of this book during its development. I thank all of you for your honest and candid feedback along the way. The book was greatly improved as a result of your efforts. Reviewers include Evie Butcher, Rick Hatton, Jill Konrath, Andrew Luan, Mike Merrill, Daniel Rich, Martin Risk, Paula Romeo, Britta Steele, Richard Strong, Wendy Verlaine, Benna Williams, and Zhiyi Yu.

Kudos to the original TRW-ESL incubator staff, wherever you may be today: Pat Sasscer, Tricia Loveland, Bruce Cole, Tets Maniwa, Bob Yee, David Freedman, and Mike Aitken. I hope that your entrepreneurial adventures and successes continue. The TRW-ESL new ventures review board members were real pioneers; I thank you all for your patience and creativity as we endured the challenges of building this whole process: Dale Lindley, Bill Clark, Luther Smith, and Fred Nikolac. Most importantly, I would like to thank Art Money, former President of ESL Inc., for believing in your vision and believing in me to carry it out.

Last but not least, a big thanks to all the entrepreneurs out there – past, present and future, whether you are independent or inside a company. Without your vision and creativity, there would be no new products, and things would be very dull indeed.

Foreword

I was reminded, as I read Catherine Kitcho's *From Idea to Launch at Internet Speed*, of the quote by Nobel Prize Laureate Linus Pauling: "The best way to have a good idea is to have lots of ideas." In over 7 years at Cisco and 16 years at Bell Labs, I have been privy to many forms of idea incubation and even more forms of product launching. Some have definitely proved more successful than others, but none would have been possible at all if there was not underlying support for idea generation and an analytical process for excavating the wheat from the chaff.

To begin, however, those ideas that have successfully survived a launch and, perhaps even more importantly, displayed sustained value, were generated and executed with a few clear concepts sacrosanct, including the necessity of embracing a deterministic process that guarantees quick, decisive action in response to new ideas that warrant execution. Additionally, in accord with a disruptive pattern of new product or service insertion, new business models based on changing market parameters are needed to establish potential and risk. Thirdly, it is imperative to utilize a team that asks tough questions, has key insights, and can recognize good ideas for what they are - just good ideas –as opposed to those that have an overriding propensity for success. And finally, the engenderment of a culture that embraces change allows for success to occur at all.

Historically, this rigorous process for reviewing ideas and taking them through to launch was not mandated in the same way as it is today. As the source of financing has changed for business, so has the successful business organization. A vertical orientation served well those companies in controlled competitive environments, whereas increasing competitive pressures have flattened many companies into horizontal models with strategic partnerships, core competencies and integrated systems. Large vertical companies typically included well-financed R & D programs that slowly and meticulously established new products and services. Over the last decade, competitive pressure and changing value chains from idea to customer have increased complexity dramatically while, at the same time, it has become increasingly difficult to fund unbounded research projects to meet these demands. Hence, the winners in today's market overcome complexity and excessive expenditure by creating intense alignment between the idea and customer via the <u>launch:</u> the imperative for Kitcho's approach.

Finally, the embrace of continuous change and development is a thread common to all companies enjoying long-term success today. While it is understandable that companies are hesitant to develop products that will render their current product lines obsolete, a pragmatic view exposes the truth: if you do not effectively develop new ideas and launch new products, then someone else with far less charitable intentions will do it for you. Therefore, successful, ongoing cannibalization of your own products is essential. And, although new product development will often be evolutionary in nature, competitors will be applying radical new thinking to these new complex problems, and so too must effective incumbents. Once again, Kitcho's approach to advancing quickly the best new ideas, minimizing risk and maximizing return on investment, are essential in today's environment.

While I expect many readers may have employed, individually, techniques and skills noted in this book, it is carrying through on the entire process that will ensure teams taking an idea all the way through launch don't miss telltale signs and harbingers of trouble that, when taken early, can often be corrected, abandoned prior to great expense, or dealt with appropriately. During good times, mistakes made during this process are often survivable. During demanding times, they are not. Kitcho's realistic framework provides the tools needed to manage the process of idea to launch well during good times and, more importantly, to win during the most demanding times.

Kevin J. Kennedy

Senior Vice President
ITD and Service Provider LOB
Cisco Systems, Inc.

Introduction

This book is for any business professional who is involved in conceptualizing, developing or launching new products. Whether you are an individual entrepreneur or an executive of a company that develops many new products, this book will help you think through the issues you will be facing, help organize the information, and help you manage the entire process from original idea screening through launch into the marketplace.

The process of developing new ideas into products and taking them to market is challenging but very rewarding. It requires creativity, patience, risk-taking, objectivity, intuition, and a lot of hard work. These skills have always been, and continue to be, necessary to the successful development of new products, but now that we are in the beginning of the Internet Era, the ability to execute them quickly is of paramount importance. The Internet Era began in the late 1990s, when Internet technologies effected a major shift in business operations and commerce in general; every company now must move at Internet "speed" in order to serve their customers and compete effectively. In addition, in the aftermath of the dot-com decline, we are witnessing the return of profitability as a key measure, not only of success, but also of business survival itself. Speed with an eye on profit has become the new mantra of those pursuing new opportunities today.

I was fortunate to have the experience of developing an entire new ventures program for TRW-ESL in the 1990s. It was part of TRW-ESL's initiative for diversification, sometimes referred to as defense commercialization. At that time, many aerospace and defense firms were seeking ways to commercialize technology that had been developed for, and subsidized by the U.S. government. The government viewed this as a way to reduce and manage its own procurement costs and was encouraging companies to begin commercialization programs. The president of ESL established a strategic goal for the company: 25 percent of ESL's sales were to be in commercial business within eight years of starting the new ventures program. Establishing this program gave me experience in applying business basics to the new idea process, and at that time, profitability was a key focus. So was speed, given the aggressive goal our president chose. The new ventures process that we used in the program enabled us to screen and validate business ideas and develop complete business plans in 60 days or less, and the process was based on models used in the high tech venture capital community.

When I started the new ventures program, ESL was a wholly owned subsidiary of TRW Inc., which is now a $17 billion automotive, aerospace and information technology company. My new ventures program was limited to ESL operations only [1]. ESL was located in Sunnyvale, California, and had about 2000 employees at that time. (Hereafter throughout this book, the designation 'TRW-ESL' refers to ESL operations only.) As Director of New Ventures, I reported directly to the president. I was responsible for setting up an internal new ventures incubator, along with the business processes necessary to screen ideas, develop business plans, find investors, and launch ventures.

[1] (ESL was a standalone company founded in the early 1960s, and during the 1970s was acquired by TRW Inc. Today, those ESL business units are part of TRW Systems Information Technology Group. For the purposes of this book, the entity will be referred to as "TRW-ESL" to distinguish it from other parts of the company. Other, separate diversification activities were ongoing in other divisions of TRW that are not discussed here.)

I had a new ventures staff of seven people and I set up and chaired a new ventures review board consisting of senior executives from finance, engineering, and business development. Over a three-year period, we were able to establish, test, and refine idea selection criteria, as a result of the many lessons we learned on how to screen ideas effectively. Any TRW-ESL employee could bring an idea forward to the incubator for screening and review by the board. Our new ventures staff established a process for idea validation and business plan generation, as well as training resources so that the incoming "intrapreneurs" could learn the business and marketing skills necessary to manage a venture. There were several decision points along the way, so that the board could review progress and the need for incremental funding. We improved the business planning process continuously, streamlining it so that we could do it quickly and in accordance with our business objectives.

How did we do? Over the three years that the incubator was in operation, we screened more than 30 ideas, 10 of them made it all the way through the process, and 3 of them are still in existence today as established companies or acquired parts of other companies. That is a 10% success rate, at the time considered by venture capitalists to be above average, for venture ideas that survive. Because it was considered successful for a defense commercialization effort, and the TRW-ESL new ventures incubator received much press and government attention. Articles were written about this effort, appearing in the *EDN Magazine, Aviation Week,* and the *Wall Street Journal.*

A 10% success rate may not be considered high in a commercial company, especially for new ideas developed into saleable products. However, success should be measured relative to the company's objectives at the time the ideas are considered. We were happy that we were able to get three ventures through the process, and felt that we had exceeded our original expectations.

The revenue potential from these ventures, even with conservative forecasts, would help us meet or exceed our eight-year revenue goal. The most important thing about this program is that *we were able to develop flexible and practical screening criteria, and a very fast validation and business planning process* – all of which can be applied to any type of company. Here are some of the business actions we took that resulted in our success:

- -Funding opportunities that had a strong tie to our core competencies
- -Acquiring expertise from outside the company in the areas of marketing, venture capital, and venture management
- -Retraining and mentoring people to teach them business and marketing skills
- -Minimizing risk by using an investor's approach
- -Using venture capital models for business plans
- -Maintaining leadership from the top
- -Maintaining an entrepreneurial environment where people are encouraged to bring ideas forward
- -Seeking strategic partners to strengthen competitive advantage and decrease time to market

These are all very sound business principles, but in our case, applying them required profound change within the organization to make this happen in less than three years. In any company, change is often painful, but unavoidable, especially when it comes to implementing innovation programs.

In the late 1990s, I left TRW-ESL and formed my own consulting company. I continued to apply the skills and techniques to my growing client base of high tech entrepreneurs and companies of all sizes. Starting with the idea selection criteria, validation techniques and business plan models that I implemented at TRW-ESL, I continued to improve and refine them, developing new tools along the way. I developed business plan templates to enable entrepreneurs to quickly think through all of the business issues for their venture. I developed partner selection criteria for companies that were seeking the right strategic partners to enter new markets. I conducted market research for clients who wanted to identify and characterize new opportunities, and, in the process, I discovered how to evaluate market trends and forecasts realistically. I developed a business model mapping technique that proved to be an invaluable tool for marketing, distribution, business operations, and channel management. I advised clients on the best marketing strategies to use for their new opportunities. I helped clients launch all types of products and services, and became a specialist in product launch, capturing this knowledge in my book, "High Tech Product Launch", which was published in 1999. From 1998 through 2000, I also integrated these tools and techniques into the graduate-level marketing and strategy courses I taught in the MBA programs of Golden Gate University and Santa Clara University. By this time, I had helped plan and launch new products and ventures for more than 30 entrepreneurs and 20 companies, from startups to giants.

The year 2000 was a year of tremendous business and economic change. The Internet Era was well underway, with companies expected to move faster and faster. New business models made possible by the technologies of the Internet were starting to take shape. Partnering and outsourcing increased tremendously. Large, mature companies took their cue from rebel startups and began to successfully convert their operations to "e-business". And suddenly, the marketing strategies that startups and large companies had used successfully in the early "Internet years" were severely tested. Customers became more powerful and central to the average company's existence. The dot-com mania started to decline, and the pendulum started swinging back toward business basics again – revenue and profit were top priorities again. This shift in emphasis means that today, we have to be more savvy about how we take advantage of new opportunities, and that's why it is time for me to write this book.

From Idea to Launch at Internet Speed follows the order of the new product cycle. The first part focuses on the idea screening process and considerations involved in establishing your own company's criteria. Chapter 2 of the book gives general guidelines on how to develop realistic criteria and how to make decisions quickly, both critical in the Internet Era. The six most important criteria each have their own chapter: strategic fit, customer, competition, market, resources, and profit. In each of these six chapters, examples are given of meaningful or proven criteria, and guidelines are presented for refining them to fit your situation or your company's environment.

Part Two is an updated look at strategy and planning for new products in the Internet Era. New marketing strategies are described here, along with examples of companies who are trying new hybrid strategies. The subject of business models is covered in two chapters; one on business model mapping as an invaluable planning tool, and the other on new types of business models for the Internet Era. Additional chapters address partnering and value distribution, speeding up product development, and how to streamline business and marketing plans.

Part Three is an update of the launch phase for the Internet Era. This is a supplement to my earlier book, *High Tech Product Launch*, and is a high-level look at ways to maintain speed through the launch cycle by leveraging the web and choosing the best marketing programs. Part Four is about maintaining momentum, and the summary chapter includes everything you need to know in order to set up and maintain a repeatable new product process in your own company. Appendices include recommended supplemental reading, as well as useful tools and templates supplied on an accompanying CD.

As you work to develop your own criteria and processes, I encourage you to provide me with feedback on your experiences. At my website, www.launchdoctor.com, I host a launch forum where I address additional topics related to my books and consulting practice. You may submit questions that I will answer at the site, or privately by email if you wish. My email address is: ckitcho@launchdoctor.com.

I wish you much success in pursuing your new business opportunities. This book will help you pursue them with speed, while maintaining a focus on profit. Also remember that every new idea has the potential to provide learning, and don't forget to have some fun along the way.

Catherine Kitcho
September 2001

1

The New Product Cycle of the Internet Era

The "Internet Era", as used in this book, refers to the business cycle that began in the late 1990s, when the Internet and related technologies started to be used on a widespread basis in the corporate world. We are still at the very beginning of this era, but Internet technology has already started a great shift in how businesses operate, collaborate, and conduct commerce. We are starting to witness the impact this trend has on how markets develop and fluctuate. Technology has increased the pace at which we do business, which in turn has created a rush to get new products developed and into the marketplace. However, in order to be profitable in today's economy, it is still necessary to employ solid business basics: controlling expenditures, serving customers, and generating demand. In the Internet Era, we still have the same product cycle to deal with, but the whole cycle is very compressed.

Innovation and new product development have always been essential parts of the life cycle of companies; when innovation stops, companies die. Before the Internet Era, companies typically followed a formal or informal procedure for defining and screening new product ideas, followed by an often-lengthy product development phase. When the new product was sufficiently developed, a promotional plan was prepared and the product was deemed ready for launch. This sequence of events lasted from 18 to 24 months – an eternity in Internet terms. Today we don't have the luxury of that much time, nor do we have the resources to sustain an effort for that long. Everything is compressed; in some companies the idea-to-launch process happens in as little as six months.

How can companies do this; must they sacrifice any semblance of process in order to do all of this challenging work in just a few months? That's not a desirable scenario. When companies don't follow a process, and instead select ideas based on the gut feel of the CEO, the VP of Marketing, or the VP of engineering, ideas quickly land in the development organization, often without any market research to justify the product specifications. During development, a marketing executive then puts together some quick promotional plans, and then the product is launched – to a market that often is unmatched to the product attributes. Everyone is in a hurry. What happens? Sometimes companies get lucky, and the product takes on a life of its own. More often, the company incurs added expense and loses time because they have to modify or completely redesign the product or a marketing campaign, or in the worst case, start over from scratch. This can be very confusing to the marketplace. Additionally, because of the time lost, competitors may enter the market and eliminate any competitive advantage the company may have had.

The only way for companies to succeed at new products in the Internet Era is to use an effective process and get to market quickly. The process must be simplified and streamlined in order to get to market quickly. The process must be driven by the business criteria that will generate profit for the company. Speed and profitability are the keys for survival and success for the Internet Era.

The four phases of the new product cycle

Before we can address how to develop products with speed and profitability, we need to review the new product cycle and what happens between idea concept and taking the new product to market. The new product cycle has four phases, as shown in Figure 1-1. These phases include idea generation, idea validation, product development, and product launch.

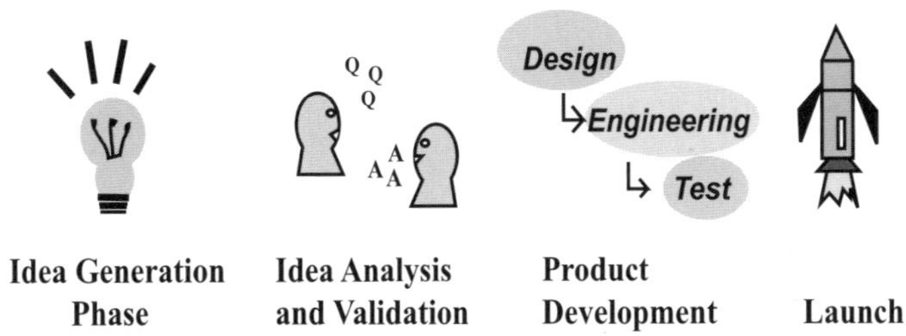

Figure 1.1: The New Product Cycle

Idea generation is the fun phase, when people submit creative ideas to decision-makers for consideration. New product ideas can be generated from many sources, such as customers, employees, or strategic partners. During this phase, the product idea is usually in the form of a concept, and there is not very much information that is known about the idea. At this stage, a product is described in vague terms such as what it is, what it does, who might use it, and why. To move through the new product cycle, ideas must be tested in order to evaluate whether it makes business sense to pursue them. Idea screening may be done by a decision-making authority during the idea generation phase, in order to find the ideas that are most worthy of further study. Those ideas that are deemed worthy move on to the next phase, idea validation.

Validation is the process of verifying whether an assumption is true. In the case of idea validation, you must prove many assumptions regarding the new product concept. The work of validation means researching the external marketplace to identify the need that a customer would have for such a product, and characterizing the market environment into which you would launch the new product. There are also internal considerations, such as whether you have the capability and competency to design and build such a product within the company. Gathering and analyzing all of this data accurately takes a substantial effort. At the end of the validation process, there is usually another screening of the idea conducted by the decision-making body. The decision-makers must have all of the facts about the product concept in order to decide whether to send the product into the very expensive and lengthy product development phase.

During the product development phase, the product is designed, built, and tested. Some time during this phase, the target customer will see the new product for the first time. Depending on the type of product, development work can be complex, challenging, and may require the efforts of a very large staff. The more complex the product, the greater the likelihood that the product will take longer to develop than expected. This creates a potential threat to the profitability of the new product and may delay its entry to the marketplace. Effective product planning and management is critical at this point, in order to keep the product development on schedule and true to the requirements of the customer and market. It is also during this phase that senior management and/or the marketing department develop the business model and go-to-market strategy. Any new partnering relationships that will be necessary to distribute or market the new product should be established at this time, as well.

The launch phase is the most chaotic and pressure-filled phase of the new product cycle because everyone is in a hurry to get to market. There is also a considerable amount of work that needs to be done during this phase. The marketing plan, which will guide the launch implementation, needs to be compiled and finalized. All marketing programs must be developed and implemented, including all marketing materials that will be used to promote and sell the product in all marketing venues. Public relations and advertising campaigns are conducted before the launch date. Sales people, channel partners, and customer support personnel are all trained on the details of the new product and the key messages being used to promote the product. This whirlwind of activity must take place in less than three months in order to make it to market on time. It takes an organized and dedicated launch team to make this happen, as well as the cooperation of senior management, partners, and the product development team. Figure 1.2 summarizes the tasks involved in the four phases of the new product cycle.

Idea Generation Phase	Idea Analysis and Validation	Product Development	Launch
-Formulate ideas -Choose ideas for further evaluation	-Market research -Identify customer need -Decide which ideas will be developed	-Design product -Build product -Customer feedback -Test	-Compile marketing plan -Develop and deploy all marketing programs

Figure 1.2: The Four Phases of the New Product Cycle

New product decisions must be made quickly and accurately Before the Internet Era, the new product cycle lasted from 18 to 36 months. Today, the cycle takes from 12 to 18 months. That is a huge change, especially when you consider that the same basic steps of process need to be taken, and that there are at least one or two major decision points along the way. Figure 1.3 shows how the four phases of the cycle have changed.

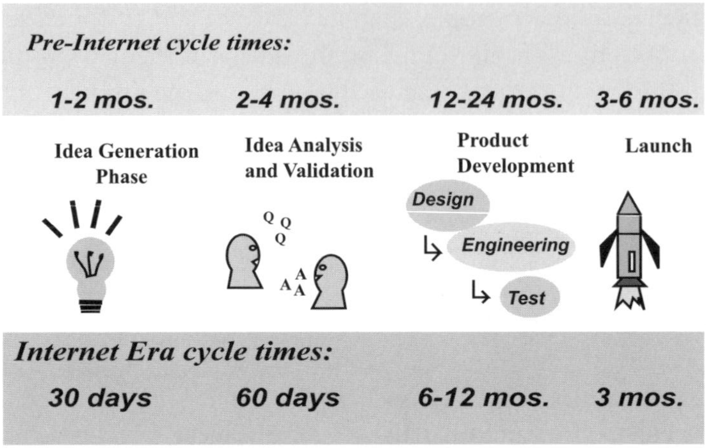

Figure 1.3: New Product Cycle Phases Before and After the Internet

Decision-makers and managers must be able to make decisions more quickly throughout the entire cycle – from idea screening to launch - including day-to-day routine decisions. Idea screening for new products is done by an individual or group of people who have the responsibility for screening the ideas that will be funded for further study or development. Screening criteria must be in place, and a process must be in place that describes how the criteria are applied. Screening of ideas must also be done accurately, which means that all of the facts and analysis must be used in evaluating the idea. The appropriate criteria that will maximize the potential for profitability must be used, and the criteria must be applied consistently when decisions are made.

A simplified and customized new product process for a compressed cycle

In order to develop and manage new products in the compressed cycle of the Internet Era, a new product process is necessary. The first step is to evaluate the existing new product process in your company (if there is one) to see if it can be modified. If you don't have a new product process yet, there are many reasons to start using one, even if you are a new startup. You won't have to reinvent the wheel each time a new idea is presented. You will have an opportunity to make sure that new products fit your current business objectives, including profitability. It will be easier for new people to come up to speed on new products. A process will improve efficiency in decision-making. You will have a basis and foundation to improve the process in response to fluctuations in the market and the economy. Table 1.1 is a summary of the benefits of a new product process.

Table 1.1:
Benefits of a New Product Process

-Repeatable process builds efficiency

-Can modify process as strategic objectives change

-Easier for new employees to learn how new products are managed

-Adds consistency to decision-making

-Eliminates confusion and saves time when new product ideas arise

The new product process must address every issue regarding new products, from idea to launch. In order to do this swiftly and to maximize profit, here are the elements of the process that you need to implement or change for each phase. There are chapters in this book that will assist you in streamlining your process, and they are noted.

Idea Generation phase

-Establish consistent criteria for initial idea screening that are appropriate for your company (Chapters 3-8)

-Educate people about the criteria so that submitted ideas can be more readily evaluated

-Take no more than one week to conduct initial idea screening

-Assign a dedicated group of decision-makers to screen ideas (Chapters 2, 18)

-Use only one decision point to screen ideas before the validation phase

Idea Validation phase

-Use no more than two decision points before the product goes on to the development phase

-Insist that all criteria are addressed by the presenter of the idea

-Take no more than two weeks for each decision point

-Apply criteria consistently (Chapters 3-8)

Product Development phase

-Speed up this phase if possible to shorten the cycle (Chapter 13)

-Use streamlined business plans (Chapter 14)

-Choose the market strategy and business model that will get you to market sooner and maximize profitability (Chapters 9, 10, 11)

-Develop partnering relationships as necessary prior to the launch phase (Chapter 12)

Product Launch phase

-Update the pre-development product information (Chapter 15)

-Use streamlined marketing plans (Chapter 14)

-Choose the marketing programs that will get you to market sooner and maximize profitability (Chapter 16)

-Leverage the web to save money and to get to market sooner (Chapter 17)

To be successful in managing new products today, companies must be organized, and focused on the bottom line. A new product process that works is the first step in becoming organized. Being focused requires the decision-makers to be willing to say no to ideas that won't be profitable or that detract from the company's overall mission. With all of the changes we are experiencing in the global marketplace and with the economy, companies must be able to respond to conditions at Internet speed, with a constant eye on profit.

2

Realistic Criteria and Fast Decisions

Whether you are an entrepreneur hoping to start a successful new business venture, or an employee of an established company who's involved in developing and launching new products (or new business units), the process of idea screening and validation is very much the same. Appropriate idea screening criteria need to be formulated, and the appointed decision-makers must have a process that allows them to use the criteria to make their decisions quickly. This chapter will help you understand the basics of the idea screening and validation process and will show you how to create decision criteria, as well as how to enable streamlined decision-making.

The Basics

As described in Chapter 1, the phases of the new product cycle include idea generation, idea screening and validation, development and launch. Successful new products come from good ideas. Ideas for new products may come from many sources, and the person responsible for idea generation is called the idea champion. Screening is done by a group of decision-makers other than the idea champion, who have the authority and responsibility to approve new products. The idea champion generates the idea and does research to "validate" the idea with the customer and market environment. Validation means doing research in order to answer all of the business questions that are related to the decision criteria that the decision-makers will apply during the screening process. This requires that the idea champion understand the criteria before the validation work is done. The idea champion then presents the idea to a group of people who screen it and make a decision according to these criteria. The decision-makers can decide to accept, reject or postpone the idea, or to have the idea champion do further validation and resubmit the idea for a future decision. In concept, the process is quite simple.

The challenge, however, is to keep the process simple. An idea may pass through the screening process several times. The initial pass may be a high-level screen that is designed to weed out the ideas that aren't worth researching further. Ideas that make it past the first screen would be funded for more research and idea validation. An initial screening decision may be made on the basis of a very high-level look at the market potential, without doing much research or validating the idea with a customer. If an idea makes it past the first screening decision, then the idea champion would do more extensive research, after which the second screening decision would then be made on the basis of the validated idea.

Figure 2.1 illustrates an example of a screening and validation timeline. The more decision points there are, the shorter the time intervals should be between them, certainly no more than 30 days between the first screening decision and the second. Opportunities are fleeting in the Internet Era.

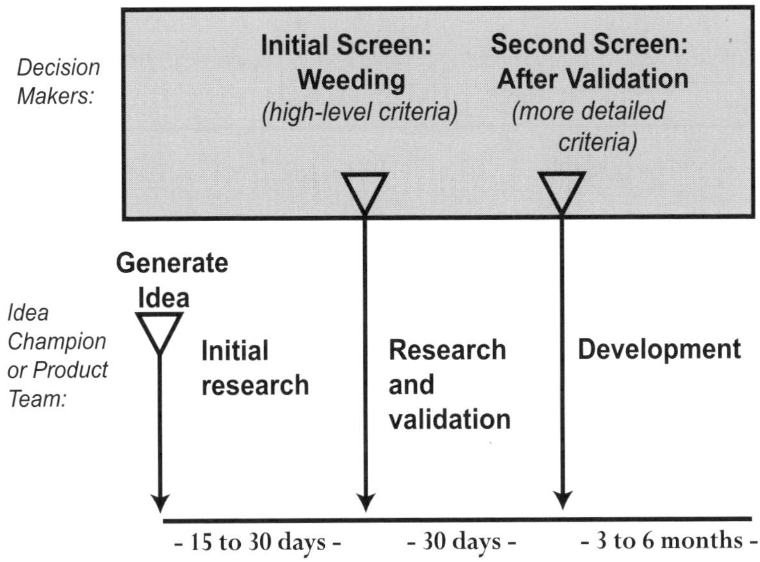

Figure 2.1: The Screening and Validation Timeline

How many ideas do you need?

What constitutes an idea? For the purposes of this book, I define "idea" as a new concept for a product or venture. A concept has not been developed into a product yet. Ideas as they exist in a person's mind or imagination are in different phases of evolution. The person who has the concept may have some idea of what this product or service would do and who might need the product or service. Sometimes the idea is an enhancement of an existing product or service but would provide different functionality or serve an entirely new market.

Not every idea that an individual dreams up will be successful, and many of them are rejected at some point during the screening or validation process. That's why it is advisable to develop as many ideas as possible, so that some will survive all the way through the process. Many companies encourage or even reward employees for developing new ideas for products. Even for an entrepreneur, original ideas may be subject to many obstacles along the way, including outright rejection. Several of the entrepreneurs that I have worked with over the years have ended up developing business ideas that are completely different than the ones that they started with, because the business concept, market conditions, or technology solution did not turn out as originally envisioned. Figure 2.2 shows the "idea funnel" – how ideas are narrowed as the screening and validation process is applied.

At TRW-ESL, the president was so concerned about having a sufficient number of new ideas to sustain enough successful new ventures, he launched a new strategic initiative called "2020", in which the top 100 or so managers in the company participated in a year-long series of off site meetings for the purposes of generating new business and product ideas. The goal of this program was to visualize and reinvent the company's activities, products and services for the future. This initiative helped begin the "idea pipeline" for the new ventures incubator, and at least 15 new ideas resulted from the work done by the 2020 participants. Once established, word about the incubator spread and employees submitted an additional 15 ideas over a three-year period. With 30 total ideas, we had an adequate pool of possibilities to explore.

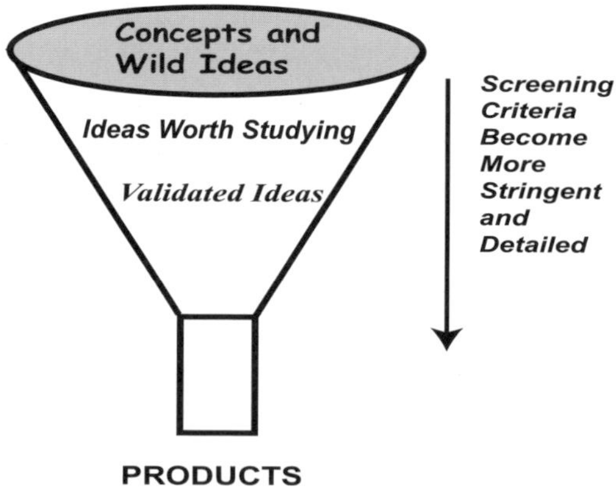

Figure 2.2: The Idea Funnel

A review body needs to screen and approve ideas

Whether it is a committee of one, or a formal group of seasoned executives, someone other than the idea champion needs to screen ideas objectively. This review body should be cross-functional, with representatives from finance, marketing, and engineering or development. You may also want to include someone from the sales organization who has current and specific knowledge of your customer base.

Tony Lustig is the CEO of Red Oak Software, a company that makes a data exchange solution for the semiconductor market. *"Typically, the business development or product development organization has the charter of pursuing new opportunities and creating new products for the company,"* says Tony. *"However, the CEO needs to establish the overall strategy and direction for the company, which in turn fosters an environment where new business and product ideas are continuously infused into next generation systems that can leap-frog technology."* A dedicated group focused on screening new ideas can also be very effective if there are resources and budget to support it.

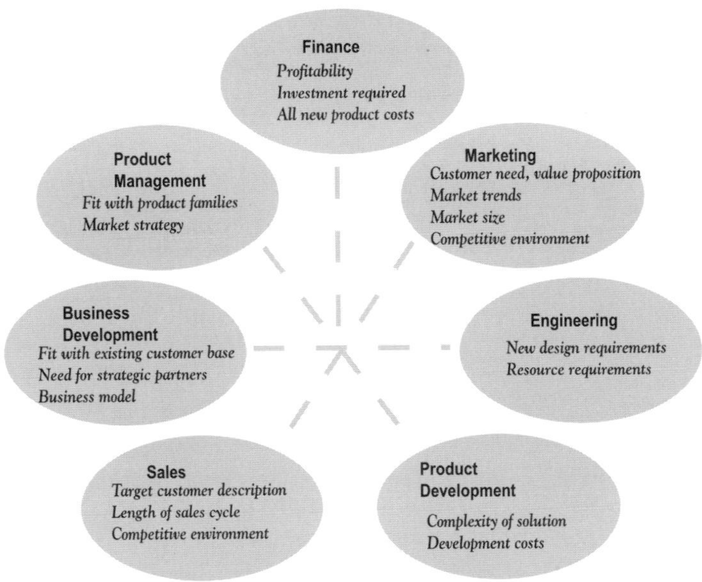

Figure 2.3: Functional Organizations and New Product Concerns

At TRW-ESL, we had representatives from finance, business development, engineering, and a senior manager from one major line of business as an "at-large" representative. We often invited consultants that the company had retained to help us evaluate specific markets and industries. It's important to have many different perspectives represented within the group of decision-makers. Although sometimes the finance person would be asking marketing questions and the engineering person asking finance questions, it does help to have enough people to raise the important business issues, without having so many people that the process bogs down. Figure 2.3 illustrates the varying perspectives on new products among the functional departments of a company.

Submitting and screening ideas should be part of a single process

Every company has some sort of process, formal or informal by which employees – and even customers – can suggest ideas for new products or ventures. Sometimes customers can suggest them as well. In many companies, ideas just evolve until they get the attention of management and receive some funding, and sometimes one of these ideas ends up as a launched product. Such ad hoc efforts have produced notable products, but the effort needs to be a bit more organized in the Internet Era; the market and economy are simply moving much too fast. Ideally, there should be one new product process that encompasses both the submission and the screening of ideas. Otherwise, there are isolated 'silos' of new product efforts; the ideas may never be validated or screened properly, and the company can miss out on some new opportunities.

Once ideas have been submitted, they must be screened. A screening process should have a minimum of two decision points. For each decision point, there needs to be a set of decision criteria that are applied to the idea. A decision should be made as to whether or not further validation of the idea is needed.

Each successive decision point should have increasingly more stringent criteria associated with it. An early decision point should be established to eliminate ideas that have little or no chance of success. This initial decision point serves as a reality check, and the criteria applied should be very general and high-level, such as: Is there a market? Would anyone buy this? Can we build this? Is this within our core business? These questions are qualitative in nature, not quantitative. Based on his experience in managing new businesses, Tony Lustig believes that there is no substitute for a formal in-depth review. *"Once an idea passes this hurdle, then more formal discussions or a presentation can be scheduled,"* he says.

TRW-ESL Pre-1.0 Questions

Here are the questions we used at TRW-ESL for an initial screen:

1. Is the customer problem real and does it exist now?
2. Who is the customer and what's their compelling reason to buy?
3. Do we understand the problem and can we solve it?
4. Is there an existing alternative already being provided by a competitor?
5. Does it fit our core competencies?

Figure 2.4 shows the decision points we used at TRW-ESL. Initially, we set up two decision points. Decision 1.0 was the "reality check", designed to filter out the ideas that didn't warrant more study. If an idea passed Decision 1.0, then the viability phase began and lasted about 60 days, culminating in Decision 2.0. At that point, a complete business plan was presented for consideration. Ventures were then "launched" after a successful 2.0 decision, which meant that we would begin the spinout process to engage investors and strategic partners.

Later on, we added Decision 1.5 as a checkpoint for market validation, because we needed more detail about the customer need and market size. When the market study was done, then a presentation was made to the board members, who assessed the market viability of the idea at Decision 1.5. If the market environment was favorable, then the rest of the business plan was developed in the second half of the viability phase. Having this additional decision point prior to spending money on a full business plan worked much better for us at TRW-ESL. Adding a third decision point to your process will give you a much better sense of the market and profit potential for your idea.

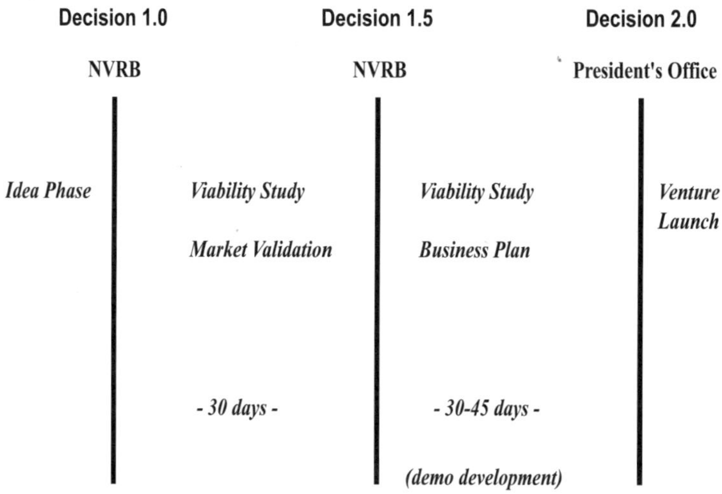

Figure 2.4: The TRW-ESL New Ventures Process

The preceding is an example of a process that we initiated and then modified to more closely fit our objectives. Decision points can be added or removed as business conditions change. It may take some trial and error to find the right number of decision points. Bear in mind, however, that the more you have, the longer it may take for ideas to move through the process (and the more meetings your review body will need to have!)

Criteria need to be established and understood

Screening criteria often take on a life of their own, with their meaning and application a mystery to everyone except the inventor of the criteria. Resist the temptation to have your local decision-analysis expert set up the selection criteria. You need to keep criteria simple and understandable for the idea creators as well as those who will be applying the criteria as judges or review authorities. If you can't describe the meaning of a criterion in two sentences or less, then it's too complicated. When idea champions present their ideas to decision-makers, the event takes place in a 30-minute or one-hour session. There is not enough time to hear what the presenter has to say, ask questions, and think about your reaction, while referring to a long and complicated list of criteria. It's not good for the idea champion or the decision-makers.

Criteria should be established by consensus; the decision-makers agree to use the criteria and apply them during the idea review process, and the list of criteria must be communicated to the individuals or organizations that submit ideas for review. Everyone needs to be on the same page and working from the same list. This may seem like an obvious step, but it is often overlooked, leading to incorrect assumptions and missed opportunities on the part of the decision-makers as well as the idea champions.

Which criteria should I use for my company?

The best criteria are those that fit your company's strategic objectives and that will help generate revenue and profit. You need to find the right specific criteria that will enable you to select the ideas that measure up to your standards. There are a wide variety of business criteria that can be applied in evaluating new product and venture ideas. I believe there should be at least three major measures of a new idea: financial, marketing-related, and strategic. Will the idea generate revenue and profit for the company? Does the idea address a real customer need and is the market ready for the idea? Does the idea fit the way you do business, and do you have the ability to take it to market?

In this book, I have described six major criteria that relate to these major measures, and there is a chapter on each one that explains why it is important and how to apply it to your situation.

THE SIX MAJOR CRITERIA

-Strategic Fit – does the idea fit your company's culture, core competencies and business objectives?

-Customer – who is the customer? what is their problem and value proposition? what is the customer profit value to your company?

-Competition – what are the alternatives and substitutes? what are the competing companies and products? what is the competitive environment for your idea?

-Market – what are the key market trends? what is your target market size?

-Resources – what is the impact of the idea on existing technology and people resources?

-Profit – what are the profit goals and metrics? what revenues are possible? what costs are required to take the idea through to launch and beyond?

"Venture capital investors use various criteria depending on their fund and portfolio requirements at the time," says Joe Becker, President and CEO of Dolphin Ventures, a Silicon Valley venture capital firm. *"However, when investors look at the executive summary of a business plan, they want to see a large and growing market, a solid management team, and potential for high return on investment. During the due diligence process, more detailed market, management and technology criteria come into play."* Even established or mature companies should view their new products as an investor would: is this new product idea worth the money, people and intellectual property it will require, and will the return on that investment improve our bottom line and enable us to reach our business goals?

Criteria need to be refined and improved

After a few ideas have made their way through the process, you may decide that your work is done, and you can use the same criteria for every new idea that comes along. Not so. Marketing and economic changes occur rapidly and affect how your company does business and how you serve your customers. Strategic goals also change in accordance with the economic environment and business performance. Venture capital investors annually re-examine their venture selection criteria, according to Joe Becker. *"Some of the changes are dictated by the nature of the fund itself; it may be targeted for certain types of technologies or companies. In general, it's a good idea to evaluate the changes in the overall marketplace and adjust the criteria if necessary."*

Whenever you make any changes in marketing strategy or technology direction, you should revisit your criteria and update them so that you can identify the ideas that will best fit your new environment. Over a three-year period, the TRW-ESL new ventures board made modifications to the decision criteria at least four times per year, to fit our evolving strategic direction. Just like business plans, the new idea criteria for your company need to be a dynamic reflection of your business.

Fast decision-making is essential

If a decision can't be made regarding a new idea in less than 60 days, one of your competitors may make it to market before you do. In the Internet Era, fast decision-making is essential for survival because no part of the new product cycle can afford to be delayed while someone studies tradeoffs for several weeks. You should do whatever you can to streamline and simplify your decision-making process.

Decision-making is also very personal and individualized. The decision-maker must have a clear idea of exactly what is being decided. Is it to commit funds to the idea in order to study it? To approve the idea so that it can move on to the next phase of validation? Or the biggest one: to send the idea through the product development process? The decision-maker must also have the right level of authority, understand his or her responsibilities, and apply the decision criteria appropriately and consistently. Sounds complicated, doesn't it? There is, however, a simple and fast way to do this.

When we started this process within TRW-ESL, a typical internal R&D proposal took about 9 to 12 months to make it all the way through the approval process. It was clear to the president that we had to come up with a much speedier way to identify and evaluate ideas for new ventures. We simplified the process by keeping the number of decision points to a minimum. We condensed the decision criteria to bulleted lists. Most importantly, we reduced the number of people involved in the decision-making process so that we could reach consensus more quickly.

Tony Lustig recommends that an internal champion own the new business idea and drive it forward to the go/no-go decision point. *"This person should have the motivation and monetary incentive to pursue the new idea, and to see it through the rest of the product life cycle."* In this scenario, the new product champion could also do pre-screening of ideas, presenting the most promising ones to senior management for final approval. This serves to speed up the initial part of the idea screening process because more research will have been done before the idea is presented to the decision-makers.

Another way to streamline the early part of the idea selection process is to have a staff of people who can pre-screen the ideas using the high-level criteria set by the decision-makers. *"Venture firms receive so many business plans and executive summaries that they must have people on staff who can read, screen and sort them into a "short stack" of the most promising opportunities – like a triage process. There's another advantage to this approach, in that these people can compare several ideas simultaneously so they are better able to compare and rank them – the ideas are fresh in their mind,"* according to Joe Becker. If your company has multiple ideas to consider, this may be worth doing as well. It will be a better use of the decision-makers' time to evaluate only the most promising opportunities.

Decisions may have several possible outcomes

There can be several possible outcomes for each idea that is considered, as illustrated in Figure 2.5. The idea can be rejected outright, with no merit and no reason to consider it in the future. The idea can also be rejected for now, and perhaps reconsidered at a future date. At TRW-ESL, we referred to this outcome as putting the idea "in the freezer"; we would then thaw it out later (hopefully before freezer burn). According to Tony Lustig, *"Sometimes an idea can be postponed, and later re-evaluated under a different scenario – such as a different business model, product configuration, or target customer."*

Another possible outcome is to take a new idea and bundle it with a different one that has been submitted for consideration; many powerful new products or product/service combinations have been created in just this way. For example, when pagers were first introduced to the marketplace, someone realized it would be a good idea to add text messaging as an additional service. That proved to be a significant differentiator for the companies who were able to offer both paging and messaging.

Sometimes an idea meets the majority of the screening criteria, but there is some information missing, so the idea is sent back to the originator for some refining. Of course, every now and then a good idea just sails right through the process, is approved and is ready for the next step.

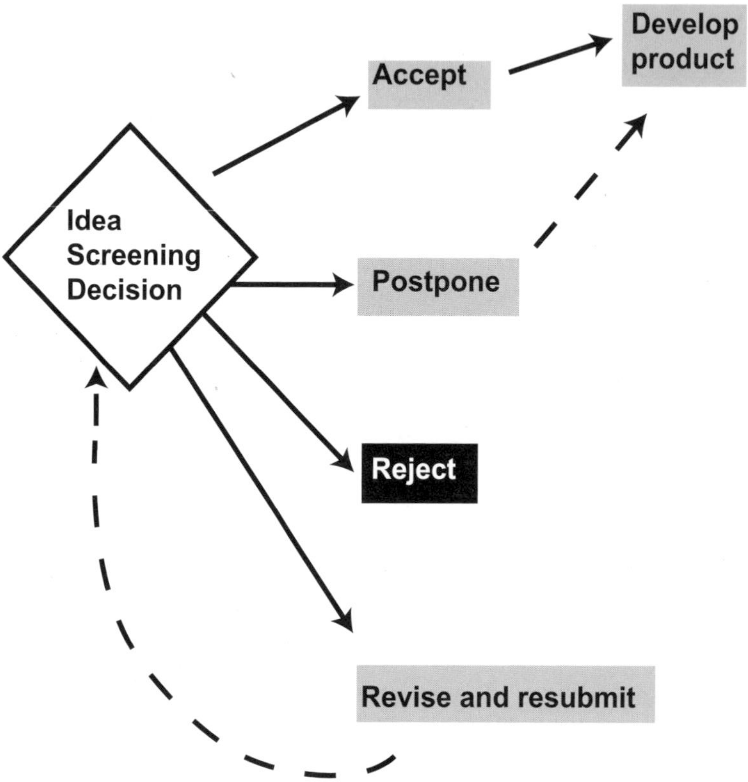

Figure 2.5: Decisions and Possible Outcomes

Regardless of the decision, it needs to be documented in some way, especially if the idea will be revisited later. This can be done through minutes of the meeting that is held, or a database of ideas that is updated, or whatever is appropriate within the company's infrastructure.

Okay, it's approved. Now what?

Once an idea makes its way through the screening and validation process, it's time to find an organizational home for it so that it can be developed into a product or a business. In the early days of the new venture process at TRW-ESL, we decided to find a line manager or business manager who could act as an "idea sponsor" so that the development could take place. Later on, when the executive decision was made to spin all new ventures out of the company, the designated home shifted to a strategic partner or new spun-out entity. Sometimes established companies decide to use an external strategic partner as a home for a new idea, or to spin it out as a separate division or company, just as we did at TRW-ESL. Then, things become more complicated. If either of these situations exists, there needs to be significant communication and discussion about how to set up the business entity (and if it's a partnership, negotiations are also involved). That takes a considerable amount of time. As soon as the decision is made to take the idea external, then a business operational plan or a partnering plan needs to be generated as soon as possible to avoid missing the market window.

Every idea that is approved needs an organizational home and someone to manage it who has the time, the commitment, the budget, and the responsibility to turn it into a product. If you're an entrepreneur, you have the same issue. You must have a development team in place and ready to go once you obtain your funding.

Using realistic decision criteria

The next six chapters (Chapters 3 through 8) focus on each of the six major decision criteria, their importance, and ways to customize them for your own company. At the end of each chapter is a list of factors to include in building your own criteria. Also at the end of each of these chapters is a list of conditions for rejecting or postponing a new product idea. This will help you understand how to apply the criterion to your internal and external situation. If you're an entrepreneur, these chapters will give you insight as to the considerations your investors may use to evaluate your ventures and business plans.

After the idea is approved, more decisions need to made

Once an idea is approved, there are many other decisions that need to be made during the remainder of the new product cycle. Decision-makers will need to choose the right marketing strategy, business model and partners, and will also need to find ways to speed up the product development phase. Those topics are addressed in Chapters 9 through 14. Further decisions are made during the launch phase, and Chapters 15 through 17 include launch solutions appropriate for the Internet Era.

Your decision-makers will be quite busy through the whole product cycle, and once they have been through it from beginning to end, you will find ways to improve the process for the next new product. Chapter 18 focuses on how to build your own repeatable new product process.

3

The Strategic Fit Criterion: Matching the Idea to the Company

Strategic fit refers to the degree of compatibility between a new product idea and your company's overall strategic direction. In order to evaluate an idea for strategic fit, it is important to examine the high-level objectives of your company at the time that the new idea is considered. You need to think about where your company is with regard to your overall business strategy, which core competencies you can apply, the nature of your company's culture, and your experience as a company with regard to business models and markets. In order to successfully develop a new idea, there has to be a fit between the idea and all of those factors. New products and ventures will define the future direction of your company, so you need to evaluate new ideas in terms of how they will help you achieve the business you want to be in.

Most of the time, a company considers new products or services when it is in startup mode or in growth mode. However, there can be other business events that prompt a search for new product ideas, such as changes in the competitive landscape, new strategic alliances, geographic expansion, and new technology developments. Whatever the circumstances, early in the screening process, you must evaluate your company's strategic fit with any potential new idea. This evaluation will raise some tough questions, and there will be many tradeoffs involved. This is true whether you are a small company with limited choices or a large company with more choices, but less capability to adapt to new ideas. This chapter presents the issues and considerations of strategic fit – the starting point for the new idea screening process.

The classic question: What business do you want to be in?

A company's business definition is a measuring stick for making decisions regarding growth, diversification, divestiture and strategic partnering. Decades ago, companies were able to define what business they were in, and then stick to that focus successfully for years at a time. Given the speed at which most companies move today, pursuing opportunities and keeping up with the competition can create subtle changes in the company's business focus overnight.

New ideas represent the business you *want* to be in for future growth. Whether or not a new idea can be developed successfully depends in large part on how different it is from your current business and whether you have sufficient resources to support that degree of change. For example, let's say that your company has been focused on developing and selling software through established channels, and now the company is considering becoming an application service provider. This shift in business focus is not vastly different from the original business and may actually provide additional revenue. If, however, your company decides instead to go into the chip business, that is a totally different business that would not enhance the primary business of the company. The first case will obviously be easier to implement than the second case. Even in the example of transitioning from software to the application service provider model, changes will be required in your infrastructure and your business model for delivering your product to your customer. Do you have the resources to do that quickly, and more importantly, do you have an understanding of that business? If not, is it possible to find strategic partners or engage in outsourcing to fill in the gaps? If so, it may be worth pursuing the new idea, but your plan must include the necessary time and money to find suitable strategic partners.

When I was at TRW-ESL, we were in diversification mode, and had a strategic goal of entering new businesses. However, we also knew from the beginning that no matter what type of venture we launched, it was going to require one or more partners, and we would not be able to develop the infrastructure ourselves. Because a new idea required us to be in a new business anyway, that by itself was not a reason for rejection. Instead, to differentiate between new ideas, we looked at other strategic factors such as core competencies, costs, market timing and fit with our strategic goals.

"If a company has a lot of expertise in an area of business, such as system integration, then it may be possible to extend that into other industries or market segments," suggests Fred Nikolac, Product Line General Manager at Acuson, a medical technology company. *"However, if you are entering a new business or market for which you don't have a core competency, you need to examine what you will be giving up to fund and staff a long, arduous process to build the new business."*

Any new product idea has the potential to shift the company into a new business, either because of the new focus resulting from the allocation of resources to the new product and resulting new focus, or because of the new product's ultimate success and profitability.

Core competencies affect the rate at which you can execute new ideas

Core competencies are the intellectual assets and collective experience that a company has accumulated from its ongoing operations. For years, companies have kept an evolving list of core competencies and technologies that reflect their recognized expertise in their industry and the marketplace. Companies have used core competencies to varying degrees in order to develop strategies, find partners, and make investment decisions. *"Almost every company attempts to identify their core competencies; however, few companies really know how to use them effectively when making key business decisions. Acuson is one of those companies; we do understand the importance of understanding and strengthening our core competencies and consider them a business asset,"* says Fred Nikolac. When faced with evaluating new ideas, companies need to revisit the most current list of competencies to assess the fit between the idea and their ability to develop the idea and take the resulting product to market. It can be argued that there are many successful examples of products that had little or no connection to the company's competencies. However, it is much easier, faster and cheaper to leverage what you know, who you know, and what you know how to do.

Carole Gum, Director of Corporate Marketing at Vertical Networks (a voice and data networking company) believes in a business strategy that has a firm foundation in core competencies. *"If you're a small company, it's critical to evaluate new opportunities in terms of the fit with your core competencies. Fewer resources constrain the ability to dabble in new markets. For a small company to grow, they must align their strategy with their core competencies, and make their new product decisions accordingly."*

At TRW-ESL, we had identified the core competencies that we would focus on for the new ventures program. Our core competencies were essentially areas of technology expertise and included digital and analog signal processing, mission and problem understanding, complex software algorithm development, and systems integration. Our policy was to stick to these core competencies when selecting new venture ideas to develop, because in our case they represented our only competitive advantage. Our technical core competencies were our primary strength, and they were the key to entering commercial markets and getting there in time.

Core competencies aren't limited to technology solutions, as illustrated in Figure 3.1. They can be any area of expertise for which the company has collectively accumulated specific knowledge successfully. Core competencies might be unique business models, knowledge of a market segment and the customers in it, the ability to deliver superior customer service, or a specific way of operating the company. Consider an example of a change in operational model: if a company has been selling servers and suddenly decides to go into the server-farm/hosting business, this represents a big change their day-to-day operations. Selling servers is a product-based business, whereas hosting is a transaction-based business. The company's infrastructure and resources may not be able to support the new business without major changes and upheaval.

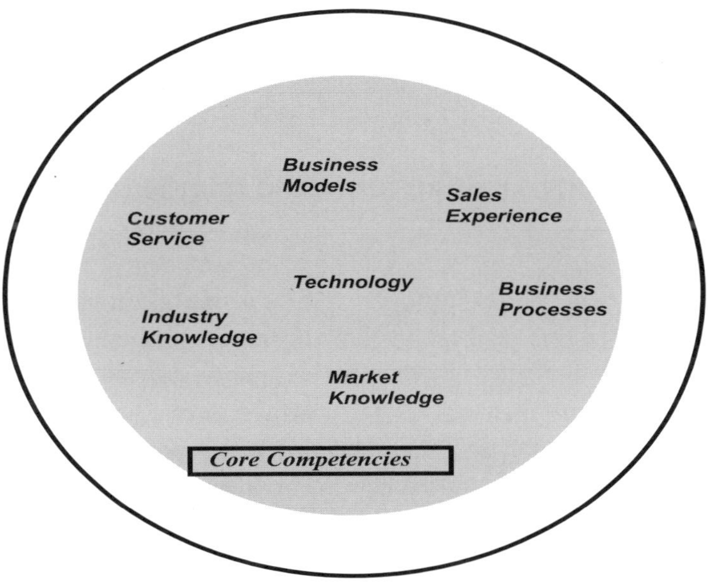

Figure 3.1: The Many Types of Core Competencies

Not only should you consider how an idea fits your list of core competencies, but you should also take it one step further and ask, "does your company have the experience and track record of applying your core competencies to the new idea being considered?" You need to be able to capitalize on the opportunity, which means you must know *how* to develop the appropriate solution. This was an important criterion for us at TRW-ESL. Even though our technical core competencies were our strength, every product idea would require us to apply our knowledge in a new way and for a different customer. This was not simply a question of having a gut-level confidence in our ability to do that. We required each idea champion to plan the technical solution in some detail before we were satisfied. *"Small companies need to focus on what they do well in order to survive,"* advises Carole Gum. *"At Vertical Networks, we have developed expertise in voice and data hardware and software, and the marketing of this technology. If a new idea would require us to sell services to our customers, we would likely reject the idea, unless the service was relevant to our hardware and software. In that case, we would probably outsource the services component."*

Your company's culture forms the foundation for new growth

When you evaluate new product ideas, it is important to assess their compatibility with your company's philosophy and way of doing business, elements of the company's overall culture. Corporate culture is something that evolves over a long period of time, and cannot be readily changed when a new product idea comes along. Often, the company culture is captured in mission or vision statements, as well as in branding campaigns. Attributes and phrases such as "dedication to customer service", "quality is our number one concern", and "leading-edge solutions for tomorrow's business environment" all say something about the shared beliefs of the company. Even a startup has some semblance of an overall purpose or vision. Companies have discovered that it is worth the time and effort to develop and maintain a unique corporate culture in order to attract and retain employees, keep people motivated, promote teamwork, and ultimately, to grow.

When new product and business ideas are implemented, they can impact the company culture, just as with any major change that occurs in a company. You need to assess the potential for an idea to disrupt the positive things about the company culture. For instance, a company that prides itself on its leading-edge technology may implement an idea that requires it to outsource the technology development to another company. What would that do to the technical staff? It probably means the "not invented here" attitude would start affecting the motivational environment, in turn affecting the overall culture in their company. If a new idea is not compatible with the culture, then companies should think twice about pursuing the idea, advises Fred Nikolac. *"Sometimes it's difficult to reject good ideas, but if the idea isn't a good fit with the current culture and it would take major change in the company to develop the product and business, then it's best to move on to other opportunities with a better fit."* Early on during the idea evaluation process, this issue may not seem that significant, but it can have a drastic effect in the long-term. New ideas should always be evaluated in the context of company culture.

"Company cultures are in a constant state of evolution," says Carole Gum. *"Our culture was very collaborative when the company was in its infancy. We have retained elements of that as we have grown and matured, but it's becoming tougher to manage. When faced with a new product idea, companies need to examine where their culture is in its evolution, in order to assess the impact of making drastic changes. If the company is ready for a change, then pursuing a new product may be an effective catalyst. However, most of the time, it's very difficult to change the corporate culture and takes a very long time."* Figure 3.2 illustrates some of the important elements of corporate culture.

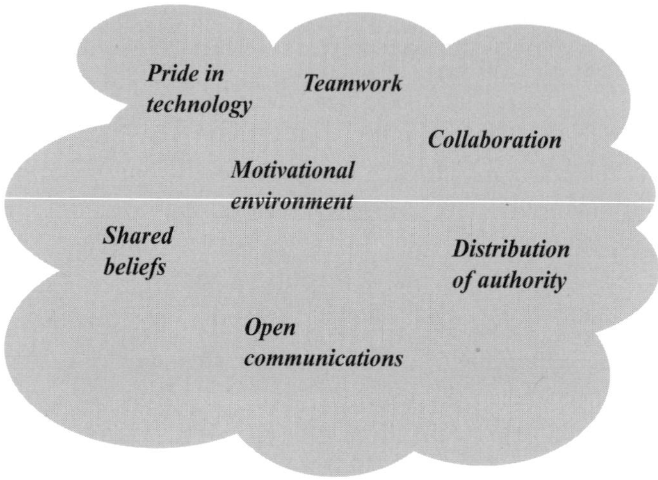

Figure 3.2: Elements of Corporate Culture

Your company's image and brand must also fit the new product idea

Another element of a company's strategy is its image in the marketplace, often reinforced in branding campaigns. Sometimes a new idea may require that the company modify its image in order to compete in a new market or to introduce a new type of product. To accomplish this may require significant investment and advertising costs. Additionally, the company may have to risk losing its reputation that was part of its old image, or risk confusing its customer base, which ultimately can reduce revenues. There is also an issue with retraining people inside the company regarding the new image and brand, which takes time. Consider a large and diversified company that sells computer hardware, whose brand is focused on the stability and strength of the company. If such a company wanted to start selling Internet-based services in a market that required it to be fast, agile and focused on individual customers, that would be a difficult transition to make externally and internally. Customers who bought hardware from such a company might be worried about whether the company is still stable or is divesting parts of the company to enter a new business. Conversely, customers for the new Internet-based services might be wondering whether such a large company can move quickly enough to serve their needs. The tradeoff here is between changing the brand and risking confusion among customers, or maintaining the current brand and facing a greater challenge in getting the new product to market. This tradeoff has to be considered early, because once you go down the path of changing the image, there is no going back. This is an important test of a new idea.

"Establishing a brand is very time-consuming and expensive. Small companies can only afford to maintain one brand – usually the company brand. As a company grows, it may be possible to develop one or more product brands, as well. However, if a new idea requires a wholesale change in company brand, that is a formidable task. Big companies may be able to pull it off with enough time and resources, but small companies shouldn't consider it," advises Carole Gum.

Your operational models must be compatible with new ideas

New products or services always have a measurable impact on a company's operations. Whether in the area of sales, customer support, manufacturing, or engineering, operational changes must be made in order to develop and market the new ideas that make it all the way through the new product cycle. These changes can be far-reaching and expensive, so at the early stages of idea evaluation, the impact to internal operations should be estimated. There are two parts to this: figuring out *how* to change the operational models, and estimating the costs of doing so.

A company's business model defines how it produces and then delivers its products to the customer, from the supply chain all the way through to final delivery to the end user. (Chapters 10 and 11 in this book address business model mapping in strategy in greater detail, but business models are mentioned here because they should be considered as part of your business strategy during the idea screening phase.) Sometimes, new ideas will require new partners, suppliers, or distributors that aren't present in the existing business model. *"We looked at the ASP model as a way to expand our market presence. On the surface, it was very attractive, but we decided we weren't in the services business, so we pursued a partnering relationship instead. That enabled us to stick to our core competencies but still pursue a new way to deliver our technology to the customer,"* says Carole Gum. It's important to consider this early on during the idea evaluation process, because it can take a long time – months or years – to identify and engage new partners that you need in order to get the new product to market on time.

"Sometimes companies pursue new business models without realizing the impact it has on existing operations, or knowing how to really implement the new model," says Fred Nikolac. *"Partnering can help in that situation, but there is a downside, also. Unless you have the resources to really manage and control the partner relationship, you could miss out on learning the new business model, and worst case, could even the lose the business entirely to a partner."* Business model decisions are very strategic, and have far-reaching impact on the company when you make changes. Every new product idea needs to be evaluated in this context.

New ideas often mean unfamiliar customers and markets

If you are taking a new product into a new market, you have a tremendous challenge ahead of you. It's also quite challenging to take a new product to your own customer base; even your existing customers may react in an unexpected way to the new product you introduce. The key question: is your company capable of successfully entering an unfamiliar market? If you have a track record of doing this, then it will be easier to do this again. But if you have never done it before, this could mean more time involved to study and know a new market. By that time, will your competitor already be there? It's a question of timing and market knowledge; to be successful with a new product, you need both.

At TRW-ESL, we identified some of the markets that we thought would be most feasible, based not only on our technical core competencies, but also on the knowledge that we had in the company. We chose three primary markets on which to focus our new venture efforts: wireless telecommunications, information processing for decision-makers, and transportation systems. The first of these three leveraged our signal processing expertise, giving us a technology edge over the potential competitors. The other two markets were based partially on core competencies, but also on collective knowledge from other TRW divisions that were in the information and automotive businesses. We felt we had the best chance for success in these markets based on what we knew. Companies that have been successful at acquisitions such as Cisco Systems, also leverage the collective expertise they gain through an acquisition when they enter new or unfamiliar markets. It pays to take an internal "inventory" of the collective knowledge and skills you have available to you when considering the potential of new markets. Your strategic partners should also be considered sources of this knowledge.

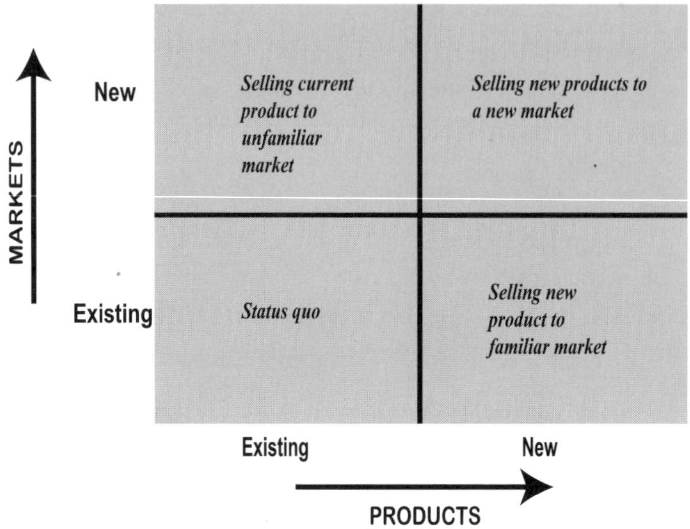

Figure 3.3: New Products, New Markets

A significant challenge exists if the new idea is "ahead-of-market" , that is, you are introducing a new product to a new market early, requiring much education of the customer (otherwise known as 'evangelism'). In this case, not only is your own company unfamiliar with the market, but the customers often don't know they need the product. Essentially, the market has not yet materialized. This is often referred to as the "new-new" quadrant of business opportunity: new product and new market. To introduce new products in this situation requires a core competency in market development, and much experience in being first to market.

Many of the venture ideas we considered at TRW-ESL were ahead of market demand. Often, our technology solutions were too "leading-edge" to make them commercially viable. We didn't want to follow a technology push strategy whereby we had a product looking for a market. That would have required us to create a new market first, and we did not have the expertise to do that at the time. Even the most successful companies have encountered this situation of introducing products too early.

Apple Computer's Newton was developed in the early 1990s, yet it took nearly eight years and the introduction of wireless phones, messaging, and then the Palm Pilot before the market for palmtop computers gained some momentum. A similar situation currently exists with low-priced Internet appliances; within an eight-month period of time, at least four companies introduced these devices, only to pull them off the market again. It's almost impossible to predict how long it will take a product to catch on, but during the idea evaluation phase, it's important to do this reality check: is the market ready, and does your company have the experience, track record and resources to pull it off? Figure 3.3 is a grid that illustrates some of the new product and new market scenarios your company may face.

Making the decision about strategic fit

The list below outlines the elements of the strategic fit criteria that should be considered in making the new product decision. You need to craft criteria that work in the context of your company. In applying the criteria, you must decide whether to develop, reject or postpone the new product idea. The "Reject/ Postpone" list is a suggested guideline for that decision, that appears here as well as at the end of each of next five chapters. These two lists can be used a quick reference for you to use in developing criteria and making new product decisions. Your own company's criteria and guidelines may be different.

Strategic Fit Criteria – categories to include:

-the business you're in and want to be in
-core competencies
-company culture
-fit with operational and business models
-new product/new market experience

REJECT the idea if:

-you have no core competencies to develop the product or service
-it would create an obstacle to meeting strategic goals
-major revamp of business operations would be required
-it would disrupt the internal corporate culture
-the new product would require a new company image campaign

POSTPONE the idea if:

-the idea is more than 12 months ahead of market
-the new product would require finding and developing new strategic partners

4

The Customer Criterion: A Renewed Focus on the Customer

There have been a great number of books published in the last five years about the importance of the customer; several are listed in Appendix A. Companies have finally figured out that customers have increasing power in the marketplace and they are not timid about wielding it. Not recognizing this can put a company out of business. Accordingly, the slogans and vision statements of many companies now include some reference to the customer. Keeping the potential customer in mind when screening new product ideas is critical. In addition to studying the potential end user of your new product, you may also have to be aware of your customer's customer, and what value your product brings to them (or, their "value proposition"). It's all part of an increasingly complex chain of value propositions that your new product must satisfy. This is especially true if your new product is a business-to-business product, and your target customer uses your product in providing products and services to their own customers. If you plan on selling the new product through distribution channels, this "double" value proposition will also be a factor. Studying this chain of value must be done during the idea selection and validation phase of the new product cycle, to make sure that your new product can deliver the appropriate value to all the stakeholders who will be involved.

Another aspect of value that comes into play is the value of your target customer to your company. Instead of merely studying buying behavior, it is necessary to evaluate potential customers in terms of their value to your company for generating *profit.* I call this the "Customer's Profit Value", or "CPV". CPV takes into account the potential profit derived from serving a new customer from the beginning to the end of the new product cycle. (It's possible to roughly calculate the CPV, and later in this chapter is a formula and discussion that shows how to apply this concept.) If we learned anything from the dot-com decline, it is that making lots of customers aware of your company is important, but you must generate profit from them. Evaluating ideas from this perspective should help eliminate the losers from the idea pile.

When considering a new product opportunity, your company needs to determine if you can sell it to your existing customer base, or if it will require new customers. If the customer is new, there will be considerably more time and expense involved in validating the new product idea. Even if you are selling to existing customers, you must still determine whether the new product will fit their value proposition. If you're an entrepreneur, you will likely be faced with a "new-new" situation – selling a new product to a new customer. Whatever the situation, there are many factors to consider in order to effectively apply the customer criterion to your new product idea.

Which comes first, the product or the customer?

Companies and entrepreneurs bring new products to market either by developing a product and looking for a customer (a very popular approach), or by studying customer problems and then building a product that solves them. There is little doubt that starting with the customer first and then developing the product is a much more profitable approach in the long run. *"In the last two years, there have been a few examples of companies who have succeeded at technology push, but only if they also happen to meet the needs of a target customer. The lessons of the dot-com boom and bust have shown us that,"* says Brooks Fisher, Chief

Marketing Officer, Intuit Corporation, a financial software company.

Companies are getting better at creating and developing products in response to the customer's need, the so-called "market pull" approach. Figure 4.1 illustrates the difference between market pull and product push. Even if an established company has been effective in using a "product push" or "technology push" strategy, adopting this approach can take considerable time and effort. It's hard to argue with success. The design team feels confident that the technology is so cool and the product is so perfect that customers will flock to it. It's a lot more fun for the developers to have this freedom to create, but the company must also be able to sell what is created. Sometimes it takes a profound change in the idea evaluation process in order to implement "market pull" thinking.

At TRW-ESL, our entrepreneurs were engineers who had very creative ideas for technology applications. When they entered the incubator, the first thing we did was to get them to start thinking about customers and the problems that needed to be solved. This often curbed the entrepreneurs' enthusiasm, but eventually they understood how important it was for the venture's success. When we screened the entrepreneur's idea, the first three questions we asked were all about the customer and their problem:

-What is the problem to be solved?
-Who is the customer?
-What's the compelling reason to buy?

If the idea could not solve an *existing* problem in the market, we rejected it. If the idea could solve a problem that no one was really interested in solving, we rejected it. If someone else was already providing an adequate solution to the problem, we rejected it. That was a lot of rejection for the entrepreneurs to handle, but we did not want to go down the path of product/technology push. We had to make sure we created products that someone really needed, and needed soon.

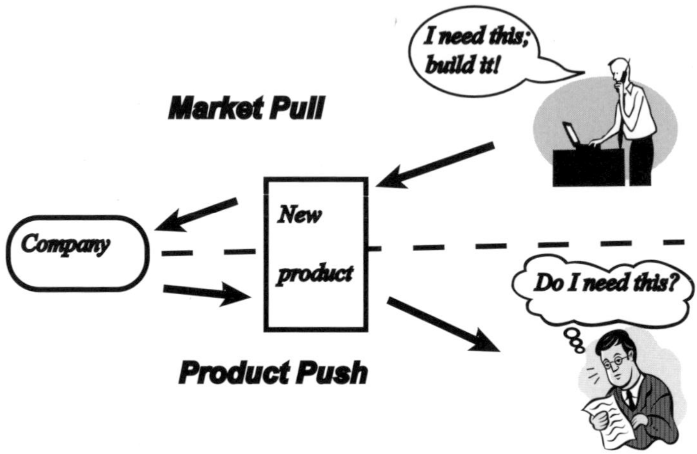

Figure 4.1: Market Pull Versus Product Push

Customer involvement is the key

With high-tech products that are very complex or expensive, customers may not know what they want. In that case, companies may build a prototype of a product and then work with the customer to further define features as the development proceeds. Bob Yee, Marketing Manager at Cisco Systems, says this is the case with some of the product lines at Cisco. *"We often create an early prototype and then work with the customer to further refine the technical requirements. Sometimes, until the customers see a basic technology mockup, they may not be able to visualize the fit with their particular problem. Having something visible or tangible helps bridge that gap. This approach also helps ensure that the product is designed and developed with the specific features and functionality that the customer wants and will pay for."*

If possible, get your customers involved in helping to develop new product ideas. That's also the best way to conduct the validation step of the new product cycle. It will help your company adjust to the market pull approach, and it will help build long-term relationships, because your customers will feel that you are listening to their feedback.

Who is the customer?

You may be selling to a known customer base or to an entirely new customer. In either case, you must characterize the human beings who have a specific need for this product or service. It's necessary to find the individual or individuals who have a problem and who are willing to pay money for the solution. This is the first step in market validation: who is the customer?

One of the things we did in the TRW-ESL incubator was to require that entrepreneurs engage in cold calling to speak with potential customers. The entrepreneurs were not happy about this, but the new ventures staff helped out by providing some training in how to formulate questions, conduct interviews, and how to sell. In one example, the venture team actually discovered an entirely new product by going through this step. The team was hoping to develop a product to improve quality of wireless telephone service at the base stations. One of the team members did some cold calling to cellular providers, and after being transferred several times, ended up speaking with someone who had the title of "Director of Revenue Assurance". That executive told our team member about the cellular fraud problem, and how much it was costing the company. Subsequently we did more research on the industry to figure out just how widespread the problem was, and we discovered a very large potential market for a solution. One thing led to another, and ultimately, the venture team developed a fraud detection and prevention system that was later spun out; it's still a successful company today. Not only does it pay to talk to potential customers to learn about problems, but also at a more basic level, this can help you define who your customer really is. It also can lead you down a whole new product path – and perhaps a more profitable one.

It takes some searching to find the target customer. Cisco's Bob Yee recommends following the food chain. *"The customer is defined as the person with the problem who is willing to pay money for a solution. If you examine the market space or industry you are targeting, and identify the entities in the food chain, you will eventually find the customer. Sometimes it surprises you, and the person you thought had the problem may not be the person who will pay the money to solve it."* Sometimes the end user of your product or service is not the person who has the decision-making authority to buy the product, but they may be in a position to influence the decision-maker to buy it. If that is the case, then you must satisfy the needs of the end user as well as those of the person writing the check for your product. Both of these individuals are regarded as customers because there is intent to buy it. However, if there is a person who has the problem that can be solved with your product, but who won't or can't pay the money to solve it, then that person is not regarded as a customer. It's a matter of intent and likelihood of sale.

Knowing your customer creates market pull

The more you know about your customer, the more easily you can develop a product that will serve their needs. Studying the customer will also help you validate your product or venture idea, and takes you one step further down the new product path. Once you know who your target customer is, it pays to use a number of different study techniques. Techniques such as secondary and primary market research, pilot tests, surveys, focus groups, and participation in user groups can all help to gather more information. At the most basic level, it helps to *talk* directly to customers.

One of the techniques we used in the TRW-ESL incubator was the "application scenario" approach that is part of Geoffrey Moore's "bible" on high-tech marketing: *Crossing the Chasm* (see Appendix A – Recommended Reading). For each venture idea, we compiled a scenario, based on information we obtained by talking to potential customers. Each scenario included the profile of a typical customer, their problem, current solution, and how our idea would solve the problem: a "before and after" look at a customer.

Another way to do this is to role-play, as if you were the customer. *"You need to look at what the customer goes through, where the problems and issues are, how they are solving a problem now, and most importantly, what their alternatives are,"* says Bob Yee. *"To do this effectively, you first need to have a thorough understanding of the customer's infrastructure and operational model, however."* If you don't know enough about your customer's business environment, you need to research it and talk to them directly.

Studying your industry and market space can also help tremendously. At Media Snap, President and CEO Kathy DeMartini gathers information about customer needs from many sources. *"We attend conferences and seminars that focus on our customer's issues. That's a good way to stay current with the problems that our customers have and how they might be trying to solve them. Information gleaned from these sources gives us more of a context for the more specific information that we gather during customer surveys and interviews."* The following table (4.1) is a checklist of questions to ask potential customers.

Table 4.1
What to Ask a Potential Customer

-What's your most pressing business issue?
-How are you addressing this now?
-What obstacles are there to solving the problem?
-When does the problem need to be solved?
-Who decides how the problem will be solved?
-Do you have the budget to solve the problem?
-Who writes the check?

Value propositions

A value proposition is a statement of the value that your product would have to your target customers, as perceived by your customers and as defined in their terms. Determining the customer's value proposition continues to be a quick and useful way to summarize the benefits that customers derive from your company solving their problem. Another phrase often associated with the value proposition is "compelling reason to buy". This refers to the "why" of the customer's buying behavior. Both expressions imply the concept of value from the customer's perspective.

A good way to think about this is in terms of pain. Your customer's level of pain, the urgency to remove the pain, and what it's worth to them to remove the pain are all components of the value proposition, according to Kathy DeMartini of Media Snap. *"Customers may be accustomed to a certain level of pain and are willing to put up with it. The relative urgency is an important factor. If you look for true pain and true urgency, and you have the solution to remove the pain now, then your product or service will sell because it fits their value proposition."* That's also an indication that at least one customer is ready for your product solution.

Once you figure out the customer's value proposition, the next question to ask is: Can we deliver to this value proposition? There are two parts to this:

-Can you solve the problem (the *how)*?
-Can you deliver the value the customer is looking for, in terms of *when* and *how much (price)?*

The first part (solving the problem) may seem obvious. After all, your company is in the business of developing solutions, right? However, the key is to develop the solution that the customer wants, not what the engineers want to develop for fun. That's why they call it the *customer* value proposition, not the *developer's* value proposition. At TRW-ESL (as with many technology-driven companies), it was tempting to over-engineer the solution and make it more elegant by adding bells and whistles. But if those bells and whistles don't have any value to your customer, or if they make the customer think that the price will be higher and less affordable, then you are missing the mark. It's critical to view the solution from the customer's point of view. At the most basic level, this means that the new product should be designed and built to meet the customer's need, from the very beginning of the development cycle.

The second part (timing and price of delivering the solution) is another challenge. You must be able to deliver the right solution precisely when the customer needs it – not ahead of time and not too late. This is not so easy to do, especially with products that have a long development cycle. Timing may also affect the eventual price of the product, since changing market dynamics and internal company financial issues play a part in determining a new product's price. What will the price have to be when the product is ready to go to market?

To understand a customer's value proposition, it is very useful to obtain feedback directly from the customer during a pilot, prototype or alpha test stage. In the TRW-ESL incubator, we required the entrepreneurs to identify an "early beta" customer who was willing to participate in a product demo. This was done during the market validation phase, and it helped us clarify the value proposition before we proceeded further with the idea.

Sometimes when you attempt to characterize the value proposition of a new customer, you can find ways to sell other services to your customers. *"It helps to keep an open mind about how you will deliver your product or service and listen to your customers describe their problem and what's important to them. You may discover a new service that you could sell as a complement to your original product that might address a related problem – like a solution within a solution,"* says Kathy DeMartini. Additional services might include an agreement to purchase latest releases of a software product, online product documentation subscriptions, recycling and upgrade programs, or moving some product functionality online so that customers can access it over a network – all of which are potential revenue-generating services.

The customer must have money to spend

What is a realistic amount of money that your target customer can afford to pay? If they don't have that much money, then they are not going to buy your product. For example, if your idea is for a product that will be priced in the tens of thousands of dollars, and you believe that the small business market needs this product, then think again. You need to make sure that your customer can be an "economic buyer" of your product. In other words, the product must be affordable for them, and they must be willing to pay the price to solve their problem. A pricing sensitivity analysis only answers part of the question – and that is, what is the range of prices that a potential buyer considers "fair"? It doesn't mean that the customer can afford to pay that price.

Kathy DeMartini believes that you need to study your customer well enough so that you can assess their budget constraints and economic considerations. *"Price is a subjective thing, and it relates to the level of pain your customer is experiencing. You should sell your product based on the solution and value you are providing, not the price. If the customer believes that the value proposition is being met, and if they are honest with you about what they are willing to pay, then they can afford to buy it. Quite often, they will come right out and tell you whether or not they can afford it."*

The key question: Will they buy your product or service?

In the TRW-ESL new ventures incubator, we used to ask the entrepreneurs, "Will the dog eat the dog food?" This was the gut-wrenching question that everyone dreaded, because it's hard to know whether a customer will buy the product. The best way to assess that is to *ask* a potential customer. We required the entrepreneurs to identify customers who would be willing to evaluate a pilot or prototype of the product, and then gain their commitment to participate. This was primarily done to assess the likelihood of customer purchase, and at what price. It also was an effective way to get the entrepreneurs to focus on the first customer sale. Learning from the first customer sale can be a tremendous help in figuring how to sell to the second and the third, and yields a lot of insight on length of sales cycle, which in turn helps forecast longer-term sales.

In an established company, you often will know enough about the general marketplace and customer behavior to have a pretty good idea of whether customers will buy the new product. *"At Intuit, we look at adjacent businesses that overlap in some way with the new idea. We have access to those existing customers, who have enough of an intuitive understanding of our product lines to give us feedback on a new idea. Once we describe the new idea, we simply ask these customers if they'd buy it and what they'd pay for it,"* says Brooks Fisher.

"With new products, it's a good idea to find an 'early adopter' who is willing to be a pioneer. You might even want to give them the product to play with and see how they use it, and what questions they ask. Obtain feedback from them on what would make them buy it, when they are planning to make a decision and who would be writing the check. After that, you'll have a much better idea about the possibility of the sale. For this to be successful, this early adopter must be candid and objective with you," advises Kathy DeMartini.

Timing is another critical element. Maybe a target customer won't buy your product now, but they might six months from now, when they have the budget or when the need becomes more critical. If you can afford to wait for a few customers to come through, that's fine, but if the majority of your target customers will be in waiting mode, then perhaps it's too early to develop this product – the market may not be ready for it yet. At TRW-ESL, one of our detailed criteria was whether the customer needed to solve the problem *now* and was willing to pay money for it *now.* If they didn't, we would either reject the idea or postpone it to re-evaluate a few months later.

It's easy to make the mistake of assuming that your customer will buy your product just because there's a good fit with the value proposition. Even well established companies become complacent and assume their customer base will buy their new products. However, it is critical to validate this notion with the customer, in order to allocate your scarce resources to the products that will generate the revenue.

Look at the sales cycle, not just marketing

When customer studies are done in the idea validation stage, the marketing factors frequently take center stage. Often an idea makes it all the way through the development process and then is dropped in the laps of salespeople who then must figure out how to sell the latest and greatest new thing. This is a mistake. You need to identify (and name!) the first, second, third, and perhaps fourth customers who will buy this new product. Then you need to examine what it will cost the company to complete the first sales cycle and then subsequent sales cycles all the way through closing. In order to do this, you must *involve* sales people during the idea screening and validation phase. Role-playing a selling situation for the new product is a great way to assess how difficult it might be to sell the product. This will give you a much better idea of what it will cost to serve the customer for this new product, which is a big factor in whether or not this new idea will be a profitable one. 'Serving' the customer means providing a satisfactory experience before, during and after the sale of the product. Sales people are in the best position to know what is required to provide that level of customer experience.

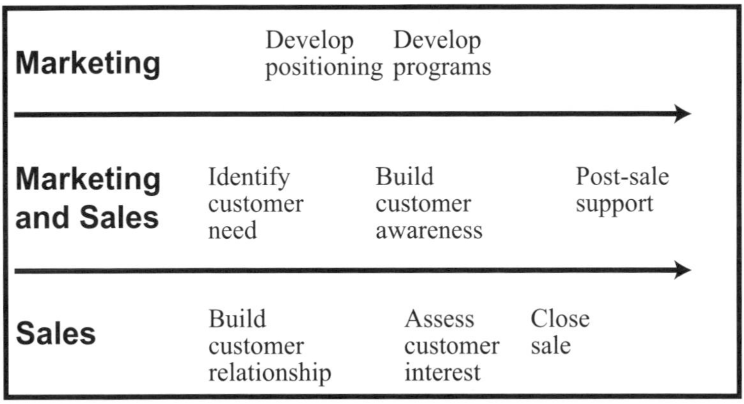

Figure 4.2: The Marketing and Sales Cycle

"The sales force is usually the first interface point with a customer," says Kathy DeMartini. *"Sales people are the individuals who build the relationship with the customer. In building that relationship, they will know more about the customer and therefore how long it will take to close a sale. They should definitely be consulted early on in the process."* Figure 4.2 illustrates the relationship between the sales and marketing cycles for a new product.

Your distributors and other strategic partners also can provide information. *"For some of our product lines, we don't have a direct sales force. In that case, we get our channel partners involved to discuss how we will handle strategy and pricing for new product ideas,"* says Brooks Fisher of Intuit.

The Customer's Profit Value (CPV) – a new screening criterion

The Customer's Profit Value (CPV) is a rule of thumb measure that can be used to decide whether this new product has customers who might generate profit for your company. The CPV takes into account the cost of serving that customer, and their likelihood of buying the product at a certain price, resulting in an estimate of the profitability for a given customer. Why should a company evaluate the CPV; after all, isn't every potential customer a desirable one to target? Not if your current infrastructure can't support certain types of customers. *"Large customers who have strong purchasing power often demand much more time and attention, or additional services and customization. This can stress various organizations, such as sales and customer support, to constantly meet the challenges. For a large company, the infrastructure may be in place to handle new customers who demand these things, but a smaller company may have to build the expensive infrastructure to do business with such customers. You really have to evaluate the customer's value to your company versus the price they will pay – and the impact on your bottom line,"* advises Bob Yee. This is something that needs to be considered at the product idea stage, before investment is made in the necessary infrastructure. It is truly a balancing act, as shown in Figure 4.3.

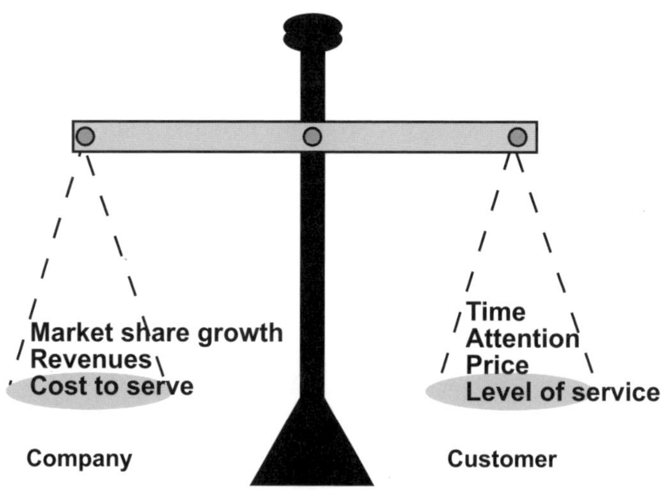

Figure 4.3: Company Value Versus Company Value

Another critical element of the cost to serve a customer is the timing. *"Sometimes customer take too long to make decisions, and you simply can't afford to wait. You need to aim for the least expensive sale, relative to dollars spent and attention focused on a single customer; or, in other words, try to harvest the low-hanging fruit,"* says Kathy DeMartini. Brooks Fisher at Intuit takes this concept one step further. *"We do lifetime value cost of our customers, especially when we are considering new products. We have learned over the years that it really pays to do this type of modeling. New companies don't have the luxury of historical data, so they would have to guess at the costs. Nevertheless, it's a great way to get a more precise handle on the cost of acquiring, distributing to and serving your customers – throughout the product life."*

The relative profitability of customers deserves some serious attention in the earliest part of the new product cycle, before the product enters the development phase. It's difficult to estimate the quantitative measure of CPV at that stage of the product cycle, especially if the target customer is unfamiliar. However, if some information can be gathered from the sales force and from the customer's value proposition, it is possible to make a rough calculation of this. The following discussion is a hypothetical example of calculating CPV:

There are three components to the calculation of CPV:

CLB = Typical customer's likelihood of buying (a percentage)
P = The estimated price of the product or service (based on value proposition)
SC = Cost to sell to a typical customer (based on sales cycle)
PC = post-sale costs for a successful sale
CPV = (P-PC) – SC/CLB
Taking an example, let's say that your product is priced at $10,000, and your cost to sell to a typical, potential customer is $2000, because of the amount of education involved in the process. If you are successful, there is an additional $1000 post-sale

cost for ongoing support. You also think that there is a 25% chance that a typical customer would buy, because it's a cutting-edge technology and therefore presents some risk for customer acceptance. The CPV = (10,000 – 1000) – 2000/. 25 = $1000.

That's a pretty small number to cover the cost of developing and producing the product or to generate return on investment for your company. Maybe this idea is too costly to sell (now) or more demand must be created to increase the likelihood that customers will buy. Whatever you use for the numbers, applying this measure can be a real eye-opener.

Customers must fit your company and profit goals

Customers do have growing power in today's economy. *"In many industries, the path to survival is consolidation, and customers will continue to have increasing purchasing power. Companies compete on the basis of having 'account control'. You also need the corporate vision, philosophy and follow-through to develop the right reputation for customer satisfaction in order to retain customers. That takes money and commitment to do it well,"* according to Bob Yee. Customers are indeed the most critical part of the new product equation. You must study them, understand them, and listen to them. Most importantly, you need to develop the new products that will meet their needs and that they will buy.

However, you should also be realistic about whether your company can truly be successful selling the new product to the targeted customer base. Your goal should not be to "obtain customers at any cost" because at some point you may not be able to pay those costs, and your bottom line will suffer. You must be willing to objectively assess the profit value you can gain from the target customer that "comes with" the new product idea, and reject the idea if it won't contribute to your profitability.

NOTE: The following chart contains categories to include when developing new product selection criteria. You need to craft criteria that work in the context of your company; these are merely suggestions. Additionally, the "Reject/Postpone" recommendations are a quick checklist to use in making new product decisions. Your own company's guidelines for rejecting or postponing a new product idea may be different.

Customer Criteria – Categories to include:

-value proposition from customer's point of view
-value propositions of your customer's customer and distribution channels
-detailed knowledge of customer and their buying behavior
-likelihood that customer will buy
-affordability of product by customer
-sales cycle issues
-Customer's Profit Value

REJECT the idea if:

-value proposition is ambiguous
-you can't deliver the value required – throughout the value chain
-product not affordable by customer
-you don't have a precise solution to the customer problem
-sales cycle too long given dynamics of marketplace
-CPV is too low

POSTPONE the idea if:

-likelihood of customer purchase low but has potential
-evangelism is involved in sales cycle
-price is too high for customer now

5

The Competition Criterion: Competitive Analysis and Constant Vigilance

Evaluating the competition is one of the key steps in characterizing the external marketplace for your product idea. Idea champions and entrepreneurs are fond of saying that they have no competition – at least not yet. However, that depends on how you define "competitor". Is it a company that is established in the marketplace selling similar products? Is it a company that has an identical product in the market? Is it a company that is in your target market space but isn't selling similar products? Is it the company that provides the alternative solution that your customer is using now to partially or mostly solve their problem? The answer to all of these questions is: Yes! Most people only consider similar products from known competitors. However, it is a mistake to overlook the other possibilities, especially during the idea phase.

Competitive analysis is a matter of studying a target that is constantly changing. You will need to keep an eye on the competitive environment from the time your new product idea is being validated until you retire the product line. Assumptions that you make when you approve a product idea for development can drastically change by the time you are ready to launch, so you will need to continuously monitor the competitive environment. Only by doing so will you be able to make informed decisions about strategy and planning during the rest of the new product cycle.

The best way to approach competitive analysis when you are in the idea phase is to gather as much information about the existing and potential competitors that you will encounter *for the new idea.* Bear in mind that these may not be the same competitors you already know and love! New product ideas often can take your company into new markets where there are companies that are new to you, and you must figure out how your company can perform in that competitive environment. Evaluating the competitive environment is the first step in applying the competition criterion to the new product idea. Once you have characterized the environment and evaluated your company's ability to compete in that environment, then you should do a company-by-company comparison for the competitors that you identify.

Everyone's moving faster, including your competition

Today's economy is moving so fast that every company is constantly under pressure to get to the marketplace; your competitors are in the same mode as your own company. A company's competitive position can change significantly overnight. Changes in the economy can eliminate a competitor. Or, a competitor can launch a new product or announce a technology breakthrough. Other possible changes include merger or acquisition, announcement of strategic partners, resignation of an executive, financial downturns and layoffs, quarterly earnings reports and analysts' reactions. Almost any news or announcement that might appear in a company press release can have a major impact on a competitor's reputation, ability to perform, customer satisfaction rating, and market share. Studying competitors indeed requires focusing on a moving target.

"Even when you monitor the marketplace on a quarterly basis, events can prompt the need for an update to the competitive landscape. If you're in an industry that has fast product development cycles like

networking or software, then you must do this continuously," says Carole Gum, Director of Corporate Marketing at Vertical Networks. Ciree J. Loftus, Software Development Manager at Luminate, concurs. *"If you are introducing a new product or using a new business model to provide products and services to the marketplace, you should do a competitive analysis at least every three months."*

Today it's more difficult to track the changing dynamics of competitors, due to their accelerated rate of change, and the Internet era has certainly contributed to that increase in pace. At the same time, however, Internet technologies also make it easier to find information more quickly so that the competitive analysis can be done.

You must study the competitive environment for the new idea, not your existing products

If your company is an established company with several product lines, you already have a lot of knowledge about your competitors for the existing products. When you evaluate a new product idea, you should not simply assume that you would be dealing with the same old competitors. Any time you make even a subtle change to product functionality or features, it creates the possibility that there might be other companies out there who could develop something identical to it, and they may not be in your market space yet. That's why it's imperative to start from ground zero when a new product idea comes along. Evaluate the competitive environment with "new eyes".

"We evaluate companies with both similar technologies and existing comparable products," says Ciree J. Loftus. *"We examine the price, market size, and customer satisfaction and usefulness of existing products. Our goal is to determine whether we can* provide a

more valuable new solution for the customer, and we look at the cost of delivering the value to that customer."

When you are in the mode of considering new product ideas, there may be companies out there undergoing a similar exercise, and you may not know about them until you have moved your idea into the development phase. Sometimes it's a matter of making predictions as to which companies might enter the new market space in the future, along with identifying those who are already there.

How to identify competing companies and solutions

As part of your analysis of the customer, you may already have some information about what the customer currently uses to solve their problem – either partially or in total. That alternative should be regarded as a competing solution. You need to give that as much weight as you would a company that has an identical product to yours. When you get ready to do your competitive research and analysis, this is the place to start: what are the substitutes and alternatives that the customer uses now?

"When you begin to evaluate a new product idea or to add new functionality, it's important to keep it broad and look at all the alternatives. You must consider the customer's point of view and need above everything else. For instance, when developing our IP telephony technology strategy, we need to consider what the customer is using today and what their expectations are. There may be several ways to implement a technology solution, so the customer's current situation is the starting point before we develop the new product," says Carole Gum.

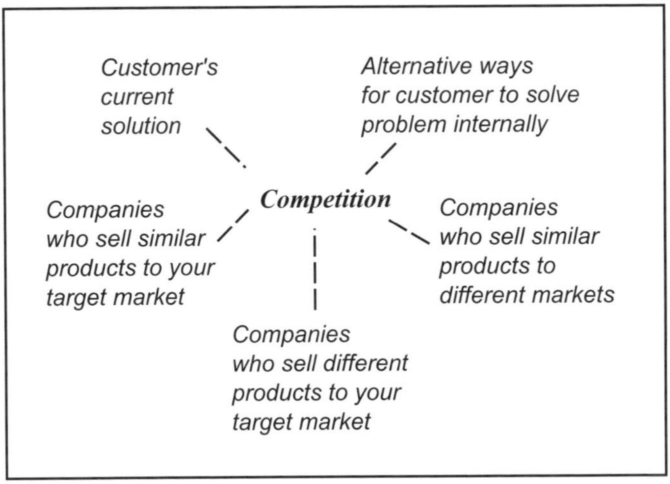

Figure 5.1: Types of Competitors

The most common type of competitor is a company that sells similar or identical products into the market segment that you have targeted for your new idea. *"We define competitor as a company that sells products or services that affect our market share,"* says Ciree J. Loftus. *"More specifically, it's a company that is selling into our target markets and where the customer base feels that only one product or service is necessary to fulfill their needs."* Even with this definition of competitor, it's important to keep the customer's perspective in mind, because ultimately it is the customer who chooses what to buy and from whom.

At TRW-ESL, we considered many types of competing solutions; they included existing alternatives that customers were using that they had developed themselves, a competitor that already had a comparable existing solution, and companies who already had products in the market that we were targeting. In our view, they were all possible threats. Figure 5.1 shows the spectrum of competition.

What to study about your competition

Now that you have some idea who your competitors might be, what information is needed in order to validate the new product idea? At the highest level, you will need information about your competitors and their companies, such as their financial status, their size, significant partners and strategic alliances, and their reputation in the marketplace. At the next level of detail, you will need information about their existing and planned products and services, along with pricing information, if available. Table 5.1 lists the information that you need to gather and evaluate. Your eventual goal is to develop a list of competitor names and then compile a matrix to compare those companies and products with your company and your new product idea.

Table 5.1:
Key Competitor Attributes to Consider

Company Level	*Product Level*
-Financial health -Company history -Size (revenues, employees) -Public or private -Strategic partners -Market reputation -Brand strength	-Features/functions -Price -Sales history -Customer success stories -Product history -Number, type of products -Familiarity with target customer

Where can you get this information? Start within your own company. *"During our pre-sales process, we gather sales information on the receptiveness of the potential customer. Whenever possible, we ascertain the issues behind lack of interest, price concerns, competing products, or lack of need. That's a good way to learn about competitors in the market space,"* says Ciree J. Loftus. This technique can help you gather competitive information for the new products you are already selling, as well as those that are currently in the idea phase.

You can also obtain a lot of information about competitors on the Internet. Company websites, trade journals, and organized database services are a great place to get very detailed information about competing companies. Companies are being more careful about the information that they post on their websites, and they will often request that you register before requesting detailed documents such as white papers or technical specs. However, a lot of information can be obtained by reading press releases and marketing information. If they are a public company, then their annual reports will also help in finding pertinent information.

Other external sources of information include industry analyst reports or media publications, and industry conferences and tradeshows. Conferences and tradeshows are a good way to get a current look at what the competitors are promoting, and the messages that they are using.

Screening the competitive environments – the first order of business

The conventional way of doing competitive analysis involves much research, analysis of attributes of the competing companies, a feature-by-feature comparison of the competing products, and identification of differentiators. You still need to do those things during the idea validation phase. However, higher-level evaluations that will help you screen your idea and look at the larger picture of the competitive environment that you will be entering should be done first. This involves identifying who is there already, as well as who could be there, and estimating the number and size of companies currently competing in the target environment. You should assess the overall environment before analyzing the companies you will compete against – company-by-company and product-by-product.

"When we evaluate new products and markets, we look at several sources of information to determine what that environment is like. Sometimes analysts will describe competitors supposedly in our market space but that never materialize. Conversely, when we look at whom we compete against in proposals and deals, we find out who else is out there in the marketplace, and those companies are sometimes not the same ones that analysts cite as our competitors. It pays to look at the big picture as well as all the sources of data," advises Carole Gum. One way to think about the competitive environment is as if you were traveling to a foreign country for the first time. Who will you encounter? How will you communicate? What will they want from you? Will they be friendly or hostile? What will they think of you? In both cases, it pays to do some homework before you arrive. Table 5.2 lists the factors that need to be considered.

Table 5-2: Characterizing the Competitive Environment

- *-How big is the market environment?*
- *-How many competitors are there?*
- *-How big are the competitors; what is the mix?*
- *-Are these companies partnering; with whom?*
- *-Who's been in the market the longest?*
- *-Who are the newcomers?*

"We use tradeshows as a venue for studying the competitive environment," says Ciree J. Loftus. *"You can quickly get an idea about who is there, who the new players are, what the new products are, and most importantly, customer reactions to the competing companies and products."* Conferences, events and tradeshows that your potential customers may attend are all venues that will help you gather information about the environment. It's important to keep a high-level perspective and an open mind, and then take the time to observe.

Although there are many possible competitive environments, there are five fairly common ones that exist today. The next five sections of this chapter describe each of the common competitive situations, and Figure 5.2 illustrates the differences among them. There also may be new ones that evolve, but these examples will help you prepare for others you may encounter in the future. Each competitive environment section contains screening criteria to apply to your new product idea.

Screening by competitive environment: if you are first-mover

Often, new products are targeted for a new market, and your company is poised to be the first to market. That's both good news and bad news. The good news is that you will get the attention and have the opportunity to set a standard (as well as the price), on your way to being market share leader. The bad news is that everyone will be coming after you and trying to take market share away. The question is, are you prepared to allocate the resources to sustain and defend your position?

Large companies are often successful in being the first-mover in a new market. *"In the case of a new market, you need some time for the market to develop, and customers need to be educated. This takes a lot of time and resources that a large company has and a small startup does not,"* according to Ciree J. Loftus. The lessons of the dot-com bust have shown that the first-mover strategy alone does not ensure bottom line success, particularly in business-to-consumer markets. The resources must be there to sustain the business.

At TRW-ESL, we were part of a big company and had the accompanying resources, but because our business strategy was to spin out the ventures, we viewed the new product ideas more like a startup would. Unfortunately, because our technology solutions were so advanced, we often faced a "first-mover" competitive environment. Our primary differentiator was the technology solution, so the only time that an idea passed the competition criterion was if the technology solution would give us significant lead time before competitors could develop a similar product, and if we also had an appropriate strategic partner with the right marketing and sales resources to educate the customers.

For this competitive environment, you need to apply these criteria to the idea:

- -Do you have the sales and marketing expertise to develop the market and educate customers?
- -Do you have the resources to enter the market quickly and defend your position?

Screening by competitive environment: if you are early entrant with strong differentiator

If you have missed the chance to be the first mover into a market niche, you can still gain a strong competitive position by getting to market early. If that's the environment in which your new product idea will be launched, then you will need a strong differentiator in order to capture some of the early attention, along with the first-mover company.

"It's hard to do this well," says Carole Gum. *"Everyone wants to be like the first company, and it's tempting to just copy. However, you must really base your competitive strategy on your unique strengths."* Defining your differentiators is still necessary.

If you have done your homework when you studied and characterized your customer for the new product idea, you will have a thorough understanding of their value proposition. If you also have some strong differentiators compared to the first-mover in the market, and if those differentiators also relate to the customer value proposition, then it's possible to compete successfully. For example, if your new product is accounting software that allows remote data entry of payroll data, and first-mover competitor Peachtree doesn't have this feature, then you may do just fine in this market. It may still be necessary, however, to apply significant resources to the effort, in order to get to market quickly and to create demand; don't count on the first-mover competitor to have completed the customer education process!

For this competitive environment, you need to apply some additional criteria to the idea:

-Do you have strong product differentiators?
-Can you get to market soon enough to be considered an early entrant?

Screening by competitive environment: if the market is fragmented

When the market niche has numerous competitors, the market share must be split up among all players, and there may not be a single player who has the majority share. This is a fragmented market environment, and it's very difficult to enter this market successfully with a new product.

"Whoever can be clearest in their differentiation will be successful, even if the market is fragmented," suggests Carole Gum. *"However, you must be sure that your differentiators matter to the customer."* You must be able to somehow get the attention of customers in a fragmented market, and it helps tremendously if those customers can relate to the differentiators.

It's easier to compete in a fragmented market if your new product is part of a product suite, suggests Ciree J. Loftus. *"If you're targeting a fragmented market with a standalone product, it's pretty hard to compete successfully unless you have a revolutionary idea or a significant price advantage. However, if the product is part of a suite that fills complementary customer needs, then it can work."*

In this situation, you may have other things to offer the customer as well, and it may in fact be an opportunity to build more revenue for the complementary products.
For this competitive environment, you need to apply some additional criteria to the idea:

- -Do differentiators match the customer value proposition?
- -Is your new product idea related to an existing product line?
- -Is there enough market share left to make it worthwhile to develop a new product?

Screening by competitive environment: if there are a few entrenched competitors

"Entrenched competitors" are companies who have built a reputation in the market segment and have been in that market for a while – like incumbents. Depending on the dynamics of the marketplace, it is possible to successfully enter this market with a new product, particularly if the product is so revolutionary that it makes the entrenched companies' products seem outdated.

Sometimes customers may want to buy their products from different suppliers, suggests Ciree J. Loftus. *"We often evaluate companies who are established in markets to see if customers are ready to buy products from someone other than the usual sources. It's certainly worth evaluating as a new opportunity, and until you consult with customers, you won't know that."*

Often companies will consider the benefits of launching a "me-too" product into an existing market. *"If the attainable market share is large enough for us to make a profit, and if it can form the basis of a competitive advantage in another market segment, then we may decide to proceed,"* says Ciree J. Loftus. *"However, it's important to remember that the decision was a strategic one, and the product shouldn't be viewed as one that can stand on its own."*

Sometimes it is possible to compete in such an environment by strategic partnering. *"Big companies are definitely a threat because they are more solid financially,"* says Carole Gum. *"In an economic downturn, big companies pose an even bigger threat because they are fighting to maintain their financial position. As a newer player in our market space, we found that partnering helped us enter the market and maintain our competitive position against the giants."*

For this competitive environment, you need to apply some additional criteria to the idea:

-Are customers ready for more choices?
-Do you have a strong technological differentiator?
-Is there enough available market share to be profitable?
-Can partnering enhance your competitive position?

Screening by competitive environment: mature markets

Mature markets include products and services that continue along without the need for major innovation. Plain old telephone service is a good example of a mature market; without deregulation, it would have been impossible for small, local carriers to compete with the baby bells. Customers may encounter high switching cost, loss of service, and less convenience when they consider a new supplier of products. In order to compete, you must be able to overcome these sales objections and hurdles, and you must be able to create a more compelling value proposition.

Mature markets can also include products or technologies that are at the end of a life cycle, such as standalone fax machines; most devices are now multifunctional and include scanning and copying capabilities. Companies who are major players in mature markets may be supporting the products only until the obsolescence stage is reached. Mature markets, however, might also represent an opportunity because as one product line ends, another one can begin. In this instance, it would be similar to the entrenched competitor environment. For this competitive environment, you need to apply some additional criteria to the idea:

-Are products at the end of their life cycle?
-Is this market ready for innovation?

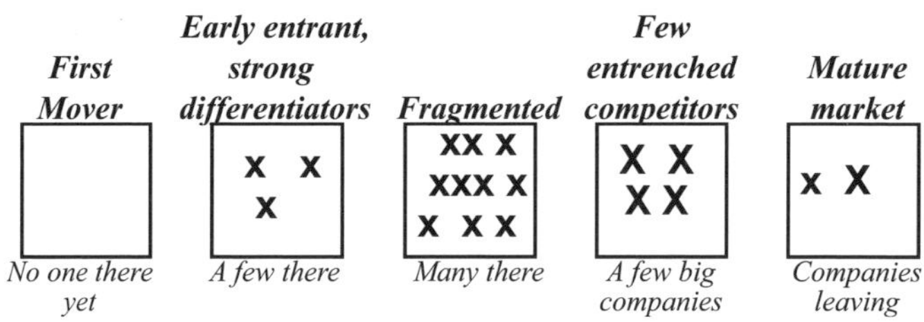

Figure 5.2: The Five Competitive Environments

Maintaining constant vigilance throughout the product cycle is essential

No matter what business you are in, and regardless of competitive environment, you will need to constantly monitor the competition. It's necessary during the development phase, so that you can make sure to build in features and functionality that will provide competitive differentiation. It's necessary prior to launch, so that you can define your market strategy. During launch, it's necessary in order to develop the right internal and external marketing programs, and to create the right marketing messages to build competitive advantage.

There are many ways to build the discipline of competitive analysis into your company's operations. *"We assign product marketing managers to continuously track certain competitors, and we also do quarterly competitive analysis reports that are distributed within sales and marketing,"* says Carole Gum.

"At Luminate, we constantly work with our sales people to study factors such as who's participating in benchmarks and field trials, and also cost of lost sales. We do an informal competitive analysis monthly with our sales people," says Ciree J. Loftus. *"We also focus on customer input, and we do market surveys with customers to learn about their satisfaction with current market offerings. We will often learn a lot about the competition from the customer's perspective."* Table 5.3 lists the things you need to do in order to keep tabs on the competition.

When you apply the competition criterion to your new product idea, your work with competitive analysis is just beginning. However, if it is done thoroughly, you will have an excellent foundation for the other strategic decisions you will encounter along the way.

Table 5-3: Monitoring the Competition
-Update market research (primary, secondary)
-Monitor competitors' websites for news
-Monitor trade publications for news
-Assess competitors at trade shows/events
-Obtain feedback from salespeople

Putting it all together

To validate your new product idea relative to the competition criteria, you will have gathered a lot of information about the environment, your competitors and their products, along with your significant differentiators. It will be helpful to compile this information so that the decision-makers can more easily understand all the competitive factors. You should characterize the competitive environment and your company's readiness to enter that market. Further, you should develop a competitive matrix that delineates the companies, their products and how you compare.

NOTE: The following chart contains categories to include when developing new product selection criteria. You need to craft criteria that work in the context of your company; these are merely suggestions. Additionally, the "Reject/Postpone" recommendations are a quick checklist to use in making new product decisions. Your own company's guidelines for rejecting or postponing a new product idea may be different.

Competition Criteria – categories to include:

-description of competitive environment
-alternative customer solutions
-names of competitors
-summary of new versus existing competitors
-analysis of competitors at a company level
-analysis of competitors at a product level
-additional factors specific to type of competitive environment

REJECT the idea if:

-the customer is happy with a competitor's existing solution
-the market is too mature to enter as a new player
-you don't have differentiators that relate directly to the customer value proposition
-creating competitive advantage means significant investment in new infrastructure

POSTPONE the idea if:

-a competitor is about to launch an identical product
-it's a new market but you don't have the resources to sustain a first-mover position
-it's a very fragmented market and you need more time to assess the competitive strategy

6

The Market Criterion: Not Every Market is a Trillion Dollar Market

Judging the potential of markets today is difficult. No one knows for sure how large the market will be when you launch your new product several months into the future. Market researchers and financial analysts are in the business of making predictions, but with the drastic economic and technology changes that have taken place in the last five years, their level of accuracy has declined. Nevertheless, in order to evaluate a new product idea, you will need to find as much information as you can, especially about market trends and market size.

You will also need to decide what type of market dynamics makes sense for your company. Is it your goal to be a big player in a big market, or are you more successful in carving out market niches? Your target market may be brand new, established but growing, flat with no growth, or declining. Which dynamics fit your company's strategy and which ones can your resources support? These are issues to think about before gathering all of the market information.

Current market forecasts are not very accurate or realistic

During the late 1990s, it seemed that every market prediction for any type of Internet-related or high-tech business was in the billions or sometimes trillions of dollars. These predictions were made by reputable analysts, caught up in the frenzy of the booming economy and its potential for changing the way we do business on a global basis. Since the dot-com bust that began in the spring of 2000, however, these same analysts are at a loss to predict with any assurance what will happen next in the Internet economy. Some predict a long-term downturn; others predict that the pendulum will swing back toward a more normal center, where it's back to business basics, such as profit and reasonable levels of growth. This uncertainty makes it difficult to assess the characteristics of the target market for your idea.

It's important to gather information from as many sources as possible, rather than just relying on one or two analyst reports. Talking to real people, especially your target customers, helps put a realistic spin on any published or printed information. When you gather a variety of information from several sources, you will see trends emerging that you can use to characterize the dynamics and size of your target market. That will help eliminate some of the uncertainty.

Market trends and forecasts-how to find information

The best way to find meaningful market trend information is to stay focused on your target market segment, and to read the news and articles that are written about doing business in that segment. Table 6.1 is a suggested list of sources. The more detailed your focus, the more useful the data will be in terms of identifying the real trends that affect the market demand. There are many different possible types of trends that may be relevant to your market. For example, trends can measure whether a market is growing and why, they can predict the rates at which technologies are adopted, or they can describe the new business models that companies are using to sell into the market. At a high level, though, most investors and company executives want to see a growing market, not one that is flat or declining.

Table 6-1:
Where to Look and What to Look For

-Trade journals, business magazines: articles about trends in technology, economy and business

-Analyst reports and publications: predictions of market size and trends by technology, industry, type of customer

-Company websites: recent news, press releases, annual reports or earnings reports

-Financial newspapers and media: earnings reports and news

-Your company's databases: changes in sales for existing products, type and number of new customers, sales leads by geographic location

-Market surveys and research reports: specific trends and size estimates with demographic information

You should look for overall demand in your target market and how it is changing. Demand may increase, decrease, or stay flat in response to various economic or technology changes. Look for the reasons behind the fluctuations in demand. You also need to consider how fast your market is changing in terms of demand, new customers, and rate of technology adoption. It's important to capture the basis for your estimates no matter how you calculate them, so that you can justify your numbers later on to the decision-makers.

Quite often, new product ideas are targeted for a brand new market that has yet to be developed. If that is the case with your product idea, you will not be able to find estimates of market demand because they don't exist yet. For new markets, you may have to infer the future dynamics and market demand. I always use the principle of "where there's smoke, there's fire", meaning that I look for similar products or technologies that people are beginning to adopt, and then project demand on that basis. Market research reports, trade journals, business publications, and market surveys are all excellent sources of information for characterizing the market. A vast amount of useful information also exists online at corporate websites, in online databases, at websites of periodicals and magazines, and at the websites of market research and analyst firms (although they are usually not free of charge). It often takes quite a bit of searching and a tremendous amount of reading to find pertinent information, but it's well worth the time.

Validation is the key to meaningful market characterization

Just because it is written, it isn't necessarily so. You should take the time to validate the predictions or forecasts found in trade journals or the press with real people in your market segment, in other words, your target customer. Very often, the trade journal articles were written on the basis of one or two examples that support the prediction, and they might not reflect the rest of the market segment. Also, if the market is brand new, it is even more critical to validate the information.

You will have information about your customer from your customer criterion analysis (see Chapter 4). To validate the market trends and size, you should compare the target customer profile with the individuals in the target market segment to identify the individuals who most closely match your customer description. You should then speak with such individuals from the market segment to find out if they have the same problem that needs to be solved, similar value propositions, and comparable buying behavior. If they do, then the market trends and estimated size will be more reliable measures of your real target market. There are many ways to conduct this validation, as listed in Table 6.2.

Table 6-2:
Ways to Validate Market Trends and Market Size

- Network and talk to colleagues
- Conduct surveys with real or potential customers
- Do focus groups
- Contract with a market research firm for a specific study
- Hire a consultant with expertise in your target market
- Develop a prototype or demo and obtain customer feedback

When validating new markets, you may encounter early adopters: individuals who enjoy being the first to try out a new technology or product. These individuals may not always be the buyers of the product, so it may require some time to get a realistic view of the market potential. According to Bob Zeidman, CEO and Founder of The Chalkboard Network, *"With a new product for a new market, I talk to a lot of people. There are those people who get excited about any idea, and others who always say they don't need anything new. The truth is probably somewhere in between, and that's why the more people you talk to, the better."*

Measures of market size: total, served, and market share

Market size is usually expressed in terms of dollars, numbers of people, or product units. There are three measures of market size that are commonly used: total available market, served available market, and share of market. The term "total available market" or TAM, usually means the total of all products and services that could be sold to a customer. An example of TAM would be the forecasted total demand for customer relationship management systems (including hardware, software and services), expressed in millions of dollars per year. TAM is sometimes taken to mean the total possible sales for your specific type of product. It's important that everyone who is involved in making the new product decision understands which definition is being used. Another more specific measure of market size is "served available market" or SAM. This usually means the portion of the total market that you could "serve" with your specific new product. Extending from the TAM example above, let's say that your company is a software developer, so your served available market would be some portion of the TAM for customer relationship management systems, because you only sell software. The SAM would be a smaller number than the TAM. This measure helps the decision makers to gauge the upper limit of the range of the market size, due to the nature of your product.

The third measure of market size is share of market (SOM), or just "market share". Market share is the portion of the market demand that you can control or "own". The market share, usually expressed as a number or percentage, will be constrained by the number of competitors, and also by the company's capacity to deliver product to that market. Extending our example once again, let's assume that there are many other competitors in the customer relationship management software market, and because of that, no company can control more than 5% of the market. That would be your maximum market share, or the upper limit. You could also multiply 5% by the SAM (expressed in dollars) to convert it to dollars instead. The SOM is usually used for an existing product and reflects market share based on actual sales, however, it can also be used during the idea screening and validation phase. The important thing to remember when using SOM to screen ideas is to evaluate the number in the context of the market environment. Having the majority market share in a dying market is not an attractive situation.

These three measures are often considered together, and abbreviated as TAM (total available market), SAM (served available market), and SOM (share of market). The SOM must be expressed in dollars, rather than in a percentage, in order to compare it with the SAM and TAM. Evaluating the numbers in this order enables the decision-maker to drill down to the smallest, and hopefully most realistic, number as the estimate of market size. Figure 6.1 shows how the three measures can be displayed on a graph for a presentation or report.

Whether you use all three measures or just one depends on the situation. *"For investors, I use all three measures starting with the TAM, and narrowing it down to the targeted share of market. By starting with big numbers, you get the investors excited. By narrowing it down to something realistic, you show them that you've got a realistic grasp of what can actually be accomplished,"* says Bob Zeidman. *"However, for internal planning and management purposes, the served available market (SAM) is most meaningful because it is a more conservative look at the market that I need to focus on. It's nice to pick a SOM as a target, but it's hard to predict for a company just starting out. And in an emerging market, the external economic factors really make it impossible to predict."*

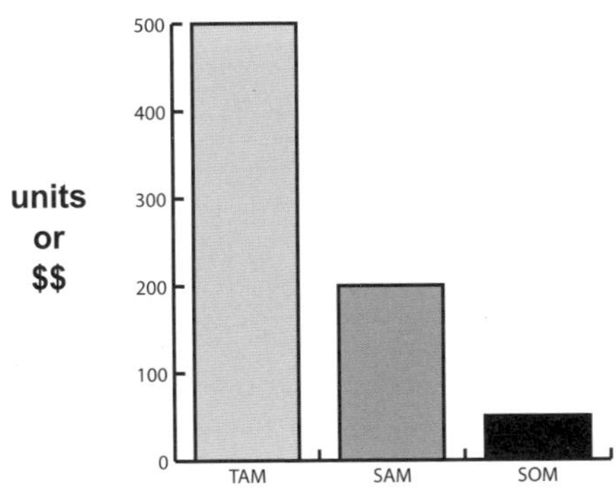

Figure 6.1: Example of a TAM-SAM-SOM Chart

If you want to simplify the market estimating process when you are screening new product ideas, it's best to do this in stages. The first level screen should be served available market (SAM). It is most realistic because it gives the total picture of the specific market niche – *for the new product idea.* In that sense, it is more accurate than total available market. You don't need to consider competition yet; just find the portion of the market that matches what the product is and does. If the SAM is a very small number, then you may not need to go to the next step. If the SAM is a reasonable number, then apply the next level screen.

The second level screen should consider the competitive environment; how many companies are selling similar products in that market? The SAM estimate will, in most cases, be reduced when you consider the competition. If you will be the first to market with the new product, then your SAM may not change at all. At the other end of the spectrum is the fragmented market with many, many competitors, and in that case, the SAM may be significantly reduced. This step will yield a number that will lead to an estimate of your share of the market.

The next step in estimating your share of market is to consider your capacity to deliver product to that reduced portion of the market as defined in the previous step. You may want to serve 90% of the market, but that means that you need to be able to deliver products on time to all of those individuals and be able to support them after the sale. Is your company up to the task? Even if you are a large company and have a successful track record of getting to market on time, if this is a new market, your true capacity to deliver may be different. You need to calculate your capacity to deliver in the context of both the new product idea and your familiarity with the target market. Here's an example:

First step: SAM based on product you're selling = $5M
Second step: SAM reduced, due to one small competitor in market = $4M
Third step: Your capacity to deliver product will limit your market share to 50%, or $2M.

This sequence is a simplified method of forecasting your market share for your target market. Executing these three steps will help you think through what is realistic in terms of the competitive environment and your capacity to deliver product. The final number may also result in rejecting the product idea, if it's not big enough to meet other new product criteria.

Market trends will help you forecast demand

Once you have an estimate of market size, then the market trend information you have gathered will help you to forecast demand over the next few years. If the trends indicate a slow adoption rate for your type of product, then your market size and revenue forecast will be flat in the first couple of years and then will grow. If trends indicate increasing demand, then you'll have an upward curve in your five-year forecast, as illustrated in Figure 6.2. Market trend forecasts and market size estimates should be used together in this way.

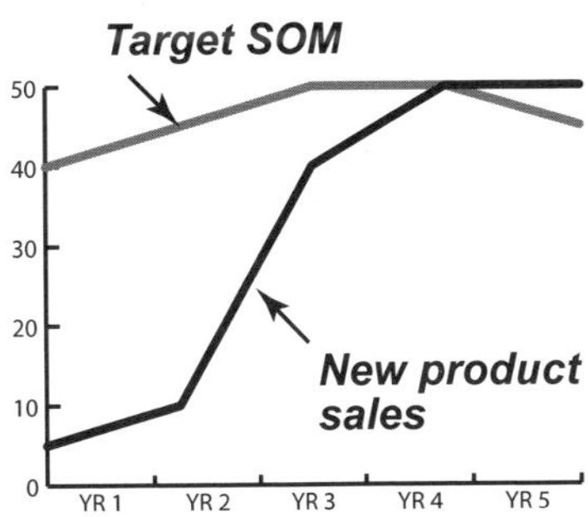

-How will you ramp up to reach your target SOM before demand peaks?
-Can you afford to ramp up quickly?
-If not, will your competitors capture your market share?

Figure 6.2: Forecasting Sales and SOM

If you are considering a brand new market, it will be more difficult to forecast the rate of change, because there are a lot of unknowns, such as product adoption rate and buying behavior of customers in that market. Companies can increase demand for their new products with significant and effective advertising, but sometimes a product is simply too early for the market, and may take a lot longer to generate demand. *"When faced with emerging markets, the timing is very tricky,"* according to Bob Zeidman. *"If you enter too early, you can run out of funds before a market exists to purchase your products. But if you wait too long, competitors can rush in before you have a market presence."* If you have done your homework with regard to customer need and value proposition, you will be able to reduce this risk. Still, it's better to be a little conservative when forecasting demand in a new market; adding a few extra months for market adoption is a wise approach.

Market expectations and metrics

Is it better to target very large markets that are growing and have lots of competitors, or can you be more successful in smaller market niches where you can capture the majority of the market share? The answer is: it depends on the stakeholders and decision-makers. Venture capital investors, for example, usually want to see a large market that will result in a large return a few years down the road, and they often have a specific number (in dollars) in mind. Your company needs to establish a threshold for market size – what size of market will fit your company's goals?

"It's easier for a startup to aim for a big market. Even if you end up being a niche player, you can still be successful and profitable. But if the market is too small to begin with, you can be squeezed out, or run out of funding before you are able to grow your market share," says Bob Zeidman. Larger, more established companies might be able to enter smaller markets, capture the majority market share and do quite well, however, due to fewer resource constraints.

The rate of market growth is a metric that should be considered when evaluating the market size. You may want to set a minimum rate of growth for the target market, such as a certain percentage of market growth per year. Your company may have established financial and company objectives that relate to market growth. If the estimated rate of market growth for the new product idea is too low, then pursuing the product may hinder the company in meeting its financial objectives. If the estimated rate of market growth is too high, and your company does not have the capacity to effectively compete, then the competitors may take away some market share, and your company's revenues will be lower. Whatever the situation, there should be congruence between your company's rate of growth and the dynamics of your target market.

Sometimes a market that is on a plateau can also be an opportunity. In this situation, the competitors and solution are established and known. According to Bob Zeidman, that doesn't mean that the customers aren't willing to consider new products, and they may in fact be unhappy with the incumbents' offerings. *"Continued growth is great to have in a market, but there may be opportunities in flat markets to generate some revenue and profit, too,"* he suggests.

It is also possible to pursue a new idea in a small market and be quite profitable, either because the margins are very large, or because your company has a significant and unique competitive advantage. Figure 6.3 illustrates these scenarios. For that reason, you need to look at the profit, and not just the revenue forecast. It may make sense to pursue an idea in a smaller market that may lead you to other related markets or related products that will grow your company in a new direction, which may be one of your company's strategic objectives.

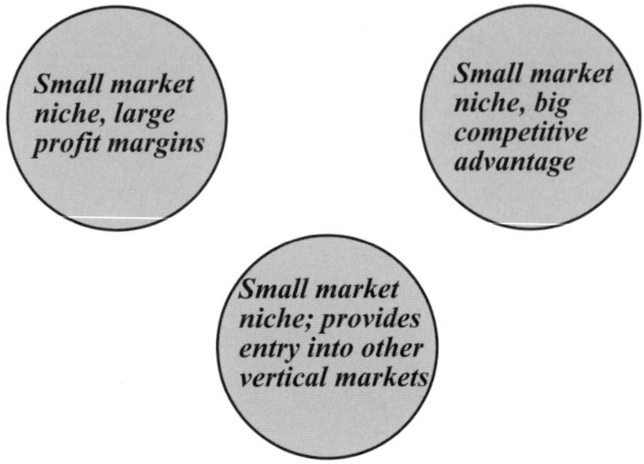

Figure 6.3: When Small is Better

Applying the Market Criterion to the Idea

In order to decide if the new product idea has a large enough market that is growing and can be profitable, you need to evaluate the market trends and five-year market size forecast.

NOTE: The following chart contains categories to include when developing new product selection criteria. You need to craft criteria that work in the context of your company; these are merely suggestions. Additionally, the "Reject/Postpone" recommendations are a quick checklist to use in making new product decisions. Your own company's guidelines for rejecting or postponing a new product idea may be different.

Market Criteria – categories to include:

-the trends you want to see in the target market
-the minimum acceptable market size
-measures you will use in evaluating the market (TAM, SAM and/or SOM)
-reliable sources of market trend data and market size estimates

REJECT the idea if:

-the market demand is declining
-the market size is too small
-the market size is adequate, but the profit is too small

POSTPONE the idea if:

-the market trend is flat in an emerging market
-the market is too small now but is expected to grow within a year

7

The Resource Criterion: People and Technology

It's never too early to evaluate resource requirements for a new product idea or venture. With a startup situation, the resource issue is automatically addressed, because most entrepreneurial efforts begin with one or two individuals, and a team must be built very quickly during the idea phase in order to attract funding. But even in an established company, this basic question needs to be answered when a new idea is presented: Do you have enough people and technology resources to execute the idea? More importantly, do you have the right resources to execute the idea quickly enough, and profitably? You must have the right resources at the right time. If you don't, you will likely want to reject or postpone the idea.

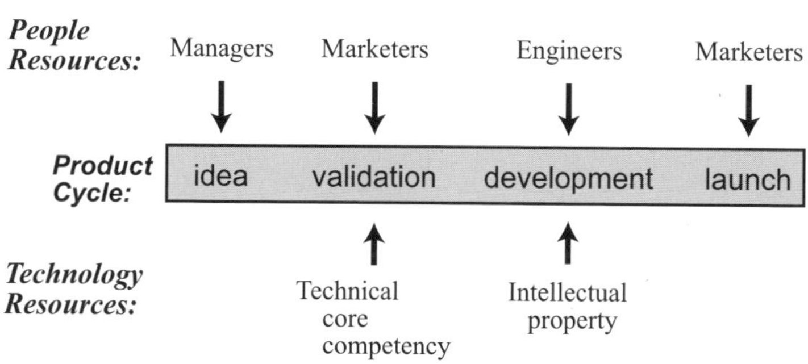

Figure 7.1: Resource Needs of the New Product Cycle

Identifying the human resource needs for a new idea requires evaluating the skills required throughout the whole product cycle. Figure 7.1 shows the skills required throughout the cycle. When you take an objective look at the whole cycle and take an "inventory" of who is available within your organization, you may discover gaps. There may be several ways to fill the gaps and each way has a different cost associated with it, which ultimately will affect your profitability.

Similarly, your technology resource needs should be identified as early as possible. The scope of technology resources includes collective (internal) technical expertise, existing technology advancements within the company, intellectual property (and which IP is protected in the form of patents or trademarks), and to some degree, your brand and image.

Shrinking time to market means more pressure on resources

In today's economy and marketplace, every company must deal with the pressure of shrinking time to turn new ideas into products and get them to market. If your company doesn't make it to market soon enough, your competitors will. According to Rob Abel, Vice-President of Strategy and Business Development at Eduprise, *"A company should stick to its long-term vision, but be nimble enough to react instantaneously to the short-term opportunities in the marketplace that align with its vision. It requires companies to turn on a dime and make decisions overnight."* In addition, awareness and acceptance of new products depends on whether your product is available at the time that your customer needs it; not too soon and not too late. As they say, timing is everything.

Finding the right resources at the right time is the key to profitability

Even in the normal course of doing business, managing and allocating resources are a challenge for any company. When a new product is being considered, the need for resources will increase as the product goes through the new product cycle. This need can be met by hiring, outsourcing, or temporarily re-allocating existing resources. Regardless of the approach, there are tradeoffs. If you outsource some part of the cycle such as development, for example, it may positively affect time to market but negatively affect profitability. There are similar tradeoffs to be made with technology resources; does the cost justify the benefits of getting to market on time? At the time that the idea is being reviewed and validated, you need to estimate the people and technology needs and compare them to the resources that will be available while the product goes through the remainder of the new product cycle. If the profit and schedule are adversely affected, then perhaps the idea should be postponed or even rejected.

Human resources are critical throughout the entire new product cycle

A few years ago, it was common practice to add resources only when a new product idea entered the development phase, and then, only if the company couldn't use its existing staff. Today, with the compression of the new product cycle, you may need additional people during the idea, validation, development, and launch phases of the cycle. You should estimate the resources required for the entire cycle when you are first considering the new product idea.

Forecasting resources is never easy, and when you are dealing with lots of unknowns, such as those associated with new products, it is even more difficult and less accurate. However, there are several ways to develop realistic estimates during the idea phase. The best method is to use past experience in your company with new products. How many new resources were added and during which stage of the cycle? If you are in a startup situation, you may not have past experience to use as a basis, but you can study other startups that have developed similar products to get some idea. It also could be argued that established companies should look at models that startups use, because the startup model enables a more entrepreneurial and less biased evaluation of a new product.

It's especially important to be realistic about ramping up resources – is it possible to recruit and hire the right people given the time to market? If it is possible, then you should go one step further and think about what will happen to the newly hired people after the new product is launched. The options are re-assigning them, laying them off, or hopefully using them for the next new product idea that comes along. With the current economy and lightning-fast reactions to Wall Street reports, layoffs happen overnight. This creates a lack of trust and loyalty among existing and potential employees. If your plans call for new hires, make sure that you can attract and retain the employees you will need to complete the effort.

Different skills are needed for each phase of the new product cycle

When should the company bring in managers, engineers, or marketing people? These job functions are needed at specific times during the cycle and require different skills and areas of specialization, as shown in Figure 7.2.

IDEA VALIDATION	DEVELOPMENT	LAUNCH
-Marketing	-Design	-Marketing communications
-Finance	-Implementation	-Public relations
-Market research	-Test	-Advertising
-Competitive analysis	-Manufacturing	-Sales
-Forecasting	-Technical management	-Project management

Figure 7.2: Skills for the New Product Cycle

It also takes a certain mentality to handle the roller coaster of getting a new product to market. *"It's difficult to find quality people who can do something new. The person has to be innovative and creative, yet very disciplined in their approach, as well as focused. Few individuals have all those attributes,"* according to Rob Abel.

During the idea evaluation phase, marketing and financial skills are essential for conducting "due diligence", which involves researching the market, technology advancements, and competition. It also involves forecasting the revenues, the costs to develop the product, and the costs to take it to market. People must be objective and must make assessments based on facts, but they also need to think creatively about evaluating the market and meeting the customer needs.

During the development phase, the product is designed, built, and tested. Whether the new idea is a high tech product or consumer goods, there will be engineers or scientists involved, and also manufacturing and operations personnel. People who do development need to be very disciplined in their approach. Development is usually the longest phase of the cycle and requires seasoned managers who have proven they can execute.

The launch phase requires marketing communications people, a launch manager, public relations and advertising specialists, and sales people. People working on the launch need to have solid project management skills, as well as the creativity to develop and execute the required promotional programs.

It is apparent that the new product cycle collectively involves all the skills found in any type of company; there are no departments or job functions that are missing from the process. This brings up the issue of how to allocate employees to new product efforts; should the people be temporarily re-assigned from doing their regular jobs to do work on new products? It may be necessary to re-assign people to work on the new products, but the impact to other products they were working on needs to be weighed in the context of the greater bottom line of the company.

Options for filling the gaps in human resources

In order to get to market on time, you will need to have the right resources available at the right time of the cycle. If those critical skills are not already on your payroll, then you need to consider some alternatives, as well as the cost of each one. Outsourcing by hiring outside contractors or vendors may be an option.

Which skill is missing most often with new products or ventures? Marketing, according to Joe Becker, President and CEO of Dolphin Ventures. *"Early stage ventures need marketing people, not sales people. Marketers will develop a strategy to create pull in the marketplace, which is what's needed with a new product. Sales people, by contrast, are more likely to try to push the product into the market, and it may not fit the customer needs for which the product was intended."* For established companies, it may be necessary to find marketing professionals who are familiar with specific markets or technologies that fit the needs of the new product, and these people might not already be on staff. Rob Abel calls these specialists "marketing architects". *"It takes a certain set of skills and a cradle-to-grave perspective to champion a new product from validation through development and into the marketplace. Marketing architects must create a strategy to fit the customer needs, figure out how to get to market, who to work with, who the partners will be and how to incentivize partners to provide value to your customer."*

Another critical skill is management. This is especially true for startups; it's difficult to find experienced and effective CEOs, and the more solid the management team is in the early stage of a venture, the better. Says Rob Abel, *"The right management team can be a key differentiator when raising money for a venture. Most venture capitalists consider the team to be number one."* This is further validated by Joe Becker: *"Investors need some assurance that the team that's in place at the idea stage has the ability to execute. If not, there are ways to fix this, but without solid and seasoned managers, the return on investment won't be there. People make the business, not just the technology."* Even established companies need to make sure that there are enough management resources to move the idea along through the whole product cycle. Figure 7.3 lists the internal and external solutions for resource gaps.

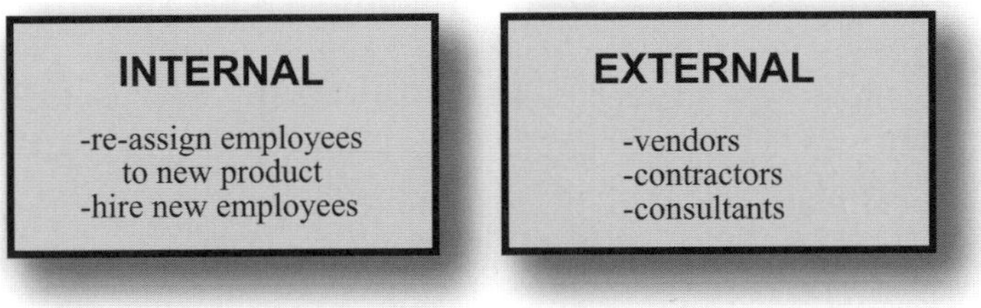

Figure 7.3: Solutions for Resource Gaps

Even if your new product idea is not a piece of technology, it's important to evaluate the knowledge and intellectual property owned by the company that can be applied to the product idea. Technology resources in the context of this chapter include technology expertise, existing technology solutions, and intellectual property (patents, trademarks, copyrights, rights to distribute, market, or sell, and export rights).

Problem-solving experience is vital

Does your company have the collective experience needed in order to build a product that will solve the technical or business problem of your customer? This is a common challenge for new products. Engineers and other employees involved in building products are a fairly optimistic bunch and love a challenge, but someone in management needs to evaluate the capabilities with an objective and realistic eye.

When evaluating capabilities of available resources, consider employees of the company, along with strategic partners, vendors, board members, and perhaps even customers. People outside the company who have business relationships may be able to lend some input to this problem-solving process. However, if you do plan to seek outside input, make sure that these people will be available when the time comes to develop the solution.

At TRW-ESL, one of the key initial criteria was whether we knew how to solve the technical problem. This was critical since we were "marketing-challenged" and our only competitive advantage was the technology piece of the new venture. With all of our ventures, we evaluated our past experience in solving a similar problem. If that looked promising, we then evaluated whether we currently had the skills to solve the problem. If we didn't, the idea was rejected.

Intellectual property should be considered

A company may have existing patents or trademarks that apply to the new product idea, or the new idea may require new intellectual property protection. There can be a sizeable cost and lengthy wait to obtain such protection. You need to consider the impact these issues will have on your ability to get to market on time as well as the effect on your ultimate profitability. The key question to ask in this situation is: How easy is it to copy this product or solution? If it's easy, then you may want to seek intellectual property protection, if it's possible. If it's not possible due to the nature of the idea, then you may need to protect it by leveraging your brand or creating a new brand around it. This means you may need a lot of money to make this happen, especially if you don't already have a strong brand presence. If the idea is difficult to copy, then you may or may not want to seek intellectual property protection, depending on the cost and estimated product life.

The costs of intellectual property protection can be prohibitive, particularly for startups. *"Entrepreneurs don't always have the money to pursue IP protection, but they should consult with legal experts to evaluate the pros and cons for their venture,"* advises Joe Becker.

At TRW-ESL, we applied for intellectual property protection of our technologies when the idea reached the validation phase. We did this to protect our only competitive advantage: the technology itself. Not every technology idea should be patented or can be patented, but the decision needs to be made very early in the new product cycle. Evaluation of this factor should be on any idea selection criteria checklist.

Finding technology resources to fill the gaps

If your company will not be able to develop the whole product internally, then you need to consider outsourcing to other business entities or acquiring parts of the solution elsewhere. You also need to evaluate the cost of doing so. The "whole product" means more than just building a widget; rather, it includes all the tasks required to design, build, customer-test, and technically support the product in the post-sale phase, including the required product documentation.

In the case of TRW-ESL, during the validation phase (and before a product entered the development phase), we looked for ways to get to market sooner. We frequently found ourselves in the position of having to simplify an existing technology solution in order to render it feasible and affordable for the commercial marketplace. That wasn't always so easy to do, and we considered outsourcing as a way to get the product built to the specifications needed by the target customer, *and no more.* Outsourcing was a way to get to market on time, with the right product at the right price.

There are obvious advantages to outsourcing technical development, but there are at least two downsides. First, you need to consider whether you will get the same quality that you would build into the product if it remained inside the company. *"It's important to evaluate your established relationships, and their value-added skills versus your own,"* according to Rob Abel. *"There may be times in a trusted relationship when it's faster to outsource, especially with the technical development of a product. However, work that relates to your own value-added core skills should be kept within the company."* The other downside is the risk of giving up the "experience curve", according to Joe Becker. *"If you outsource the first product, and do your second product in-house, you will lose any learning from the first product. It delays or in some cases eliminates the building of skills internal to the company. If you don't learn enough about the business and market you're in, it's tough to be a successful player."*

Another way to fill a technology gap is to acquire parts of the solution by using off the shelf components or complementary products from partners. You can also extend this idea further to include the acquisition of an entire company to provide a partial solution. Many companies have leapfrogged into new markets by using this approach. *"Acceleration comes from designing products that are complementary to other existing technologies,"* says Joe Becker. *"It's a great way to develop the whole product rapidly."*

Getting to market profitably and on time

There are many considerations related to people and technology resources, and it's tricky to evaluate their impact. If you decrease time to market you can adversely affect profitability by spending too much on extra resources to get to market sooner. However, getting to market sooner may also mean more revenue, which eventually will create profit. Figure 7.4 identifies the possible impact of these decisions.

Resource action	Expenses	Time to market	Competitive advantage
Outsourcing	↑	↓	↑
Patents and IP protection	↑	↑	↑
Hiring for new product	↑	↑	↔
Licensing or using off the shelf technology	↑	↓	↔
Training employees on new product	↔	↓	↑

Figure 7.4: Effect of Resource Actions on Profitability and Time to Market

The important things to do when evaluating resources are to be realistic and to do the math. You must think through what resources the new idea will require versus what you already have to work with, and assess the impact on profit. In order to realistic, you need to keep the new product team "lean and mean", and fill gaps with external resources in order to stay on track to the market.

NOTE: The following chart contains categories to include when developing new product selection criteria. You need to craft criteria that work in the context of your company; these are merely suggestions. Additionally, the "Reject/Postpone" recommendations are a quick checklist to use in making new product decisions. Your own company's guidelines for rejecting or postponing a new product idea may be different.

Resource Criteria – categories to include:

-human resource gaps and total resource requirement
- key skill gaps
-core technologies and existing collective knowledge
-intellectual property protection requirements
-feasibility of outsourcing

REJECT the idea if:

-you have less than half of the required resources in-house
-the missing skills would take more than 6 months to hire
-you don't know how to solve the technical or business problem
-there are no identifiable outsourcing options
-the idea is easily copied and you have no established brand identity

POSTPONE the idea if:

-internal resources would need significant training to facilitate product development
-the intellectual property protection would take more than 12 months to obtain
- new strategic partners would need to be located for the development phase

8

The Profit Criterion: Serving the Market Profitably

Now it's time to get back to business basics. The potential for profit is the most important criterion for evaluating new product ideas today. Profitability has always been a key part of formulating business strategy, but at the beginning of the Internet Era it took a back seat to the attractiveness of the new technology. With the return to economic reality, profit is again king.

The dot-com pioneers were able to convince investors to take a risk on a new wave of innovation that promised to change the way we do business. Such leaps of innovation gathered momentum, and no one wanted to be left behind. The new pioneers scoffed at conservative "bricks and mortar" thinking; the future looked so bright that revenues and profits were sure to follow, so detailed business plans were virtually discarded. Now, with countless new-economy companies either dead or on life support, the typical bricks and mortar company is still standing, and its income statements showing black ink. The primary lesson here is that you must have a detailed plan of how to make money before you leap into innovation mode. That plan begins when the product or venture is in the idea phase. The other lesson is that business leaders must have the courage to say no to entrepreneurs and developers who can't demonstrate that their ideas will ultimately turn a profit.

This is not to say that assessing the profit potential of a new idea is easy. Planning of any sort calls for divining the future, and we'd all be living in Las Vegas if we were that good at it. What's more, even though you may have a profitable idea at the product level, other economic or market factors can affect the profitability of the company as a whole. The best that you can do is to carefully assess the revenues and costs associated with the new product idea at the very beginning, in order to determine whether it will meet the profit hurdle.

Many companies make the mistake of comparing new ideas to the profit models of existing products. If the new idea fits the existing model in terms of similar profit margin, similar market size, and/or similar distribution, the idea gets approved. However, that approach leaves out the step of assessing the true cost for the new idea, as well as the specific value proposition for the new idea's target customer. The factors that applied to the existing product may no longer apply when a new idea comes along. For example, let's say that a software company has three major software product lines that are sold to large companies, and the new product idea is for software that is similar, but intended for small business customers. The profit expectations may need to be modified (the small business market might have a higher or lower profit margin), the market size will likely be different, and there may be different distribution channels used to get the product to the intended market. Any of these three factors will change the profit equation. The better approach is to view each new product idea as if it were a new company – with a clean slate. That way, the specific costs and revenues for that product can be calculated.

Predicting potential profit requires estimating revenues and costs. Estimating revenues is a fairly straightforward process once you establish the price and develop the demand forecast. Estimating costs can be more of a challenge, and many new product costs are overlooked during the idea phase. Development costs are obvious, but there are many other categories that need to be considered and estimated at this stage.

Maribeth Lazich is a veteran of implementing new high-tech products. With product management and marketing experience from Aspect (call center technology provider) and Entegrity (Internet security systems), she currently is principal of Market Keen, helping companies take their new products to market. *"Companies are tempted by the R&D money they have earmarked for new products or that they have obtained from investors, and they tend to rush into the development cycle too soon. Companies need to be more quantitative in evaluating the new ideas, particularly when it comes to potential profitability,"* she says.

It pays to err on the side of detail during the new product idea phase. Gather all the information needed to construct the whole profit picture. Analyze it and consider the tradeoffs before making critical decisions. During this stage of the game, remember that a company will not survive for long without profits. Don't be afraid to say no if necessary.

The profit mentality: view each new opportunity as a new business

Employees get more excited about new and innovative products than they do about reducing expenses or increasing sales for existing products, or about figuring out ways to increase profit in the company. However, people should approach a new product idea as if they were creating a whole new business, not just a cool product. You have to be able to get the cool product to the customer who also thinks it's cool and will pay money for it. You have to be able to produce, market, and sell the cool product at costs that will give you the required profit margin. Who will do all of these steps, what will it cost you and how long will it take you? Can you get your cool product to that customer at the right price before your competitors do? These questions need to be addressed for every new product idea.

If this "whole business" point of view can be instilled in employees, it helps everyone understand how their own jobs contribute to profitability. That's good for morale, and it's good for the bottom line. When new product ideas come along, people will be better equipped to understand the tradeoffs involved in deciding which products will be developed and launched. When they work on new products, they will be better equipped to make day-to-day decisions that will help reach the profitability goal.

Using the right profit metrics

There are numerous ways to measure profitability, and the choice of method largely depends on who's doing the measuring. A company's finance organization might use ratios such as return on assets, return on investment, or more complex ratios developed for internal company use. Investors look at return on investment, return on equity, and simpler metrics such as gross profit, taken from the pro forma income statement. When you measure the profitability of a new product idea, you are looking at the future, which means that you are making an educated guess. Regardless of how the calculation is made, you will need to estimate expected revenues for the new product several years out, along with all the costs associated with the product, forecasted out the same number of years.

The primary three factors that influence profit are product price, product demand, and cost to produce the product, as shown in Figure 8.1. Your company can control the price and the production costs. Your competitors can influence the price you set for your product. Your customers control the demand, but your company can influence demand through effective marketing.

PRICE - Estimated product price, influenced by:
1) competition 2) what customer will pay

DEMAND - Number of products you can sell, based on:
1) extent of customer need 2) competition

COSTS - All costs to develop, produce, launch and support the new product

Figure 8.1: Forecasting Profit During the Idea Phase

Most companies have an established method of calculating profitability. Fred Nikolac is the general manager for a product line at Acuson, a company that builds medical ultrasound systems. *"At Acuson, we know the ultrasound market pretty well, and we can calculate the realistic market share for a new product. We know our target customers well enough to determine the appropriate price. We also try to control our cost of goods sold by setting target limits. With those three measures, we can estimate the profitability for a new product idea. From there, the finance people may also calculate their ratios, but all the basic information is in place."* Understanding the market, the customer and the competitive environment will improve the accuracy of your profitability assessment.

Assessing the profit potential of new ideas

The research that is done to characterize the customer, market, competition, and resource needs will provide important input to the profit calculation. You must first consider revenue, which is driven by market factors and effectiveness of marketing and sales. You must also consider many different areas of cost, such as the costs to attract customers, market to them, distribute products to them, and sell to them. There are other internal costs, such as development costs, and the costs associated with changes to infrastructure to accommodate the new product.

"It's pretty basic," says Maribeth Lazich. *"You need to consider all of the costs to research, develop, launch, support, and obtain personnel for the new product. The other side of the equation is calculating the value of the customer's 'pain relief' and what the lifetime will be for that target market. Evaluating the profitability is like developing a very short business plan and then making a decision based on the bottom line."* To begin this profitability assessment, it's a matter of gathering the data, making the calculation, and then assessing the number that results from this exercise: how will this profit number fit with our business objectives?

Dealing with the revenue side of the profit equation

To estimate revenues, you need to know the anticipated product price, the timing and ramping-up of sales that will occur during the first year or two that the product is on the market, and the targeted market share per year that you estimated when the market criterion was assessed (see Chapter 6). The price of the product is used in combination with the estimated timing and ramp-up of sales, to estimate sales by year going forward. You should then compare the sales by year to the target market share number by year; will your sales ramp-up high enough to meet your market share goals? If not, then perhaps a more aggressive sales acceleration should be implemented. These are the steps to follow in forecasting revenue for your new product.

Establishing the price range for a product in the idea stage can be very complicated. Quite often, you must guess what the price should be, based on customer value proposition and market factors such as competition. If you have actual price sensitivity data from customer surveys or market researchers, it will help you be a little more accurate as to the product price.

There are many books written on the subject of pricing; it is an art and a science. Pricing issues begin when a product is in the idea phase, and they continue until the product line is rendered obsolete. The price of a product is one of the two determinants of revenue; the other is the estimated demand for your product. Pricing and demand are also often closely linked, and one can drive the other. If prices are low, demand may increase, and vice versa. However, that doesn't mean that demand will always decrease if your price is higher, or if you increase prices; it depends on the value of your product as perceived by the customer. *"If a company is considering increasing the price of a product in order to increase profit, the pricing sensitivity of the customer and their value proposition still needs to be the determining factor. The concept of 'whatever the market will bear' still holds true. The customer's perspective still should take priority,"* says Fred Nikolac. Perceived value from the customer's perspective drives demand. Supply can also affect the pricing dynamics. Sometimes if there is high demand for your product and you are the sole supplier, customers will buy at whatever the price, because the perceived value of a scarce commodity commands a higher price.

Competitive pressures complicate the pricing picture. If you price your product lower than a competitor's, then you may outsell your competitor as long as the customer perceives your product's value to be the same as the competitor's product. But customers' switching costs can also influence this; it may be more convenient for a customer to stick with the competitor's product rather than buy yours, even though yours has a smaller price tag. Can prices ever be too low for a product? *"You need to be careful not to price your product in the bargain basement range,"* warns Maribeth Lazich. *"It's very easy to lose credibility with your customers that way."* If your product's price is too low, the perceived value of your product may be diminished from the customer's point of view.

If your product's price is:	Demand will increase if:	Demand will decrease if:
Higher than competitor's	Customer-perceived value >competitor's	Customer-perceived value = competitor's
Same as competitor's	Customer-perceived value >competitor's	Customer-perceived value <competitor's
Lower than competitor's	Customer-perceived value = or >competitor's	Customer-perceived value <competitor's

Customer's perception of value for the price affects demand for your new product.

Figure 8.2: The Pricing Game

Fluctuations in demand, supply, and competitors' pricing strategy complicate the pricing game, as illustrated in Figure 8.2. However, if you focus on the customer's value proposition and have some idea of the pricing sensitivity of your target customers, you will be much better prepared to establish a product price that will help you get to market and maintain competitive advantage.

When you estimate revenue, you need to include everything that you are selling to your customer. Not only do you need to know the price of the product, but also the price of any related services that they might buy from you, such as customization or maintenance contracts. Once you have the prices of everything established, then you need to examine the sales cycle. The price and the timing of sales will enable you to assemble your revenue forecast.

The revenue side: ramping up sales

It may take a few weeks or several months to sell the first new product to the first customer. It may take additional weeks or months to sell to the second customer. The length of the sales cycle, and the rate at which sales ramp up, are critical factors in measuring profit potential for a new product idea. The expected product life is another important factor. If it will take one year to close the sale with your first two customers, and the product has a useful life of two years, then your revenues may not be sufficient either to cover your development costs or to result in any profit.

The easiest way to gauge the sales cycle and ramping rate is to create a timeline such as that in Figure 8.3. Obtain input from sales people as to the length of the sales cycle for the first, second, and subsequent customers; the sales cycle should get shorter as time goes on. If the new product will be a large and expensive item, then the sales cycle might be longer, and you may not have just a few sales in the first year. However, if your product is small with a small price tag, or is a commodity, then you may have hundreds or thousands of sales in the first year. At TRW-ESL, our ventures were large, expensive systems, so we required the first and second sales to occur within six months of market launch, regardless of venture. This forced the entrepreneurs to think about the reality of how long it would really take to close the early sales. So, think about the sales process and timing, and then plot each of the early sales on the timeline, using the price you estimated earlier. Extend the timeline out several months or years to show product life expectancy.

The last step is to plot your target market share (in dollars) on this timeline. The challenge is to ramp up sales to achieve the market share goal; the curve on the timeline may look like a hockey stick with a sharp upward bend toward the market share number. You will need to do some smoothing here; how fast can you ramp up sales to deliver product to all of your target market? This will depend on your sales and distribution strategy; if you only have one salesperson and don't plan on hiring any new ones, then you should decrease the forecast to reflect what one salesperson can handle. If you plan on having resellers or distributors sell your product, factor that into the timeline, but be realistic in estimating how much they can sell.

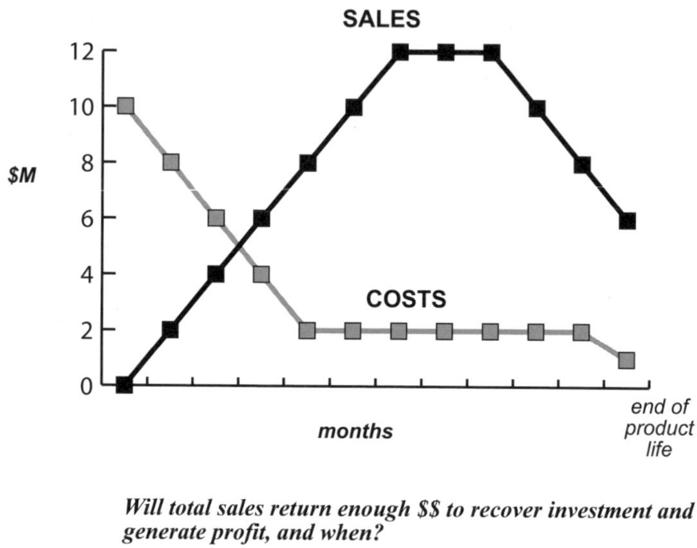

Figure 8.3: Sales Timeline

This timeline will give you a forecast of sales by month and year. Later on when you've calculated your costs, you can plot the costs on this same timeline and then calculate the date when you will break even and generate profit.

Dealing with the cost side of the profit equation

Forecasting costs is more complicated than forecasting revenues. There are many types of costs that need to be considered, and each of them occurs at a different time during the new product cycle, as summarized in Figure 8.4. The following section outlines some of these costs and how to use them in calculating profit potential.

The cost side: cost to develop the product

Development costs are often the only costs considered when thinking about new product profitability because development is usually the single largest cost associated with a new product, due to the length of time involved and the number of resources required to complete all the work. It's important to consider all of the costs involved at each step, from initial design through product test, including:

-Pre-development research
-Product requirements analysis and development
-Product design
-Product management
-Testing at all stages
-Production
-Quality assurance
-Beta test and subsequent modifications

The cost side: cost to change business or operational model

Can your infrastructure support the new product idea? If not, you may need to make changes to your business model or operations. Here are the costs to consider:

-Additional staff to support new operational functions
-Training of new staff
-Additional equipment or assets to support infrastructure changes

The cost side: cost to find paying customers

If your new product idea is in the "new-new" category, you will incur significant costs to develop the market. If you will need partners to help you enter the new market, those costs also need to be factored in. If your target market isn't new, you still have costs associated with marketing efforts to develop awareness of your new product among your customer base. Subsequently, you will have costs to find buyers for your product. Here are the costs to consider for this category:

-Marketing or advertising campaigns
-Lead generation
-Lead qualification
-Market development costs
-Partnering efforts

The cost side: cost to sell new product

The various modes of distributing products to your customer have associated costs. This is true whether you have a direct sales force or use channel partners. There will always be costs for training a sales force or channel partners about the new product. Here are the categories to consider:

-Sales tools for sales force and channel partners
-Training programs for sales force and channel partners
-Sales incentives and promotions
-Costs of acquiring additional distribution channels
-Channel partner management

The cost side: cost to implement market strategy

Your strategy to compete in the market may be simple and familiar or new and complex. The costs of implementing the required market strategy are also critical to profit, because marketing will help to create and increase demand for the product. The market strategy begins after you have developed some awareness of your new product among your customer base. The costs of implementing your market strategy include the entire launch phase, plus the continuous marketing activities needed to achieve your market share. Here are the costs to include in this category:

-Marketing programs and materials
-Launch events
-Company-internal marketing and sales materials
-Marketing programs for channel and strategic partners

The cost side: cost to serve customers

If your customers for the new product idea are different than those in your existing customer base, then you may have some new costs to consider: the costs of providing service to your target customer after the sale. Here are some of the specific costs to consider for this category:

-Training programs for customer support representatives
-Additional customer support representatives
-Warranty, guarantee, and return policy costs
-Account management for key accounts

The cost side: risks of cannibalizing other product lines

There may be a risk that the new product may take sales away from existing product lines, because customers may view existing products as obsolete or at the end of their life cycle.

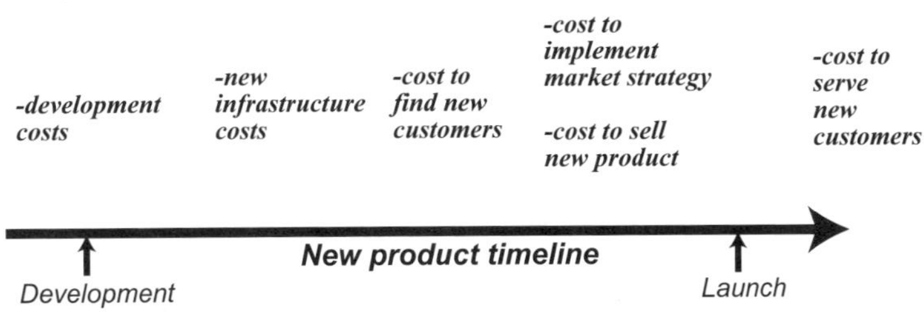

Figure 8.4: Types of New Product Costs and Timeline

Sometimes this is done intentionally and is part of the overall strategy for the new product in the context of all of a company's product lines. *"In some markets such as electronics, you can sometimes increase your profit by lowering your costs and your price. This is particularly common when a company enters a new global market and must lower the price in order to compete. However, there is always a danger that your other existing markets will suffer due to different pricing structures. It's wise to consider this impact before you enter that new market or build that new product,"* suggests Fred Nikolac. If you think there is some risk of doing this, compile a list of existing product lines, along with where each one is in its life cycle, the customer's price sensitivity, the price, costs, and profitability of each. If the new product would adversely impact any one of those factors, then the impact needs to be considered when making the new product decision.

How much profit do you need (and when)?

Determining profit hurdles is a very subjective exercise. It's a matter of managing the expectations of shareholders, investors, and employees, as shown in Table 8.1. What does that number have to be in order to satisfy all parties, keep the company in business, and keep it growing? Profit hurdles need to be realistic. If the company is depending on the new product to pull it

Table 8-1: Factors Affecting Profit Goals

-Investors' expectations - exit strategy and rate of return
-Shareholders' interests - stability, dividends, rate of return
-Employees - retention, motivation, satisfaction, productivity, skills mix
-Type of industry company is in and typical profit margins
-Company's planned growth rate
-Economic environment

out of a loss situation and into profitability, that's too high an expectation for a new product and too risky. New products should be viewed as opportunities to contribute to profitability or to increase the rate of profit growth, not be the sole supporter of the profit.

Sometimes, the typical profit margins for a given industry constrain the profit potential. For example, if your company is in an industry that operates on very thin margins, then that will narrow the range of profit that you can aim for when you evaluate new products. In such situations, companies may not have much leeway to either raise prices or reduce costs in order to improve profits, even with a revolutionary new product. In this case, it is a good idea to seriously question a new product that has a forecasted profitability well above or below the industry standard.

In addition to considering how much profit a new product will generate, you also must decide on the timing. At what point after launching the product will you measure the profitability? You must know this ahead of time, before you evaluate the profit potential for the new idea. At TRW-ESL, the venture had to be profitable within five years after spinout, to satisfy the internal and external investors. All ideas were evaluated accordingly, and we rejected those that did not meet that hurdle. If a product won't be profitable for two years, and your shareholders are expecting profit next quarter, then it may not be wise to pursue the new product. When it comes to profit, timing is everything.

Predicting profitability of new products

There are no guarantees with regard to profitability of future products. Economic and market conditions can rapidly change the profit picture for a new product. Examine past product successes and failures and their associated costs, along with pricing strategies and sales cycles to determine profitability patterns. If the product was not profitable, what could be done better the next time? *"If possible, evaluate the success or failure of meeting the customers' need,"* suggests Maribeth Lazich. *"Talk to the targeted potential customers who didn't buy the product and find out why."* If the product was profitable, what were the factors that made it so – on the revenue side and the cost side? If you are an entrepreneur developing your first product and your company at the same time, you won't have a history to learn from, but you can read articles and cases about similar products in the business literature to gain some insight.

Sometimes a company can launch a new product that is wildly profitable, and then the next product fizzles. To prevent that situation, Maribeth Lazich suggests involving your customer in your product line plan, or "migration" plan. *"Bringing the customer into the new product process early can help the company decide what products should be part of the migration plan, as well as building credibility with the customers to sell it when it's ready for market."* That's why it's important to view the company as a "profitability portfolio". There may also be times when it makes sense to develop a new product with marginal profit potential, if it might help boost sales of an existing product. That will add to the accumulated profit across the company. *"Companies today have no shortage of ideas. The difficulty is in determining which ideas should be funded. It's necessary to look at the whole product roadmap, as well as relative profitability of each product, in order to decide which new product would add the most value to the portfolio – in terms of profit as well as technology advancements,"* advises Fred Nikolac. Taking the portfolio approach helps you keep every new product decision in the context of the greater good of the company.

NOTE: The following chart contains categories to include when developing new product selection criteria. You need to craft criteria that work in the context of your company; these are merely suggestions. Additionally, the "Reject/Postpone" recommendations are a quick checklist to use in making new product decisions. Your own company's guidelines for rejecting or postponing a new product idea may be different.

Profit Criteria - categories to include:

-price as determined by customer value proposition
-length of sales cycle
-market size target (demand)
-all possible costs associated with marketing, selling, developing and supporting the product
-company profit goals
-the profit metric and how it's calculated

REJECT the idea if:

-the estimated profit is less than the company's minimum acceptable target
-the product would cannibalize another product line and decrease overall company profit

POSTPONE the idea if:

-the sales cycle can't be shortened without acquiring new channel partners
-the demand is too low in the short-term to recoup costs soon enough
-the break-even point or profitability point occurs too late (due to long sales cycle)

9

Market Strategies for the New Economy

A market strategy provides the high-level, overall framework for how you will get to market and how you will position your company and product in the market environment. People often confuse "market strategy" with "promotional strategy". For instance, when you ask a businessperson what their market strategy is, they might say, "Oh, we mainly use the web. It's cheaper than doing print ads." This response describes one marketing program used by the company to promote the product – using the web for marketing collateral. Market strategy is very high-level and encompasses more than just the list of promotional programs you will use when you launch the product. A complete market strategy must describe how you will capture the target market share and maintain competitive advantage, and the timing of market entry. Promotional programs are some of the detailed tasks that need to be done in order to implement this framework. Market strategy is, as its name implies, strategic in nature, while promotional programs are tactical. Strategy is how the war will be won and why; tactics are the details of who will do what to accomplish the overall objective. Figure 9.1 illustrates these differences.

Market strategy *IS NOT A:*

-promotional program
-distribution channel
-business or operations model
-marketing message
-differentiator
-partner strategy
-business objective

Market strategy *IS A:*

High-level statement that describes how market share will be captured and how competitive advantage will be maintained. Also, if it's a new target market, it includes the timing of market entry.

Figure 9.1: Definition of Market Strategy

An example of a market strategy is the "First-mover Strategy". This describes a situation in which the company intends to be the first to introduce a product to a new market – this describes the timing of market entry, i.e., as soon as possible in order to be first. The First-Mover strategy also implies that the company will be recognized as the first to market and will therefore have greater awareness among the customers in that market, leading to a greater market share. Finally, the company's increased recognition and reputation for being the first is how the company will maintain its competitive advantage.

Developing effective market strategies in the Internet Era is a matter of learning from strategies of the past to identify what worked and what didn't, especially the strategies implemented by dot-com companies in the last few years. Today, it may be a matter of combining the best elements of what has worked before with newer elements to formulate 'hybrid' strategies. It is also important to be willing to change strategies as external conditions change.

When to develop your market strategy

During the idea and validation phases for a new product, the preliminary market strategy should be formulated at a high level, using generalized information gathered about the customer, market, and competitive environment. The market strategy should be further expanded and refined while the new product is in the development phase, in response to changes that occur in the external market environment. In the month before product launch, the market strategy should be finalized, so it can be included in the marketing plan that is written prior to launch. The market strategy then forms the basis of the marketing plan for the product and contains the specifics of the customer, market environment, and competition, positioning, and marketing programs to be used in launching the product. All of the elements of the marketing plan should support the implementation of the finalized market strategy. Later on during launch or after the product is already being sold in the marketplace, the market strategy may change. If that occurs, it will likely require changes in the marketing plan as well. The market strategy always drives the marketing plan. Figure 9.2 shows the timeline that should be followed.

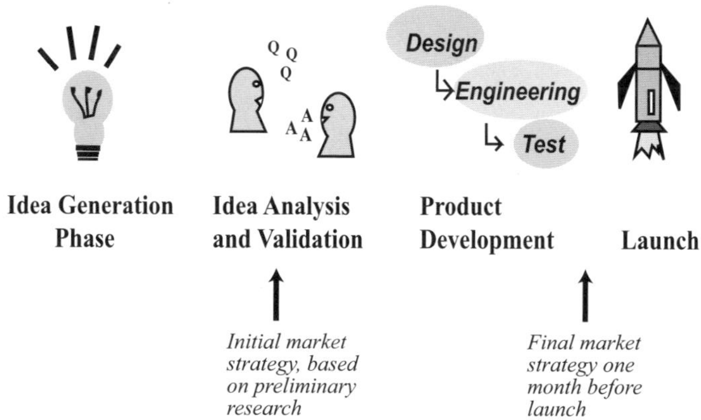

Figure 9.2: Timeline of Market Strategy Development

Market strategies old and new

Establishing an effective market strategy takes some science, some art, and a little intuition. Companies have experimented with various market strategies for decades. A market strategy that works in one industry may not transfer well to another. For example, using the same strategy to sell semiconductor equipment and Internet services would not be effective because the dynamics of the markets are different, as are the sales cycles. The same is true for consumer and business-to-business markets; a strategy that succeeds in a mass market may fail miserably in a business market and vice versa. There are, however, a few elements of older strategies that can work in today's economy. There are also some new strategies spawned by the Internet that have roots in some of the older strategies. This section explores some of the market strategies that companies have used successfully, and Table 9.1 is a summary of these strategies.

Table 9.1:
Market Strategies Yesterday and Today

-Low price leader	-First-mover + dominate
-Quality leader	-Market segmentation
-Technology leader	-Coopetition
-Differentiation	-One to one marketing
-Branding by itself	-Word-of-mouth
-Merger or acquisition	

In the days of the industrial economy, some of the most effective market strategies were based on price differentiation (low price leaders) or cost differentiation (lower costs due to economies of scale.) There are many examples of low price leaders in the consumer products arena, such as Kmart, Bic, Motel 6, and airlines such as Southwest that still use low price as an element of their strategy. These are all companies that have been around for years or even decades. Now that we are in the information economy when the customer is king, price is not as much of an issue in the marketplace; customer satisfaction has become all-important. Companies may need to combine the elements of customer satisfaction with their low price leadership to continue to be competitive. Examples of companies who use cost differentiation effectively are UPS and Wal-Mart; they have extensive infrastructures or distribution networks that lower their costs and make them strong competitors.

The quality leader strategy stemmed from the total quality management movement that began in the 1980s. The companies that could maintain measurable quality standards had a decided edge in the marketplace over the competition. Some companies, such as Ford Motor Company, even used slogans to proclaim their quality emphasis: "Quality is Job One". However, the quality movement was a good news-bad news situation. The good news is that it forced companies to improve the quality of their products and services in order to remain competitive. The bad news is that customers have come to expect very high levels of quality in products and services, and therefore it is no longer a competitive advantage for companies.

Product or technology leader strategies were based on the level of precision or sophistication of the technical solution. Silicon Graphics, for example, was well known for its high-end graphics systems targeted for graphics-intensive market segments. In the early days of high-tech industries, being the technology leader was a key strategy. Now it's expected, and the sophistication of the technical solution can reach a point of diminishing returns. At the point where the technical solution exceeds the customer's value proposition, customers become reluctant to pay extra money for the higher degree of sophistication.

More recent strategies are focused on competitors and the market environment. Differentiation is a market strategy that emphasizes the differences between your company's products and services and those of your competitors. Even today, this market strategy is successfully used on its own or as an element of a larger market strategy. Apple Computer has been using this strategy in its recently redesigned product lines, even using the slogan "Think Different" as part of its advertising campaign.

Branding has become an increasingly popular element of strategy, or is sometimes used as a single strategy. Branding of companies and products means the proactive promotion of the company or product 'identity', which may include its logo, slogan, or reputation. The objective of branding campaigns is to build widespread awareness across a large market. If you have invested the time and money to establish and strengthen a brand in the overall marketplace, it may indeed be an effective single strategy. Examples of strong brands that work as strategies are Nike, Microsoft, and Sony. When you see these companies' logos or hear their company names, there is an immediate association made with the types of products, as well as levels of quality or customer service or technological innovation (and perhaps some negative traits as well!) Brands such as these are established and have widespread recognition, and the companies are market share leaders in their targeted markets. In that respect, their brand acts as a market strategy, helping these companies introduce new products to the market very quickly, and helping to maintain their competitive advantage. For a new company, or one whose brand is unknown in a market segment, branding will only work as an element of a larger market strategy. You will need other approaches, such as differentiation, to help you establish your market position.

The first-mover and market domination strategy became very popular in the 1980s, and many companies still believe that this strategy works today. This strategy implies that the company is the first to enter the market, and does so with the intent to dominate the market and become market share leader. Examples of companies who have used this approach as their initial strategy are Oracle in the database market, and Motorola in the cellular phone market. Today, both of these companies have increasing competition from newcomers in the marketplace and have had to use other elements of market strategy to maintain their competitive position. Motorola, for example, lost a lot of market share to Nokia – a relative newcomer to the cellular phone market. Motorola has had to use differentiation of product features, such as lighter and more compact phones, in an attempt to regain their competitive position.

Another market strategy used today is market segmentation, which means dividing up the available market into smaller portions. The market may be divided in several ways: by demographics of the customers, by industry verticals, or by consumer versus business. *"The difficulty is determining how to segment the market,"* says Rob Abel, who is Vice-President of Strategy and Business Development at Eduprise, an e-learning company. *"You need to segment at a micro-level, not a macro-level, and you must divide the market by customers who buy things for the same reason. In my experience, that's the most effective segmentation approach."* Companies may do this in order to better focus on their true target market, but they may also use this as a market strategy, focusing on smaller and smaller pieces of the market that they can dominate – one at a time. This is sometimes called the "niche" market strategy. It can be a powerful way to enter and grow market share in an unfamiliar market, especially if additional niches are added incrementally. For startup companies, this is often the only way to enter a market and build competitive position – by focusing on a very small piece of it. Kinko's is an example of this strategy. When they first started their copy centers, they focused on consumers and students who didn't have routine access to photocopiers. Later, they targeted traveling professionals who could use Kinko's for business services as their remote office, thereby moving into the business market segment.

Coopetition is a term that was coined many years ago, and it is derived from combining the words "cooperation" and "competition". It means (legally) cooperating with the competition to more equitably divide up market share or to increase the size of a market. This is a market strategy, as well as a form of partnering. When coopetition was first formulated, it was based on the theory that competitors are attracted to the value you bring to the market, because it can have the effect of generating more revenues for everyone who is competing in the marketplace. *"Eduprise uses coopetition as an element of our overall positioning,"* says Rob Abel. *"Because we provide the services in our marketplace, and our competitors provide products or technologies, we collectively can deliver a more complete and whole product to the market, and on a much larger scale."* Coopetition efforts can sometimes lead to a merger or acquisition. When companies begin working together in the same marketplace, they may find that it makes more sense to merge efforts to achieve a larger combined share of the market. An example of this situation is Agile and Ariba, two companies in the B2B exchange market who decided to merge. Companies also use mergers and acquisitions as an intentional market strategy without engaging in coopetition first, especially if they have the size or investment capital to do so.

Personalization, or one-to-one marketing, is one of the market strategies that has seen widespread use in e-commerce and in doing business over the Internet. Personalization is a philosophy of focusing on the individual customer, one at a time, throughout the entire marketing, sales and support cycle. This is not an entirely new concept; companies such as Nordstrom have used the idea of one-to-one marketing for many years. But because doing business online over the Internet can be somewhat impersonal due to the lack of human contact, this strategy requires that extra measures be implemented to extend individual attention and service to the customer. Dell Computer has been successful at using this strategy from the beginning, selling customized computers to individual consumers and business professionals via their website. Dell had to make the process of configuring and ordering a system online easy and fast for the customer in order to compensate for the lack of direct contact.

Another popular Internet Era market strategy is viral marketing. This refers to the spread of marketing information about your company or products, via email or links among websites. This basically means "word-of-mouth" or referrals, except viral marketing occurs online and not in person. It is "viral" because it takes on a life of its own, and there is nothing that the company can do to control it. Word-of-mouth is actually a very old strategy that companies have used in whole or in part for decades. Tupperware is an example of industrial economy viral marketing; word about the company's products spread via homemakers and their friends. Examples from the Internet Era include Napster, which spread via email; and Amazon.com, which grew via website links and referral incentive programs.

Dot-com market strategies and lessons learned

The dot-com companies deserve a lot of credit for teaching the rest of the business world some lessons about market strategy. A lot of strategies were tried, many of them didn't work, but it was a great experiment in testing some new ways to approach the market.

The problem with the dot-com approach was not the types of market strategies used; rather, it was the reliance on the strategy without putting into place the other basic business elements, such as a realistic business model or the infrastructure needed to carry out the strategy. Also, some dot-coms chose strategies that only work for an established company, not a new company targeting a new market with a new product. An example is

Webvan; their strategy was to have the fastest response time with the broadest selection among grocery-delivery companies – a differentiation strategy. To fulfill that strategy, however, they spent most of their venture money on warehouses, inventory and procurement systems, and a fleet of delivery vehicles. They decided to build expensive infrastructure first, at a level that only large companies could afford to do. Those functions could have been outsourced or leased while the overall business concept was being tested; then if the market was strong enough those capital investments could have been made later. *"The dot-com demise had a lot to do with a lack of solid business fundamentals,"* says Tony Lustig, CEO of Red Oak Software, a company that makes a data exchange solution for the semiconductor market. *"You can't just announce that you are in business and expect everything to magically fall into place. You must be able to build a product your customers need and will buy, and then you need to scale and build the business from there."* A company can have a brilliant market strategy, but if it can't execute the strategy from a business or management perspective, it won't be in business very long. The market strategy must fit the company's infrastructure, operations, and financial situation.

The most common market strategy used by dot-coms that failed was the First-Mover strategy. The leaders of dot-coms made their case to investors by claiming that all they had to do was set up a website and people would flock to it – just because it was new and they were the first. In a lot of cases, there was no solid business model in place for generating revenues, and sometimes these companies even gave away information or services without charging customers money. *"It's amazing to me that all those companies put forth a business model where they would give away things free of charge. Over the long-term, those dot-coms only attracted customers who didn't want to pay for things, making it impossible to 'monetize' their business model. AOL, however, was a first mover but didn't give away free service (except for initial promotions); instead they emphasized ease of use and simplicity for newcomers to the Internet. They had a money-making business model from the beginning,"* says Rob Abel. The first-mover strategy must be supplemented with other elements, such as differentiation. In the case of AOL, they understood the customer value proposition of simplicity, and they differentiated themselves from others in the market, even though they were the first.

The second most common strategy used by dot-coms was branding as a single strategy. With many newly funded dot-coms, as soon as venture capital investors delivered the checks, the money went into ridiculously large advertising campaigns, in futile attempts to build a brand quickly. There were no projections done on the anticipated return on the advertising dollar. In most cases, that analysis would have shown that the expenditure on branding campaigns would have exceeded the expected lifetime revenues from the target customer base. Building a brand does not happen overnight from one Super Bowl ad. Many advertising agencies made a lot of money during this dot-com heyday, but they were the only companies who did. In the absence of other market strategy elements, such as market segmentation or personalization, branding does not work well as a single strategy, particularly for a new company with a new product in a new market. It is necessary to first build a customer base and then build up a brand incrementally.

Table 9.2:
Market Strategy Lessons Learned from Dot-com Boom and Bust

THE PAINFUL:
- Missing some basics: market strategy with no revenue model or infrastructure in place
- Lack of execution: no resources to implement
- "First-mover" as a single strategy (failed)
- Branding as a single strategy (failed)

THE GOOD:
- Word-of-mouth strategy makes a comeback
- Web as medium forces greater customer focus and personalization

From the dot-com experience, we did gain insight on how to apply some new strategies, as summarized in Table 9.2. Word-of-mouth marketing made a comeback – as viral marketing. Personalization came about through the necessity of providing human contact over a highly impersonal medium. Together with other strategy elements such as differentiation and niche marketing, we are on the verge on many successful hybrid strategies that can guide us into the future.

Hybrid strategies for the New Economy

A single market strategy is no longer sufficient to create profitability; one strategy is not enough for today's demanding customer, competitive environments, and dynamic economy. It's much better to use a hybrid strategy that applies the successful elements of what we have learned from the past and the dot-com experiments.

"Establishing an effective market strategy today requires a multi-faceted approach," says Tony Lustig. *"You need to clearly identify what it will take to meet the demands of your customers and deliver a solution for them. It's important to test out your market strategy ahead of time, using market surveys, focus groups or pilot projects. You should also have a backup plan handy and be able to implement it quickly."* Focusing on your customers and their needs is a great way to develop the market strategy that will work, for that is the test of a market strategy. If you can build and strengthen your customer relationships, it will also be easier to modify your strategy, if necessary, because you will have more knowledge about what is happening in the marketplace. It all begins with the customer.

Effective market strategies apply to the whole product, including how you deliver it to the customer and how you support your customers after the sale. *"Today, it's critical to have a well-rounded market strategy that supports all elements of the product and its life cycle. You also need to be nimble enough to modify your strategy quickly in response to market and economic factors,"* advises Mike Oitzman, Product Manager at Remedy Corporation, a company that develops customer relationship management solutions. A company can't maintain its competitive position in the marketplace by focusing solely on the product. Today's environment requires a higher-level view that includes the level of service throughout the product cycle.

In the next four sections are some hybrid market strategies for you to consider; they are summarized in Table 9.3. These strategies contain elements of some past and current strategies that apply to today's environment. All four have an element of customer focus, as well as consideration for the whole product. There may be other hybrid strategies that also emerge from continuing changes in our economic climate, so keep an open mind and try to find other elements that make sense for your company to use.

Strategy: Divide and conquer through partnering

Although partnering is widespread in today's economy, it is not generally considered a market strategy. In practice, however, it really is a market strategy. Partnering with the intent to divide and conquer is similar to the older coopetition strategy, but today, such partnering is used to develop new markets (rather than to divide up an existing one), or to enter a market that is new to the company. Partnering is also an attractive market strategy because technology and the speed of business enable these relationships to be assembled faster today than in the past.

Companies can partner to develop a new market, building market demand and market share for the respective parties. This approach works best when both parties envision the potential of the new market and have equitable resources and commitment to develop the market accordingly. Application service providers (ASPs) have used this model successfully, whereby the ASP provides offsite hosting of an application developed by a partner. Together, these partner teams created a whole new market, each gaining market share in the process.

More often, companies use this strategy to enter a new market niche, where the partner has different product expertise or knowledge of the market than the company. *"At Remedy, we are market leaders in some areas, but for markets that are unfamiliar to us, we consider partnering to provide us with the other 25% of what we need to deliver the whole product and necessary services,"* says Mike Oitzman. The partnering strategy forces a company to examine where the gaps are and to fill them, in order to provide a complete solution.

Every effective market strategy must be linked to the customer's needs and value proposition. Sometimes your own knowledge of your customer is different than that of your partner, which makes the partnering strategy more difficult to implement. According to Rob Abel, *"With a new product or service, it's hard to find partners who already know how to sell or get to the target market. Sometimes it's easier to use a direct sales force first, and then train your channel partners to expand the market coverage. At Eduprise, the services we sell are targeted to the academic and executive officers at higher institutions of learning such as universities. The channel partners we could use only sell to the IT people within universities. Selling to IT people and selling to the academic side of an institution are vastly different, so we would have to train prospective channel partners on how to sell to a different constituency in order for the partnering relationship to be effective."*

Strategy: Niche differentiation

It has always been a good idea to identify and promote your differentiators when developing your market strategy. Differentiation as a market strategy can still work in today's economy, except it must be extended down from the broader market to the level of a very specific market segment or niche. This is called "niche differentiation".

First you need to define your target market niche, which is a portion of a larger market with very specific customer characteristics. It will be necessary to understand the detailed buying behavior and value proposition of the customers in the target niche. You must also know the competitors who also serve that niche, as well as the competitive environment (see chapter 5).

The next step is to develop and understand your differentiators before you enter a niche market. *"Differentiation is the most critical part and the most difficult part of the market strategy for a product manager,"* says Mike Oitzman. *"Sometimes it's necessary to introduce a 'me-too' product to a new market in order to stay competitive, especially when the market is crowded. In this situation, you need at least two or three major differentiators to build a story around. You also need to 'deliver' on your promise; you must have the infrastructure and business model in place that support the claims you make through those differentiators."* Your key product differentiators may or may not relate directly to the customer's value proposition. Differentiation is more effective as a market strategy if there is a match with the customer value proposition, because that demand will help 'pull' your product into the market.

Niche differentiation is not the same as the older market strategy, niche domination. The reason is that if differentiation is used effectively, it's possible to be profitable without dominating the niche as long as the market demand is sufficient. Entering a market niche is also easier for startups, because less capital is needed to serve a niche as opposed to a larger market. Success in one niche may mean that it is possible to target another niche.

Strategy: Incremental personalization: building one customer at a time

One-to-one marketing means focusing on the customer down to the individual level and providing personalized service. This strategy involves building up a customer base, one individual at a time.

"Lots of companies say that they have a personalized sales approach to customers, or that they deliver individualized customer support. Those are just two elements of personalization. You need to take the time to build a trusted relationship with customers, from initial contact, through the sales stage, and support stage. That personalized relationship doesn't end with the first sale; it merely builds from there," *says Mike Oitzman.*

Using the incremental personalization strategy requires the ability to simultaneously manage many individual customer relationships, and that is not so easy to do. It may require revamping of every business process in the company that involves interface with the customer. From the first customer that you target, you need to be sure that all people that have direct interface with the customer provide consistent levels of attention, responsiveness, and quality of service with each customer interaction. Thereafter, each subsequent customer is afforded the same level of attention, responsiveness, and quality of service. In practice, this strategy may require retraining of people to work with customers at this level, and it may also require the hiring of additional people to maintain this strategy over a long period of time. The primary objective of this market strategy is to strengthen the customer relationship over time, creating longer-term loyalty. This approach is consistent with the idea of viewing each customer as a 'lifetime' customer, which refers to a customer that you can sell your future products and services to – over their entire product-buying lifetime. Regardless of the market strategy you use, that is a good way to think about customers in general.

Strategy: Viral evolution: growth through referrals

One of the new strategies prompted by the dot-com world is viral marketing. Many books have been written on that subject (see Appendix A). The Internet has strengthened the practice of referrals among people who are connected by web and email. The downside of this wave of viral marketing is lack of control on the part of the company. *"Viral marketing is a little bit like public relations. You can implement a public relations campaign, but you can't control what the media or analysts will write about your company or products. Viral marketing can't be controlled, either, and it's almost worse, because the information spreads much faster online than in print media,"* says Mike Oitzman. However, there is a way to influence the referral community, if not control it. That is by implementing a proactive strategy to build a referral community and then create incentives for people to use it.

Amazon.com was among the first to use an online 'affiliate' program – that provided a commission for referrals through website links. By being proactive, Amazon could control how the marketing information was displayed, and they could establish the process and rules that defined how the affiliate program worked. This market strategy can work well offline or online; the referrals can take place by humans actually talking to each other and giving referrals in person, or through email. The important element is to find willing participants in the community and to provide them with something of value for their participation (money, goods, services, or discounts).

Table 9.3: Hybrid Strategies for Today's Economy

1: Develop and conquer through partnering
-mutual commitment of resources, common business model and target market

2: Niche differentiation
-use differentiators to capture target market share but without domination

3: Incremental personalization
-focus on one customer at a time to build lifetime customer base

4: Growth through referrals
-proactive referrals, incentives with control

The changing role of branding in today's market strategies

When it comes to branding, companies either obsess over it or grudgingly figure out some way to deal with it. It's the rhinoceros in the middle of the room that cannot be ignored. Whether you love it or hate it, you will have to decide what role branding will play in crafting your market strategy.

There is confusion about what branding really means. *"Branding shouldn't be regarded as just a nice logo or an advertising campaign,"* says Rob Abel. *"Think of brand as the total experience a customer has with your company and product. You need to clearly delineate your position in the marketplace from the very beginning, so that customers are clear about their choice. Over time, you need to defend and maintain that position to build brand awareness."* The word 'brand' is an intangible concept. It is an impression held by buyers or potential buyers in the marketplace regarding your company or products. It's something that you can influence, but there is never any guarantee that the buyer's impression will, in fact, change to reflect your intended message.

For startups or companies new to the target market, branding is a huge challenge. Building a brand takes a lot of time and money. It is a necessary part of any company's strategy, however, even if it is executed on a small scale. *"Branding creates the perception of value that's important for growing the company,"* advises Tony Lustig. *"In the case of a startup, you may need to build a brand one customer at a time. Once you have a first customer, you have a reference account for the next one. These are incremental steps in the branding process. This approach works well for us at Red Oak Software."*

Branding efforts will help to reinforce your market strategy over time. Favorable impressions of your company, reinforced through branding, will help you establish and maintain your competitive position in the marketplace. Branding may also help to increase market share as more people become aware of your company. The important thing to remember is that branding should be done in the context of your company size and what you can afford.

When to modify your market strategy

The market strategy needs to be in place when you launch a new product. Thereafter, the strategy should be changed in response to external conditions such as the market dynamics, competitive environment, and the overall economy. Sometimes you may have to anticipate what those changes will be in order to react quickly. When a market strategy is established before launch, you should assume that it will be in effect for the first six months after launch. At that point you will have an idea whether it is working and can make modifications if it isn't.

Short-term and long-term market strategies

Market strategies should be developed for the long-term, but monitored in the short-term and modified as necessary. Long-term means that the strategy lasts several years. Short-term refers to just a few months. There may be instances where one short-term market strategy is used to launch a product, and then a different short-term strategy or a long-term strategy is used as the market share begins to grow and the market position must be defended.

Each new product that your company develops may have a new and different market strategy, but the strategies need to be managed in the context of the whole company. *"Each market strategy needs to be optimized for the organization; there has to be a fit,"* says Rob Abel. *"The long-term market strategy often becomes the leadership strategy for the company. Because of that, you need to make sure that your market strategy is based on the market position that you can defend. Once it's in place, the market strategy needs to be pervasive throughout the company, and people need to be trained in how to implement the strategy – down to their day-to-day responsibilities."*

Regardless of whether your company uses short-term or long-term market strategies, they need to be consistent with the company's overall business objectives. If many different strategies are used, or if they are changed too frequently, it can create confusion among customers; that is something you need to avoid. Above all, you want to apply market strategies that will help you create revenues and generate profit; that is the ultimate guideline.

10

Business Model Mapping

A business model is a framework that describes how your company does business and how you get your product to your customer. A business model map is a diagram of this framework that shows your company, your customer, your suppliers, and other partners involved in getting your product to your market. A business model map looks like a flow chart; several examples are presented in this chapter. Business model mapping is an effective planning tool for a new product because it helps you to understand the external environment and to identify the business relationships that must be in place when the new product is ready for launch.

During the dot-com boom, the term "business model" became the magical pair of passwords to open the door to venture capital. If an entrepreneur could convince the investors that his or her venture had an innovative new business model, it was sufficient to bring out the venture capital checkbooks. Unfortunately, a lot of the business models developed during the dot-com boom were just buzzwords and had no substance. Many people failed to understand what a business model is and what to do with it.

Business model mapping can be used for many purposes during the strategy and planning phase of the new product cycle. The process of business model mapping helps you address these questions:

-How does your product get to your customer?
-Will you interface directly with your customer and end-user, or will another entity do that?
-Which entities need to be part of the process of getting your product to your customer?
-Is each entity in the process:
  -cost-effective?
  -necessary?
-Are there gaps or missing links that need to be filled?
-How does money flow back to your company from the end user customer?

Creating a business model and thinking it through forces you to find the gaps where you will need to establish new business relationships with partners or suppliers. Business model mapping helps to refine your overall market strategy, so that you can readily identify the path of how you will get to the market and who will be needed to get to market. It's also a good way to compare different distribution channels, in order to choose the partner that will be of greatest economic benefit to your company. Later on, when the product is launched and the business model is being followed, the business model map can be used to evaluate channel performance in order to decide the optimum mix of partners for profitability. Business model mapping is a key planning tool for the entire new product cycle.

The business model is a map of how your company operates in the external world

Sometimes people confuse 'business model' with 'operational model'. The two terms have very different meanings. An operational model refers to the processes that are in place internally in your company, such as how the various internal departments work or "operate" together. An example of an operational model is a "project" model, where people from the technical departments work alongside marketing people for the purposes of building and launching a specific product. A business model refers to how you operate in the external market environment. Your external business relationships with suppliers, distributors, or partners are reflected in the business model, as well as their roles in getting your product to the customer, including post-sales support, training, and other services. Every business entity involved in the whole product cycle should be considered part of the business model.

The basics of business model mapping

The first step in business model mapping is to create a diagram with your company on the left hand side, and your customer on the right-hand side. Below your company, you may also want to add 'suppliers' if you will need them to develop your new product or service. Leave room in the middle, or add some boxes with question marks to be filled in later. Your basic business model map should look like Figure 10.1 below.

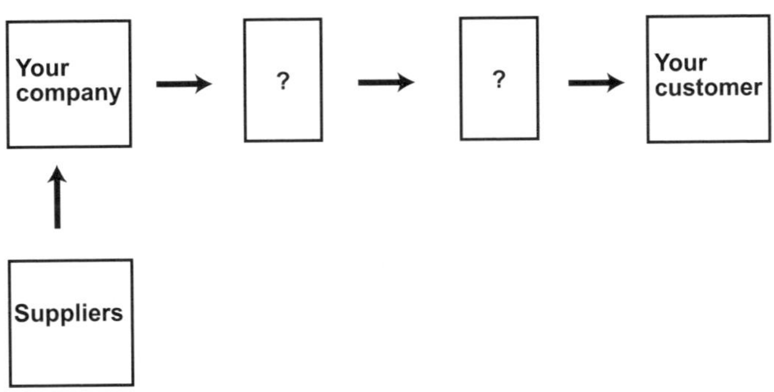

Figure 10.1: The basic business model map

Once you have this basic business model map prepared, it's time to start the thinking about process, either by yourself, or with your new product team. Begin with the question: who else do we need to help us get our product to our customer? There may be several choices that make sense for your product. Other business entities may include distributors, development partners who add further value to the product before it gets to your customer, wholesalers, resellers, or other types of channel partners. For every business entity that you identify, add it to the map in the form of a box. Don't worry about adding the flowchart arrows until all of the entities are on the map; you may discover that the interface occurs in a different place on the map than you originally thought.

Planning distribution

The next step in developing your business model map is to characterize your need for partners that will help get your new product to your end user customer. These types of partners are called 'distribution partners' or 'channel partners', because these partners act as a pathway for your products to your customer. Companies may sell products directly to a customer using their own sales force instead of having channel partners. Sometimes companies who have their own sales force also engage channel partners to help increase sales or market coverage. Regardless of which approach your company uses, the distribution method should be shown on the business model map.

For illustration, let's say your company has been in the business of developing data messaging systems and services for cellular phone users, and your new product is a wireless email application for palmtop computers. In this example, assume that your company has a direct sales force that sells to corporate accounts, and channel partners such as retailers who sell to consumers. For your existing business, your business model would look like Figure 10.2:

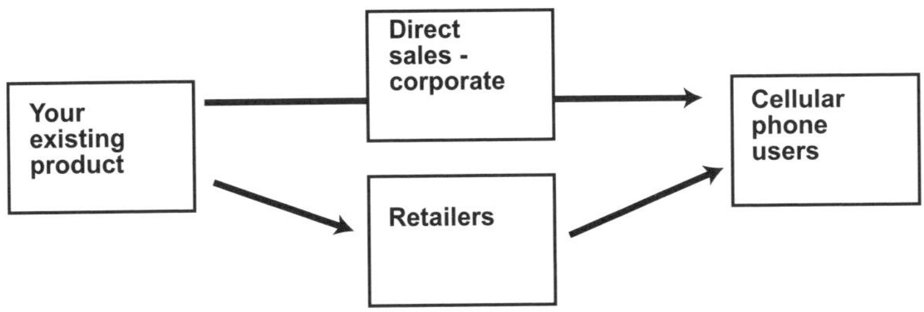

Figure 10.2. Existing Business Model for Wireless Company Example

In this example, you have two distribution channels: your direct sales force and retailers. For the new product, your customer changes slightly; the end users will be palmtop computer users who need wireless email applications. For the new business model map, modify the customer box to reflect that change. Now the question becomes: can you use your direct sales force to sell to corporate accounts? Based on your market research, you believe that corporate employees also use palmtop computers, so the answer is yes, your direct sales force can sell to these customers also. You can include the direct sales box in the new business model map also. Now think about the indirect channels. The retailers in your existing business are cellular phone retailers who resell wireless services such as yours, but they don't sell palmtop computers and related applications. For your new product, you will need other types of retailers or distributors who do sell those products. Here is how your new product business model would look in terms of distribution (Figure 10.3):

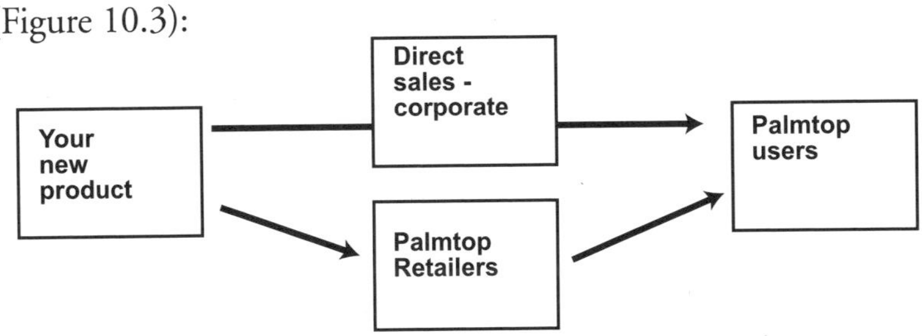

Figure 10.3. New Product Business Model for Wireless Company

At this point of the business model mapping, you have identified the need to develop at least one new business relationship. In addition, you also know that some retraining of your direct sales force will be necessary in order for them to understand the slight differences between cellular phone users and palmtop users in terms of how they use applications and their specific needs for functionality and features.

Other types of partners

In addition to distribution partners, there may be other types of partners involved who will help you develop the product or supply you with components or pieces that you need for the 'whole product'. Another important step in developing the business model map is to add these supply chain partners. In our continuing example of wireless email for palmtops, assume that your company already has at least one partner, who supplies a basic email software application that your company enhances. Your company adds value to the basic email application by adding additional features: a wireless interface from cellular phone to desktop email records, and wireless ISP interfaces and links. Now your company must add the features and functionality to a new platform, so two other partners are needed in order to test the application: a palmtop manufacturer to supply the hardware, and an operating system vendor to supply the operating system for the hardware (assuming that your company is not in the operating system business). Because these partners are used only in the testing process, and these partners add no value to your new product, they are usually drawn in with a dotted line. The next figure shows your supplier and development partners on the business model map (Figure 10.4):

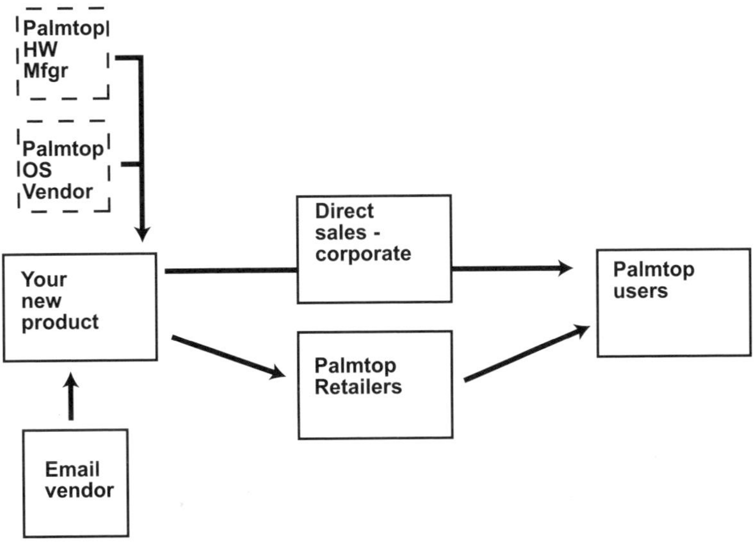

Figure 10.4. Business Model Map with Supply Chain and Other Partners.

Once again we have added necessary business relationships to the business model, but in this case these relationships must be in place before the development cycle.

Other types of partners may be added to the map to show other types of business relationships. For instance, sometimes companies have marketing partners who help with promotional programs or referrals but don't actually distribute or sell products for the company. Partners who do routine tasks for every product a company launches, such as advertising agencies or public relations firms, don't need to be added to the business model. However, if your company has a new strategic partner who will be helping you gain market entry for your new product, it helps to add them to the model. If the partner is playing a significant role, you may need to develop special marketing programs or materials that will help facilitate the process. Adding them to the model serves as a reminder of the new programs and processes that need to be put into place to implement the whole business model.

Clarifying customer interface points

The process of business model mapping can clarify whom your customers and end-users really are and can highlight the degree of customer interface that will be required as you take your new product to market. You might discover that you will not be selling directly to the end-user of your product, and another business entity such as a channel partner or marketing partner will be doing that instead. This does not mean that you should modify your product in any way, because it still needs to solve the ultimate customer's problem. However, it may mean that your marketing programs and strategy may have to be more extensive or complex, in order to develop awareness of your product and get your customers to buy it, regardless of how they purchase it and whom they purchase it from. Your channel marketing programs that educate and create incentives for your channel partners to sell the product will require effort and resources to be effective. The more channel partners you have, the greater the investment and commitment. Developing the business model map during the planning phase helps in budgeting and allocating resources for channel partners, so that all is in place at the time of product launch.

Planning the whole product

Another application of business model mapping is to make sure that the whole product will be delivered to the end-user customer. That means the product itself, plus any services that the customer may expect before or after the sale. This needs to be evaluated before the product is launched. For example, if you have more than one sales channel, the customer can be confused as to where to go for technical support. Sometimes your company's suppliers also offer technical support to ultimate end users of their components, making it even more confusing. Business model maps can be used to identify potential points of conflict so that they can be resolved before the product is launched. Using our continuing example, here is how to evaluate the customer support issue; for each 'node' or box, ask the question: is this entity the primary provider of customer support for this product? (Figure 10.5)

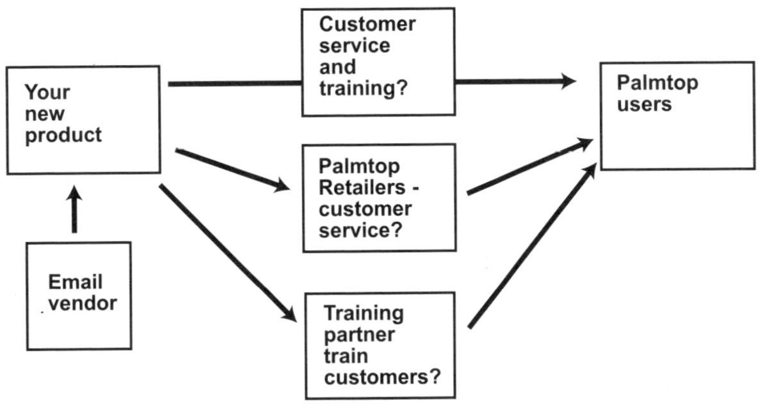

Figure 10.5: Which entity will be providing direct support to the customer?

Evaluating performance of potential channel partners

Business model maps should be used to compare channel partners, especially in terms of the financial issues. It's important to 'follow the money' through the business model. That means evaluating the economics of doing business with various channel partners. What discount must you extend to do business with them? How much revenue are they likely to generate? How effective will they be at reaching your market and increasing your market share? Comparisons can easily be made using business model maps by mapping in the dollars and then deciding which channel partner will be more effective (Figure 10.6):

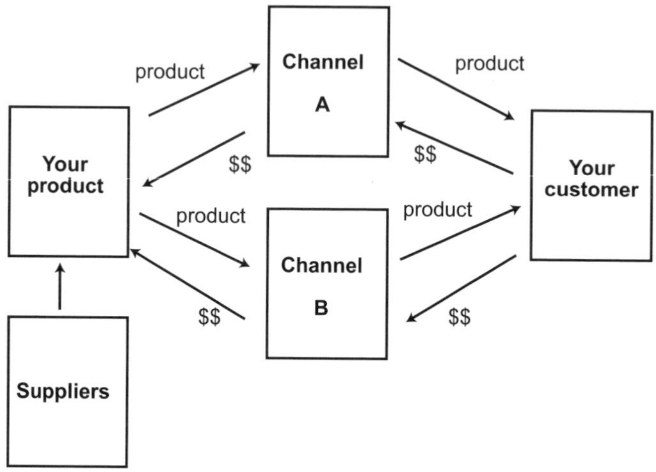

Figure 10.6: Use business model maps to choose the best channel partner.

This same map can be used after the new product is launched in order to compare the financial performance of channel partners (assuming that you are using more than one). Again, map in the dollars in terms of the net sales that they contribute. Sometimes, you may find that the original channel partners are not performing as you expected, and you can use the business model map to evaluate new ones.

Comparing profitability of different models

When planning a new product effort, it is important to do some 'what if' analysis using business model maps, in order to identify which business model will be most profitable. For instance, there may be more than one way to develop the product, using different suppliers. If your original intent was to only do direct sales of your new product to your customer, you may want to consider the impact of adding channel partners; will that help you reach your revenue and profit goals sooner? Also, you need to consider the return on investment for establishing those additional channels. Part of your strategy may be to sell indirectly through channel partners until you have entered the market, and then gradually build up a sales force. In that case, you could construct two different business model maps showing the initial and future business models, as well as the economics of each. By mapping in these entities and relationships, and then mapping in the dollars, you can use business model maps as a quick way to evaluate these different scenarios.

What to do with the business model map

When you have completed your basic business model map, you may think you're done and you can place it on a shelf, next to the dusty business plan. Wrong. The business model map will always be a work in progress. Once you have the basic business model in place, you will have a baseline to use. At some point during a new product's life cycle, you will want to make some changes to the business model. You can also use the business model map as a basis for many other day-to-day business decisions.

You can use the business model map to evaluate sales and channel performance on an ongoing basis. A good example is the case of a networking products company that needed to evaluate a slip in sales for one of its product lines. They weren't sure what to do and had several options that they were considering, including expanding the sales force, getting rid of channels, providing more training for sales people, or reorganizing sales territories. Here was their business model in place at the time (Figure 10.7):

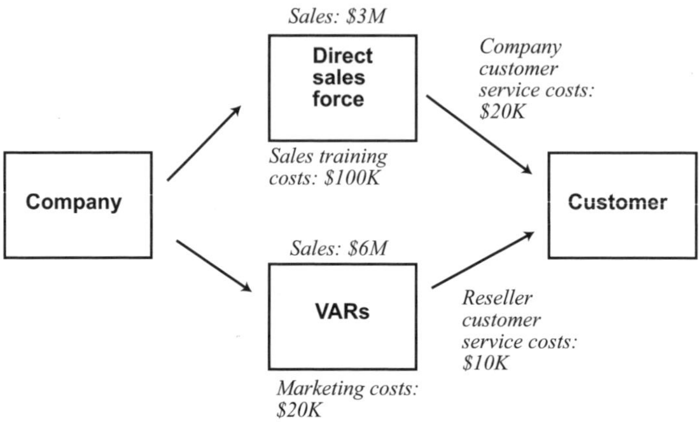

Figure 10.7: Evaluating Sales Channel Performance.

In the process of evaluating the sales figures, the company discovered that far more sales occurred from their channel partners than from their direct sales force. Because they were about to spend a major portion of their budget on sales training in that particular product line, they decided instead to spend the money on a promotional campaign for their resellers, and to redirect their sales force to sell other product lines where resellers were not as effective. Six months later, the sales for the product line returned to target levels. By diagramming the situation and mapping in the associated sales, the responsible manager was able to make an informed decision quickly, with a visible improvement to the bottom line. Although a similar exercise could have been done using a spreadsheet, plotting the information on a business model map makes it much easier to visualize.

Changing the model when new ideas come along

Once you have a working and successful model for your new product, that doesn't mean that every new product that comes along will fit the current business model. In fact, it is the other way around. The customer and the new product should drive the business model that you put into place. Part of the value of the whole product that is delivered to your customer is how it is delivered – which is your business model. Begin each new product effort with a fresh look at the business model that will work best for the new situation.

11

The Business Model Palette of the Internet Era

Several decades ago, there was only one basic business model that every company followed. No company dared to experiment with creative and innovative ways to get their products to their customers; after all, if it wasn't broken, why fix it? In the last few years, the beginning of the Internet Era, there has been a dramatic increase in the variety of business models that companies have chosen to use – some successfully and some not so successfully. Today, there is a large palette of business models from which to choose.

As business models have evolved and become more creative, the business relationships between entities are also changing. There is more focus on the role of the customer today. Resellers and distributors are finding new ways to add value. Internet technology is providing a new venue for the buying and selling of goods and services. All this change means good news and bad news. The good news: more choices than ever before. The bad news: managing and evolving these complex business models require more time and resources than ever before.

Dot-com lessons learned

The mantra of the dot-com boom was "business model". If an entrepreneur could dream up a new way of using the Internet to get a product to a customer or to provide a new service, venture capital checkbooks were open. Business models that arose from the dot-com boom were quite innovative. The problem was that entrepreneurs and investors were using the wrong definition of "business model". In the last chapter, I defined a business model as a map of how you will get your product to your customer, a map that identifies other business entities that may be involved, and that also shows how money flows back from the customer to your company. It's this last part of the business model that was missing in the dot-com era: the money flowing back to the company. That's why many dot-coms did not survive; their business models were incomplete.

We have learned a lot, however, from the new ways of thinking, and also from the ubiquitous connectivity that the Internet and related technologies provide. A lot of these business model elements still make sense, as long as there is also an emphasis on profit. The business models of the post-boom Internet Era are an interesting blend of the old and the new. Supply chains are still with us, but today suppliers might link directly with your company over a network, or they might participate in a global online exchange. Distributors and other channel partners still resell products, but with many new business models the role of channel partners has been curtailed or eliminated, as companies instead sell directly to customers online. In many cases, distributors have stayed in business only by becoming more creative and offering value-added services such as inventory management or customer support. Companies still sell directly to customers and also through indirect sales channels, just as they have in the past, but they may be changing their mix of sales channels by selling more products directly to customers online, as does Cisco Systems.

Every new product needs its own business model. During the idea validation phase of the new product cycle, research done to characterize the customer, market, and competition will provide valuable clues as to which business model would be most effective for the new product. When the new product enters the development phase, the business model needs to be chosen, and all relationships with external entities should be established. Sometimes an existing business model used by the company will work for a new product, and if it does, great. However, companies should view a new product as an opportunity to examine the current business model to see if there are ways to introduce efficiencies and provide more value to the customer. The innovative business models of the dot-com boom provide an interesting palette from which to choose, as described in this chapter.

Evolution of business models

Why do business models change? The basics of business really haven't evolved all that much in decades; you need a product to sell, distribution channels, customers, and perhaps suppliers. It's quite simple, at least in terms of identifying who needs to involved in your business. The challenge is in the implementation. How do you deliver a better product to your customer faster and cheaper than your competitors? It all depends on your business model, and how your company can manage the external entities that make up your business model – suppliers, distributors, and customers.

Increasing competitive pressure is one reason that business models must evolve. Other reasons are technology advances that impact how we build and operate our companies, and increasing customer focus. Narry Singh is Vice-President of Global Trading for Rapt Inc., a provider of solutions for dynamic commerce management. Narry believes that four influential people tell the story about why and how business models have evolved. *"There are four laws proposed by these individuals that have shaped the business models of today's economy,"* Narry says. *"Any business model can be described using a combination of these laws – which are related to trends in technology or business philosophy. Some of these laws are very old and have been around for decades, but still apply today. It's useful to think about how your chosen business model fits within these four laws, to discover how the model can evolve and be improved in response to changes in the market environment and economy."* These four laws are:

1. Metcalf's law (Robert Metcalf): The value of a network increases in proportion to the square of the number of nodes in the network.
2. Moore's law (Gordon Moore): The data density of integrated circuits doubles every 18 months.
3. Simon's law (Herbert Simon): An economy of plenty with a wealth of information creates a poverty of attention (to customers).
4. Coase's law (Ronald Coase): Companies should reduce transaction costs, and only perform the functions in a value chain that they can perform more efficiently than anyone else.

These four laws describe the impact of technology, communications, efficiency, and customer focus on how we do business. A company such as Dell uses a business model that combines laws 1 (the exponential network) and 3 (personalization); they compete by using the efficiencies of the Internet as a distribution channel, and by delivering personalized service to each customer. Bricks and mortar companies such as UPS have successfully followed law 4 (efficiency leader) in their business model, but more recently have incorporated law 1 (the exponential network) in order to provide more of law 3 (personalization). Intel's successful model is based largely on law 2 (technology value versus cost), especially since Gordon Moore was a co-founder of the company. Intel combined law 2 with law 4 (efficiency leader), but has also recently incorporated law 1 (the exponential network) into their business to enhance relationships with their suppliers, distributors and customers. Figure 11.1 shows examples of companies and how they can be mapped on this grid.

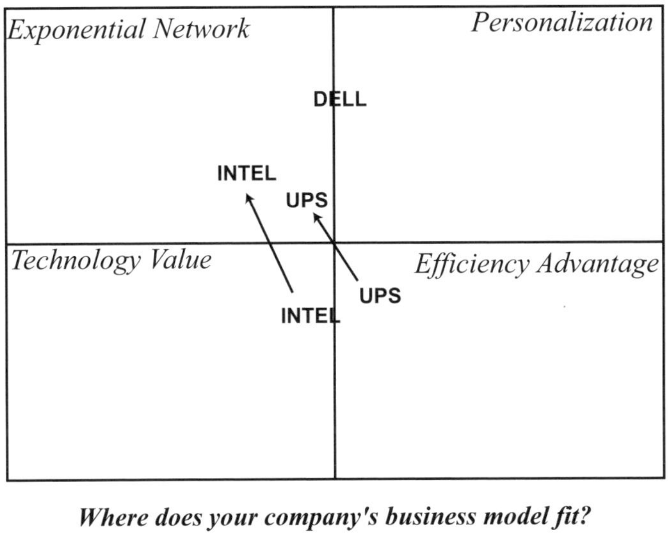

Figure 11.1: Four Laws Governing Business Models

It may be a useful brainstorming exercise to use this chart to examine your own company's business model to see what has worked in the past, and to find ways to change it in order to be better, faster, and cheaper for the new product that you will launch. If your company is new, or in the startup phase, you might want to use this chart to find elements of business models for companies similar to yours. When it comes time to change or update your business models, this chart can also be used to simulate new elements to add to the model.

The time for innovation – technology stimulates business creativity

The dot-com boom and increasing reliance on Internet-related technology resulted in many new ways of doing business. Indeed, the technology itself provided a new venue for doing business, and new ways for companies to market, sell, and deliver products to customers. That's why so many variations of business models were developed and implemented during the dot-com boom – the Internet provided a 'clean slate' for business creativity. Figure 11.2 illustrates some of the beneficial changes.

Brooks Fisher is Chief Marketing Officer for Intuit, a financial software company. *"The Internet represents a powerful way to extend the product life cycle curve,"* he says. *"Companies had to completely rethink commerce: how they delivered products and provided service to their customers. Companies today are finding ways to capitalize on the access and the efficiencies that the Internet can provide. Eventually, the Internet may become invisible, evolving to be a natural part of the way every company does business."*

Some of the business models weren't entirely new. For example, before the late 1990s, the idea of providing services to customers free of charge and making money through advertising was rare, but it did exist. The only Old Economy examples were media such as broadcast television and newspapers; their primary source of revenue was advertising. However, for the dot-com era, it was not a model that could be sustained for very long because web advertising did not prove effective for the advertisers. Indeed, many dot-coms who had such a model did not survive. However, some companies such as Yahoo have been successful by expanding their online offerings to include fee-based services, in order to supplement any revenue derived from web advertising.

One of biggest areas of innovation was in customer access. The Internet and related technologies made it possible to find target customers down to the individual person – regardless of where they were located around the globe. Dell Computer is able to do this easily, based on the business model that they use. One-to-one marketing and customer service is not only possible, it is becoming an expectation.

The faster communications made possible by the Internet and email have changed the way companies deal with suppliers, distributors, and customers. Customers expect speedy responses and receipt of goods and services. Suppliers and distributors can process procurement and accounting transactions using electronic commerce. Today, companies must provide email and website access for their customers and business partners to communicate with them, or they won't be in business very long.

Collaboration among business partners, suppliers, and even customers also has evolved through Internet technology and is playing an increasing role in today's business models. Participants in an online network can find each other more easily and can work together on mutually beneficial efforts, while reducing travel and other overhead costs that were part of the old way of collaborating.

-Internet capabilities forced new thinking and creativity

-Increased customer access and personalized service

-Better and more efficient communication among all participants in value chain

-Collaboration capabilities and reduced costs

Figure 11.2: Beneficial Changes Resulting from Dot-com Experiments

Because of increased access, faster communications, and the ability to collaborate, new efficiencies in doing business became possible for the first time. Today, the companies that will be able to attain and sustain competitive advantage are those that can figure out how to capitalize on those efficiencies. Today's business models must work in this new environment.

Customer-centric business models

A positive trend emerging from the dot-com business models is the idea of the customer being the focus of the company – no matter which business model is used. It's almost as if the customer is in the middle of the business model, and all entities in the business model revolve around that customer, as in Figure 11.3.

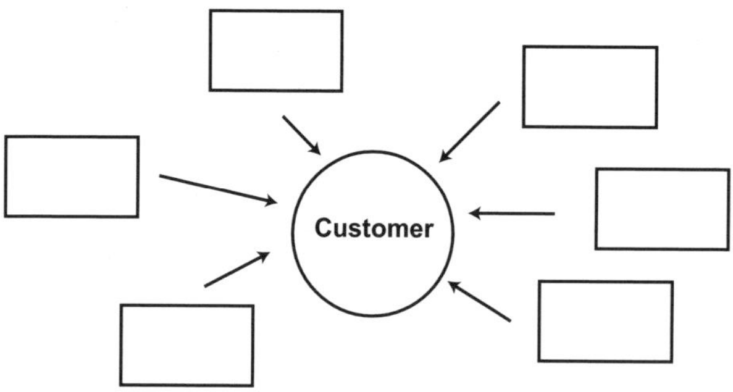

Each box might be the company, a supplier, a channel, a marketing affiliate, or a partner.

Figure 11.3: Customer-centric Business Model

In Figure 11.3 any supplier or company or business entity has equal access to the customer, especially reaching that customer via the Internet. Customers can interact directly with companies instead of communicating through distributors or resellers. That's the downside for distributors and resellers. Competitors can also find your customers more easily; that's the downside for your company. Because of universal access, the Internet truly has leveled the playing field for suppliers, companies, and distributors alike. More pairs of eyes are now focused on your customer.

It is no accident that the customer is in the center of this business model. Customers' power has been increasing, and companies who don't understand that won't be in business very long.

David Stoner is a Principal Consultant with DNV, a firm that provides training in ISO 9000 processes. *"Customers now demand just-in-time delivery of their goods and services, whether it's a business-to-consumer or business-to-business environment. Customers now drive the cycle times, not the suppliers. Companies must figure out how to meet the timing needs of their customers, and business models need to be driven by those needs,"* says David.

The Internet also enabled a fast and powerful way to receive feedback from customers. *"Customers today are accustomed to providing feedback to companies via email and the company's website. In fact, customers expect to have that communication channel provided to them. Companies used to spend millions of dollars implementing targeted customer surveys that would take weeks or even months to complete and analyze. Now, in a matter of hours, companies can get the same feedback, with very little cost. The customers have newfound power and the company gains more insight. It's a win-win situation,"* says Brooks Fisher.

Managing customer relationships is key to any business today, but in the new business models of the Internet Era, it's a matter of survival, as several books (see Appendix A) from the last five years have claimed. *"The companies who survive and are profitable are those that can achieve and sustain customer loyalty better and faster than their competitors,"* says Narry. *"Customers have evolved significantly in response to the capabilities of the Internet and related technologies. Customers' expectations in terms of value, privacy, and service will continue to increase; it truly is the age of the never-satisfied customer. Companies need to plan their business models to focus on the customer and their growing needs, or they won't be able to compete."* Figure 11.4 illustrates how customers can impact the business models of companies.

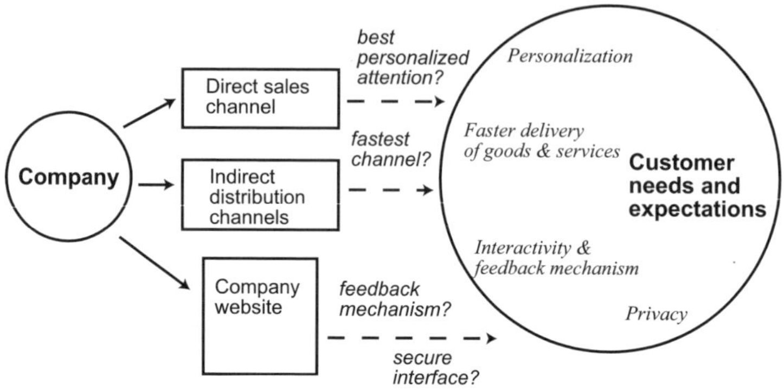

Figure 11.4: How Customer Needs Impact Business Models

Regardless of where your customer is located in your business model, you must understand how their growing power and influence can impact how you build and deploy your business model. Customers have become the most important constituent of the company's business model, and all other entities must provide and transfer value to that customer accordingly.

Direct to the customer: how distribution channels are impacted

With so much attention focused on the customer today, there is much more competition over who will have direct interface with your customers. Historically, resellers and channel partners played a significant customer interface role in selling. Today, it is much easier to deal directly with your customer, given the ubiquitous nature of the Internet.

The direct-selling business model was probably the most successful and most widely adopted of all those spawned by the dot-coms. Disintermediation, which is the elimination of channels or intermediaries in a business model, began to occur as a result of increased direct selling. Setting up a storefront website and selling directly to customers online is a way of eliminating many other entities (intermediaries) and significant overhead from the business model, and thus, it can greatly increase profits – as long as the target customer is comfortable with buying online. E-tailers selling consumer goods directly to customers (such as Amazon.com) set the trend for this model, and soon after, business to business companies adopted the model, including established companies such as Cisco, Apple, and Dell.

The online direct selling model also helped many small businesses grow and expand their sales reach, with very low startup costs. If a company could set up a website and accept credit cards, it was very easy to benefit from this model. This is likely to continue into the future.

Online marketplaces and supply chain models

In the past few years, many online marketplaces, supply chains, and exchanges were set up in order to exchange goods and services between companies. Most often, these exchanges were specific to a certain industry, such as automotive, chemical, electronics, or consumer goods.

Online marketplaces were also developed for consumers to buy and sell goods and services. In the case of eBay, it was a marketplace to buy and sell used goods. Figure 11.5 shows the business model for eBay. Who is eBay's customer in this model – the buyers or the sellers? eBay provides services to both, but only collects a transaction fee from the sellers. In the strictest definition, eBay's customers are the sellers, because they receive revenue only from them. The buyers are the sellers' customers. However, for this model to work, eBay must provide the highest levels of service to both buyers and sellers (and so far, they have been able to survive and grow their business successfully).

In a sense, the buyers also need to be treated as if they were customers, because eBay needs to make sure that the buyers can find the sellers.

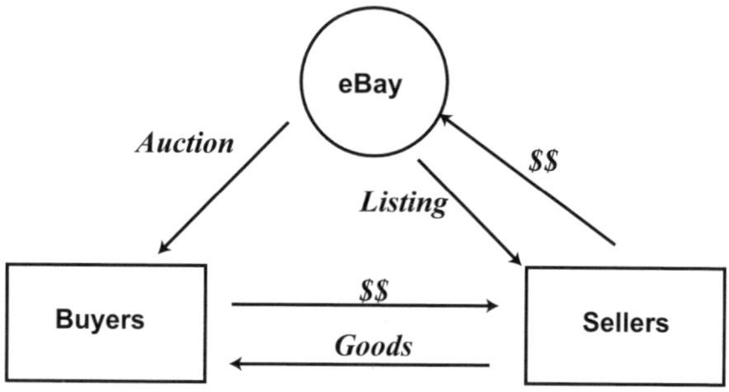

Figure 11.5: eBay Business Model

Another innovative model is that of the online buying cooperative, where buyers can control the price by virtue of collective demand and buying power. Mercata was an example of this model for the electronics marketplace, until they folded in January 2001. Priceline uses a similar model, enabling customers to name their price for certain goods or services. Other companies have developed 'demand aggregation' software or systems to help buyers participate in exchanges; an example is MobShop.com. The buying cooperative business model is shown in Figure 11.6. In this model, the customer has the power, and the company acts as the broker, managing the price that will be paid for the goods. The company also must find the right supplier, so that it can make money, and it also provides fulfillment to get the goods delivered to the customer.

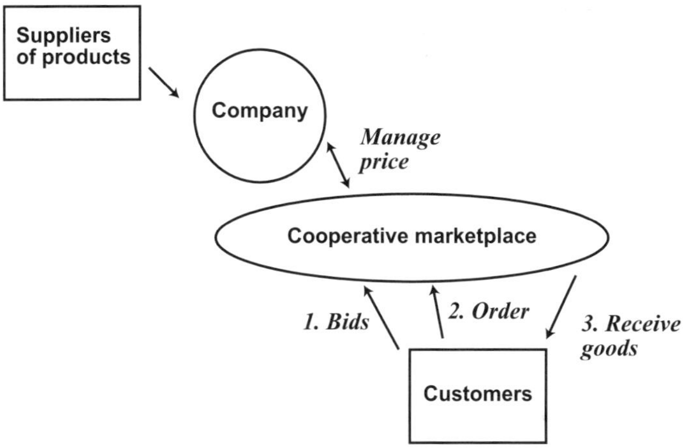

Figure 11.6: Cooperative Business Model

"Online supply chains today are all about collaboration and efficiency," according to Narry Singh. *"However, if you're just automating a system that's already a mess, you are no further ahead by moving the supply chain transactions to an online environment. Exchanges will only work if it makes money or saves money for all participants. Companies that provide infrastructure, software, or services for exchanges and online supply chains need to demonstrate the financial returns to the participants beforehand. Rapt, for example, only makes money if they save their customers money. In working with a large client, Rapt was able to reduce supply costs and increase profits. Before participating in an online exchange, a company should evaluate the financial returns they hope to achieve, and only participate if it will result in real bottom-line benefits."*

The concept of cooperative and online marketplaces can benefit your company and should be considered when choosing a business model for your new product. There may be ways to introduce more efficiency and more value to the customer by participating in an exchange.

What has happened to vertical integration?

A vertically integrated company is one that has invested in infrastructure and internal resources in order to provide all (or nearly all) of the services and pieces of a new product to a customer without using any external entities. Many years ago, this was considered a desirable goal, mainly because the company could control all of the processes. Some experts claim that the days of the vertically integrated company are behind us, perhaps permanently. This is because it is far cheaper and faster to engage other partners to do things for you, and it's much easier to communicate and do business today. But what about the companies who set up a new business online, offering their customers the opportunity to place an order directly, pay for the product, and have it shipped to them? And suppose that this same company has back office processes in place that produce (internally or externally) or ship the item on a just-in-time basis triggered by the customer's online order. This is really vertical integration, deployed via the Internet. In this new version of vertical integration, the Internet provides the glue of connectivity that enables efficiency in communicating the transactions among all the participants in the value chain. In this case, all the participants happen to be different departments within the same company. Figure 11.7 shows the "before and after" of a company with conventional distributors that moved their operations online.

Vertical integration - before Internet		Vertical integration today - deployed via Internet	
-Internal infrastructure -Facilities, technology -People resources -R&D -Production -Marketing & sales -Inventory, warehousing -Fulfillment -Customer support -Billing and accounting	-External: -One or two distributors	-Internal infrastructure -Technology -People resources -R&D -Marketing	External: -Facilities -Equipment -Production -Distributors -Inventory -Warehousing -Fulfillment -Customer support Billng and accounting

Figure 11.7: Evolution of Vertical Integration

Says Narry Singh, *"Before the Internet, a company would pursue vertical integration if it was worried about competitors and needed more control of the supply chain. Vertical integration required investments in infrastructure and resources, which often was out of reach for many companies. Today, the Internet and the communication it enables, in effect provides a virtual infrastructure that allows people in different departments to participate in the value chain to provide products and services to the customer using the same network."* David Stoner says, *"The established bricks and mortar retailers and e-tailers were among the first companies to successfully implement a vertical integration model. Using the Internet and its global reach, retailers can promote their products, take orders that trigger the manufacture and/or shipment of an item, and complete the financial transaction – all from one website. Companies in business-to-business markets can use the same approach. The Internet has enabled vertical integration from top to bottom, and it can help companies regain their competitive advantage by doing everything internally."*

A checklist of new business models

With a new product, you have a golden opportunity to put the dot-com innovations to use in crafting your business model. You need to consider several issues relative to the basics of your model: the product, suppliers, distributor, and customer. It's also an opportunity to consider how technology advances can improve access to your customer or make your model more efficient. Figure 11.8 is a checklist of questions for your business model planning.

1. *Do you need all the distributors and channels that are in your existing business model?*
2. *How can access to the customer be expanded?*
3. *Can another entity deliver your product or service more efficiently?*
4. *How can the Internet and related technologies improve efficiency or customer access?*
5. *Does your company have the network infrastructure to sell directly to your customers online?*
6. *Does your target customer use the Internet to purchase products and services?*
7. *Does your customer purchase from specific channels?*
8. *Are there exchanges or online marketplaces that your company can use to reduce supply chain costs?*
9. *How do your competitors sell their products to the marketplace?*
10. *How can you deliver superior customer service within your new business model?*
11. *How can you use the Internet and related technologies to reduce channel support and management costs (i.e., extranets, collaboration, data sharing)?*

Figure 11.8: Business Model Planning Checklist

Investments in new business models can be huge and can take a great deal of time to implement. How can you tell if the one you choose is the best one for your company? *"At Intuit, we have learned that it's wise to do some what-if analysis and modeling ahead of time,"* says Brooks Fisher. *"The first questions to ask are whether the company is in the right business to be able to implement the chosen business model, and how the company makes money. Map it out and follow the money through the model. What are the tradeoffs that must be made regarding investments in infrastructure, finding channel partners, and reaching the customer?"* It's very important to take the time to analyze the business model before investing in expensive process and infrastructure changes. The ultimate goal, of course, is profitability. *"The right business model is the one that shows a clear path to profitability,"* according to Narry Singh. *"Sometimes profit happens in the short-term, sometimes in the long-term, but regardless of the timing, you have to make money with your business model."*

When do you change the business model? *"If an existing business model is not profitable, it's time to change it,"* advises David Stoner. *"Keep this in mind if you have a new product and you are considering using a business model from an existing product. Will that model work in your new target market, and what is the cycle time expectation of that target customer? If you can't meet the needs of the customer, you won't be competitive and you won't be profitable. The same approach should be used for existing products; the model should be evaluated every few weeks or months, depending on how fast the market changes."* It is necessary to have success criteria for your business models and to evaluate them periodically. Financial factors such as revenue and profit are common measurement criteria, but there are others as well. Customer retention levels and customer satisfaction ratings are also key criteria. If there is manufacturing involved, then quality issues, yields, and manufacturing cycle times should be measured.

Transferring value throughout the chain

Business models today are less linear. The shape of them is more like a hub with spokes, often with the customer at the center of the hub. With the innovative business models we have today, it is not so easy to deliver and measure value all the way through the business model or value chain. It's particularly difficult to make sure that all of the necessary processes are in place to support the model. David Stoner believes that companies should take an integrated systems approach when implementing a new business model, to ensure that value can be distributed. *"Companies will often develop and perfect one process at a time, but the processes aren't linked. Each process must be developed using the customer requirements as a basis, and must work efficiently, but also must link to all other processes in the system including the supply chain. The collection of processes needs to be linked and seamless in order to transfer the value to the ultimate customer."* Crafting a new business model on paper is one thing, but developing and deploying the business processes that will make the model work is a serious and often expensive effort. In your planning effort, it is important to take the time to evaluate the business processes that are already in place or that need to be in place by the time the new product is launched, and then to factor that into the overall product budget.

If you have other business entities in your business model, value transfer becomes more complicated. *"The key to value transfer is to create incentives for your channel partners, even your suppliers,"* says Brooks Fisher. *"If you have cash and customers, you will have greater leverage to make sure that your partners are delivering your products and services the way that customers want them delivered. If your partners don't deliver the intended value, their bottom line and their reputation will be adversely affected."*

Managing multiple business models

As your company grows and develops new products, it is possible that you may have several different business models to manage simultaneously. And because the corresponding business processes must support each business model, you may run into conflict or resource issues in trying to keep everything running smoothly. *"The internal challenges are huge when it comes to managing several business models,"* says Brooks Fisher. *"It is necessary to examine the infrastructure of multiple internal departments to make sure all the skills are in place and to make sure that all the back-end processes are in place to support different operations. In particular, it is imperative to be able to share data, and the back-end systems need to provide the access and the updating of information on customers, products, suppliers, and channel partners."*

The other important element of business model management is flexibility, especially the willingness to change business models if they are not profitable. Each business model needs to be evaluated in terms of its own level of profitability. One business model may be profitable on its own, but if maintaining that model is stressing the infrastructure and processes of the other business models, then perhaps it needs to be changed. The profitability of the company as a whole needs to be considered, and the business models need to work in that greater context.

12

The New Breed of Partners: Distributing Value

The need to get new products to market faster than ever before is prompting an unprecedented degree of corporate partnering. There is much value to be gained from partnering – for your company, for your partner, and most importantly, for your target customer. Few companies have the resources – financial, intellectual, or geographic – to do everything themselves. It's faster and easier to use a partner's resources to get to market quickly. Any time that you venture outside your company to use another company's expertise or resources, you are forming a partner relationship with that company to one degree or another, even if it's just a supplier or vendor relationship.

Partnering has multiple benefits, but it's also very challenging to build and manage partnering relationships. Companies are recognizing the need to ensure that value is transferred through the partner relationship to the ultimate customer or end user of the product. Companies are gradually learning to do a better job of selecting and managing partners to help reach their goals of profitability and speed.

The need for partners becomes clear during the process of mapping a business model for a new product. Companies must begin the process of finding partners well ahead of product launch date, in order to have the proper relationships in place by the time the product is ready for launch. It can easily take months to determine the type of partner that is needed, to find candidates, screen them, negotiate with them, and sign a contract. Companies are sometimes able to put a deal together in a few days or weeks, but only if the candidate has already been researched and identified, and if both partners are ready to move quickly.

The rising popularity of partnering

Why has partnering become so popular in recent years? It is largely due to the changes in the economy, technology advances, and accelerated new product cycles, which result in a shortened time to market. For new companies and startups, acquiring investment capital is often a challenge, forcing them to be creative about getting more done with fewer resources. As a result, companies are changing their business models to include partners. It is no longer feasible to maintain a huge staff that can provide every aspect of getting a product developed and sold into the market. In many cases, it is far quicker and more economical to have another company share the burden with you. It enables companies to remain lean and mean, and to concentrate on what they do best.

Technology advances, such as Internet connectivity, make it easier to find partner candidates and to communicate with them. Specialized software applications that can be deployed over the Internet can also enable collaboration among partners. Such collaboration and communication tools make it easier to track the status of cooperative efforts and manage partnerships.

The shortened time to market is the major reason that companies are turning to partnering today. During the development phase of a new product, partners may help to package or prepare the product for the market, speeding introduction. When the product is ready for launch, engaging the right partner with the right contacts can pave the way for a company to enter a new and unfamiliar market, often before competitors get to market. Partners can also help expand market coverage in the target segment, or provide entry into additional market segments, helping the company reach market share targets sooner. Sometimes partnering is also done as a preemptive move to block competitors or reduce their market share.

Today, companies of any size may have already had experience with managing several or even dozens of business partners. As companies increase their partnering activity, they accumulate knowledge about how to implement and manage partnerships. This makes it easier to engage the next business partner, and it speeds up the process.

Partnering for many purposes

There are a multitude of reasons to partner with another company, depending on the gaps in your own company's resources and capabilities, as shown in Figure 12.1. The most common partnering relationship is that of a channel partner who resells your product to the customer, with or without adding value. Channel partners are sales partners. But there are also partnering relationships for the purposes of investment, technical development, operations and manufacturing, marketing, customer service and support, and training. Your company's suppliers and vendors are supply chain partners. Essentially, any type of service or component that adds further value to your new product represents an opportunity to partner. Partners may be engaged at any point during the new product cycle, from pre-development through launch, depending on the type of partnership (Figure 12.2). The details of the partnering relationship may be formalized and captured in a signed contract, or they may be informal, as in a vendor or supplier relationship with simple business transactions that guide the buying and selling of services.

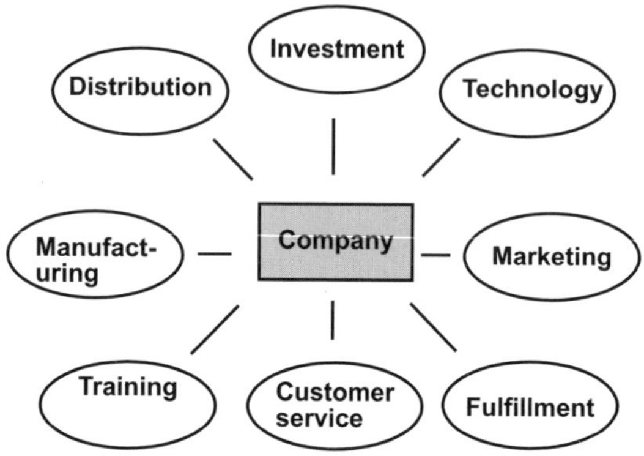

Figure 12.1: The Types of Partners

Investment partners are individuals or companies who invest in a new company or startup, or in an established company as part of a growth strategy. Although many people would not include investment partners as active business partners, the role of investors has changed over the last few years. Today, key investors may be involved in formulating strategy, serving on the board of directors or a board of advisors, or providing key contacts for market entry and expansion. Many of the venture capital firms in Silicon Valley, and even the angel investors do this for their portfolio companies.

Partners may be engaged to help develop a product or service, or to provide key technology that adds value to your own company's product. Development partners can significantly reduce the development time for new products, and many companies routinely use such partners, especially for high tech products. For instance, large software companies such as Microsoft and Oracle, as well as smaller software companies have formalized partner programs for independent software developers that leverage each other's technology in the marketplace.

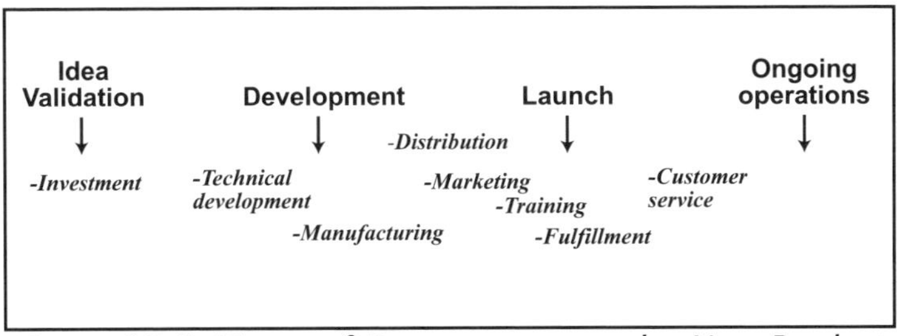

Figure 12.2: Types of Partners versus the New Product Cycle

Manufacturing is often handled by strategic partners, especially if the company does not have the infrastructure or internal resources to mass-produce the new product. If manufacturing is required, the partner should be involved during the latter part of the development cycle, so that production can begin when all product testing has been completed. Even large companies use manufacturing partners. In the semiconductor or chip business, companies such as Applied Materials and Intel have global manufacturing partners to supplement their own operations.

Marketing partners can help achieve entry into a new market, or help develop a new market segment. This type of partner is generally used when the company is targeting an unfamiliar market and needs to build awareness quickly. This is sometimes a difficult partnership to develop, because there needs to be some type of significant incentive for the marketing partner to help with another company's product. If the marketing partner has complementary but not competing products to sell, and is established in your company's target market, they might enhance their company's image if your products can provide a more complete solution for their customers. Another incentive might be an arrangement whereby the marketing partner is seeking entry into a market in which your company has significant presence, hence mutual benefit. There are many types of incentives and scenarios that might work, limited only by the creativity of the two companies involved. The important thing is to make sure that each company is receiving mutual benefit from the relationship.

Customer service and support partners are often engaged when a company does not have the infrastructure to provide those services, or needs proven expertise that might only be available from a partner already in that business. This is a common type of partnering, and a very critical one, because, with the exception of the sales force, no other group will have as much direct customer contact. It's very important to make sure that there is a way for the customer service partner to gather and report customer feedback to your own company.

Training partners can be sought if there is a significant amount of customer training that needs to be provided for your product or service. Just as with the customer service partner, training partners have significant direct contact with your customers, and there needs to be a feedback mechanism as well as a level of trust in the training company.

In Chapter 10, the supply chain part of a business model was defined as the collection of vendors and suppliers who provide pieces of your total product – before, during, or after development. Vendors and suppliers should be regarded as strategic partners also, because they are vital to maintaining speed and profitability of your new product cycle. They are usually referred to as 'supply chain partners'.

Benefits of partnering

The primary benefits of partnering are speed, filling in the gaps in the 'whole product', and opening up markets. These benefits are significant and compelling to any company, regardless of size. Maribeth Lazich is a Principal of a marketing management consultancy called Market-Keen. She says, *"How can you **not** partner today? The financial, marketing and technical benefits are huge. Partnering has shown us that there truly is strength in numbers. It can significantly reduce your cost of doing business and also reduce time to market. Today, no one company can pro-*

vide the whole solution, and it makes good business sense. Partnering is becoming a core business skill for companies today."

Speeding up the development cycle or time to market is a significant benefit of partnering. Leveraging the resources of a partner's company means that your company doesn't need to spend the time to recruit, hire, or train people to do what it will take to get your new product to market on time. That alone can reduce time to market by weeks or even months.

The 'whole product' concept refers to all the services and support necessary to develop, produce, launch, and support the new product. Customers now expect companies to deliver all the value of the whole product at the time it is launched. Unless your company is very large or 'vertically integrated', you may need to look to partners to fill in some of the gaps in delivering the whole product to the marketplace. Such partners might include a customer support organization that is already supporting other product lines, or a manufacturer who has the capability of mass-producing the new product quickly and efficiently. In some cases, you may need to look for new partners to fill in the gaps, especially if your company has no plans to add the required infrastructure or resources internally. Whether you engage existing partners or find new ones, the ability to fill in the whole product gaps represents a significant benefit for your company. *"The right partners managed effectively can act as an extension of your company,"* says Bob Yee, Marketing Manager at Cisco Systems. *"At Cisco, we have done extensive partnering. We identify the areas where we can best leverage the partners' resources and strengths. It's about doing more with less, but it's also being strategic about how best to deliver value to the customer."*

There are many marketing benefits of partnering. Through partners, it is possible to quickly expand market coverage to new vertical markets or expand presence in an existing one. When two companies partner, one can leverage the brand presence of the other; it's a way of gaining more market awareness through association. *"Credibility rubs off,"* says Maribeth Lazich. *"Associating your company with a partner who has strong brand presence is a great way to leapfrog into the marketplace."* Partnering can change the competitive landscape because it increases the combined competitive advantage of the two companies. Through a partner, it is possible to learn more about the market and the products that the customers need. Partnering also creates an opportunity to share marketing expenses, ultimately enhancing the bottom line of both companies.

The challenges of partnering

There are a lot of benefits to partnering, but there are also significant challenges that need to be considered. These include: giving up control or interface with the customer, brand dilution, and need for effective management.

If your partner will have direct contact with your customer, this can create a perception of less control, especially among the sales force. *"It's a matter of trust,"* says Maribeth Lazich. *"There will always be some level of mistrust among the direct sales force because they see a partner as competition toward meeting their goals. However, it's important that the sales force understand where the line of demarcation is with regard to interfacing with the customer. If that understanding is clarified at the very beginning of the partnership, conflict is reduced."*

Partnering with another company can create brand confusion among your customers. If you are a small company partnering with a big company with a recognizable brand, your own brand can be easily overshadowed. The upside, however, is that you may be able to 'piggy-back' on the other company's brand, which can create more awareness of your company and products in the long-term. *"Brand dilution is always a risk when partnering,"* says Steven Puthuff, Chairman and Founder of Sybersay, a wireless voice-enabled mobile communications company. *"I have found that the best defense is a good offense. If you have a solid plan to build your own brand regardless of which company you partner with, you will win in the long run. Don't expect another company to build your brand for you; you must do that yourself or you won't make it in the marketplace. You may choose to be just an OEM type of company, but the Silicon Valley graveyard is full of those companies who became too dependent upon one big partner."*

Another challenge is effective partnership management. *"Partnering is not free,"* says Bob Yee. *"It takes a lot of resources to set up partnerships and manage them effectively. That must be taken into account before partners are even identified. If a company does not have the resources to meet this challenge, then they should not consider partnering."* Companies must recognize that managing a partner relationship is a significant challenge, different than simply managing another department in the company, and it will require dedicated resources and unique processes.

Distributing value through partners to your customer

Every partner that you engage for your new product must contribute or increase value to the ultimate customer. This is not so easy to accomplish, especially if the partner has more direct interface with your customer than your company does, as shown in Figure 12.3. How can you ensure that another company communicates and transfers the value you built into your product? *"You must choose your partners very carefully,"* says Steven Puthuff. *"The objective is to find a partner that can add value that complements your product or service rather than competing with your product or service. The right partner can help strengthen channels or broaden the scope of the total market (and therefore the value) for everyone. If done correctly, it's as if one plus one becomes much greater than two."* The partner's complementary products effectively provide more value to the target market, and therefore more value is ultimately delivered to the customer. For example, companies that integrate business computing and networking systems for companies often provide a mix of products and services to their customers. These "systems integrators" resell many different hardware and software products in the course of completing an integration project. If the systems integrator was reselling your company's software product, you would want to make sure that they were able to not only integrate your product into the overall solution properly, but to make sure that their customer understood your product, how to use it, and its value. In this situation, you must trust your partner, the systems integrator, to deliver the value that you intended for the end-user of your product.

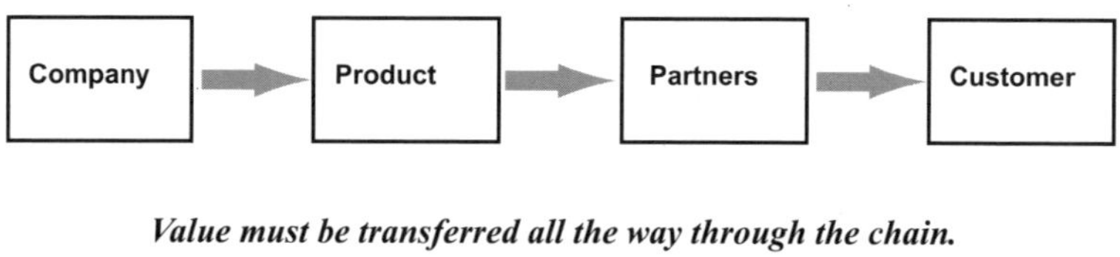

Figure 12.3: Transferring Value to the Customer

When selecting a partner, it's important to assess the level of importance they place on their customer relationships, and how they deliver value to their own customers. *"Partners need to have the same priority – a happy customer,"* says Maribeth Lazich. *"This means that partners have the necessary processes in place to support the customer during all interactions. The processes used by your partner need to be consistent with the high level of standards you use in your own company before you even begin the partnering relationship. Once the relationship is in place, then the two partners must act as a team and communicate constantly to make sure that that level of value is delivered in every customer interaction. That should also be documented in a partnership agreement."*

Finding the right partners is like screening new product ideas

Your company will not be compatible with every potential partner candidate. Finding the right partner requires research, resources, and patience. The search for partners is like screening new product ideas in that you must have a set of criteria established before you begin your search. The company must also designate one or more persons who will evaluate and select the partner candidates based on the chosen criteria.

Partnering is a strategic exercise, and more often than not, it involves the top executives of each company. Sometimes executives will make the initial contact with their counterpart in the candidate partner company in order to begin discussions. Thereafter, the process may be conducted by another senior level manager or business development executive who can conduct discussions with the partner to gather more information about the partner as part of the screening and selection process. Once the screening criteria are applied and the partner or partners are chosen, the chief executives may once again become involved in approving or signing the final partnership agreement. Figure 12.4 is the basic framework for a partner selection process.

1. Define type/ role of partner	2. Develop criteria	3. Research candidates	4. Evaluate candidates vs. criteria	5. Conduct discussions to narrow search	6. Select partner / begin negotiations

Figure 12.4: The Partner Selection Process

Table 12.1: Partner selection criteria

- -Compatible goals and philosophy
- -Cultural compatibility
- -Interested in mutual and equal benefits
- -Level of commitment
- -Resource availability
- -Have core competencies that fill critical gaps
- -Market influence
- -Partnering experience and history

Developing partner selection criteria

Unlike the six criteria for products (strategic fit, customer, market, competition, resources, and profitability), the criteria for selecting partners are related to the potential compatibility between two companies. Table 12.1 lists the major high-level criteria most commonly used to screen candidate partners.

Compatibility between two companies can be measured in many different ways. Both companies should have business goals that are compatible rather than competing. In a partnership, one company may achieve greater market share for its product, and the other company may achieve market entry for a new product, if they combine their marketing efforts. Those goals are not identical, but they are compatible. Operating philosophy is another way to judge compatibility. A very small company, for example, may have few formal business processes in place, whereas a big company may have very formalized operations with several reporting levels and consensus decision-making. It's important to assess how a potential partner operates, because it will directly affect how the business of the partnership is conducted.

Cultural compatibility deals with the company culture, which includes the work environment, work styles of employees, vision, and belief system. This may not seem as important as the other measures of compatibility, but if two partners have vastly different cultures, even simple events such as meetings held on each other's premises could be a source of friction. If that's not something that can be tolerated for several years, it can get in the way of conducting business. Cultural compatibility is a key partner selection criterion.

A partner should be interested in achieving mutual and equal benefits from the partnership. This criterion is difficult to assess, and even if the partner states their intention to benefit equally, there are no guarantees that will actually happen. The best thing to do is to research the partner candidate to make sure there aren't other motives involved, such as an unfriendly takeover, or an attempt to learn more about your company's products or assets. It all comes down to whether you can trust the partner candidate or not. On the flip side, your company must assess how the partner will benefit from the relationship; what's in it for them? *"A partner will be more committed to making a partnership work if they have a strong business incentive to help you succeed,"* advises Maribeth Lazich. *"It's not just a one-way commitment. You need to think about what you can offer them."*

How can you ensure the commitment of a partner to the relationship? One way to demonstrate commitment is by taking an equity stake of the partner company. *"Cisco has been very successful at partnering for many different business purposes. The equity stake arrangement is done frequently, especially when the target partner is strategic to developing a new market segment,"* says Bob Yee. Commitment, however, is a two-way proposition, and the arrangement can't be one-sided. Both companies must commit equal resources to the relationship. Those resources might be in the form of money, time, or dedicated personnel. The important thing is that both partners are satisfied with the value of the resources that they contribute and receive as part of the relationship.

Another important criterion to consider is whether the partner candidate has resources that they are willing and able to assign to the partnership. If a candidate doesn't have resources, or if they don't think that this is an important issue, that should represent a red flag. It may mean that the partner candidate has no prior partnering experience, or that your company may be expected to do all the work. This criterion can be assessed during discussions with partner candidates.

Partner candidates should have the core competencies, core technologies, or core resources that will help you fill in the gaps in your whole product. Sometimes it is useful to first characterize what you need to fill the gap and then find the partner candidates who have a reputation for a particular strength in that area. During discussions with those candidates, it's a good idea to make sure that their core strength is still present and will be made available to the partnership.

"It's important to consider the market as a whole and look for the powerful or important players. Who are the true influencers? Which companies must you partner with in order to be recognized as a player at all? Sometimes those companies who have the most power or influence are not the big companies, either. The ideal situation is to look for a partner who has market influence that you can leverage," advises Bob Yee. When assessing a partner candidate, it's advisable to study the market environment and where that candidate fits in, and then to make sure it's the same market environment that you are targeting.

Companies that have prior partnering experience will be more valuable to your company. Those companies are more likely to have the processes and communication links in place to manage partnerships effectively. *"Track record is very important,"* says Maribeth Lazich. *"There are always lessons learned from partner relationships, and your company can benefit from another partner's experience."* It will save your company a lot of time and effort because it won't be necessary to develop and agree on all of the operating processes that will drive the partnership. You will still need to make sure that they have a compatible operating philosophy, however.

These criteria are key to selecting and screening partner candidates at a company level. You may have additional, more specific criteria that relate to your new product, such as familiarity with the target customer or knowledge of the related technology. The best approach to find the ideal partner is to screen partner candidates at the company level first, and then apply your list of product-level criteria.

Managing the partnering relationship takes time and attention To be considered successful, a partnering relationship must shorten the time to market and increase profitability. There is a lot at stake, and it takes full-time management attention of one or more persons to effectively build and maintain a successful partnering relationship. A checklist of management factors is shown as Figure 12.5.

-Dedicated resources to manage relationship	**-Commitment demonstrated through action**
-Management attention	**-Written partnering agreement in place**
-Consistent communication process	**-Exit strategy in place**
-Collaboration among partner teams	**-Success metrics established and applied**

Figure 12.5: Checklist of Effective Partnership Management

Some companies even set up a small organization dedicated to supporting and managing a partnership. *"At Sybersay, we have*

OEM partners and distribution partners who have complementary products. For each partner, we assign a program manager who is dedicated to managing the partner relationship across both organizations. This is actually funded by the partner, as well. This has proven to be an effective way to accomplish the goals of the partnership and to make sure it is moving forward," says Steven Puthuff.

The three 'Cs' of effective partnering management include communication, collaboration, and commitment. These three elements must be at work from the beginning of the partner search, all the way through to the end of the partnering relationship. All three elements take a lot of time; partnering is work and shouldn't be viewed as something that one person can handle by sending an occasional email or making a phone call.

To be effective, communication needs to be honest, clear, frequent, and responsive. In the early stages of partner search and selection, clear and responsive communication can make the difference in terms of whether your company can capture the attention and interest of a potential partner. During the negotiation phase, clear and honest communication becomes even more critical, as the terms and logistics of the relationship are discussed and formulated. When the partnering relationship is in place, communication needs to be frequent and responsive to ensure that the collective work of the partnership is moving forward.

Collaboration between partners means that the work of the partnership is accomplished as a team effort. Representatives from each partner company should work together to share information, resolve issues, make decisions, and take action. This happens through continuing dialogue, meetings, discussions, events, and projects. Collaboration can take place in person, online, or via teleconferencing. The important thing is to make sure collaboration is part of the partnering process.

When two companies partner, they are in essence making a business commitment to each other to accomplish specific business goals together. This commitment is discussed during negotiations and is captured in the partnering agreement. However, commitment needs to be more than a few sentences in a written agreement. Commitment needs to be demonstrated through action, and supported by the highest levels of management within each company. Commitment also means that partner companies take the partnership seriously and assign priorities to partner-related issues accordingly.

The initial discussions and negotiations between the partners set the stage for managing the ensuing relationship. It is customary to capture the terms and conditions of the partnering relationship in some type of written agreement. One of the important issues that needs to be discussed and captured in such an agreement is the expected duration of the partnership. Most partnerships last less than five years but can last longer if the relationship still serves the needs of both partners. *"I've implemented many partnerships during my career,"* says Steven Puthuff. *"I think that the minimum length of a partnership should be two years, and the average is about three years. However, it's also important to have an exit strategy that is clearly specified in the partnering agreement. If you begin a new partnering relationship and it's not working out in the first few weeks, there should be a way to terminate it. This is easily done by adding a 30-day termination clause to the agreement. Letting a partnership linger if it has no chance of providing value is a waste of time and money."*

Trust plays an important role in how the partnering relationship is managed. There is a lot at stake in most business partnerships, and one company must trust another company to actually carry out the work that was agreed upon. *"Each partnership may be different in terms of how the day to day operations are managed,"* says Bob Yee. *"If there's a lot at stake, it is tempting to get on the phone every day to check on the status of what's being done, but it's hard to do that without being pushy. It's best to de-*

velop a working relationship that both parties can be comfortable with, especially when it comes to reporting status and results, or resolving issues."

In every partner relationship, metrics should be established that measure the effectiveness and success of the relationship. Depending on the purpose of the partnership, measurement factors might include increase in sales over a period of time, customer satisfaction levels, percent of technology development complete, or decrease in time to market. *"It's extremely important to set up success metrics at the beginning, and then honestly assess progress on a regular basis,"* advises Maribeth Lazich. *"If the relationship reaches a point where the challenges outweigh the benefits, or where the relationship becomes one-sided in terms of benefits, then it may be time to end the partnership."* Sometimes, external factors may impact the partner relationship. Markets can mature, or new competitors can limit further market growth. Economic changes can decrease demand for products and services. For many reasons, it is important to periodically evaluate whether the relationship still makes business sense, and to have the wisdom and courage to end the partnership if it no longer serves the needs of the partners or your customer.

13

Speeding Up the Development Phase

The longest and most costly part of the new product cycle is the development phase. Product development can be a very complex process, involving multiple teams of people to complete all the tasks involved. There are entire books devoted to the subject of managing product development that provide detailed information on design approaches, processes, tracking, managing workflow, and documentation. This chapter is focused on only one aspect of development: speeding up the development phase.

Today, product life cycles are becoming shorter than ever, and time to market is decreasing. Companies want to make sure that development doesn't last longer than originally planned, because it means greater expense and an even longer wait before realizing some return on their investment. Cost, however, is only one of the reasons for speeding up the development phase. Other reasons include competitive pressure to get to market faster and the increased rate of technology evolution. Companies must find ways to get to market sooner, with products that leverage the most current technology developments, especially in today's high-tech economy.

There are two things that companies must do in order to shorten the development phase: increase customer focus and streamline their development processes. To increase customer focus throughout the development cycle, the customer needs to be more involved in the process early on. There are many different ways to streamline development processes, and those discussed in this chapter will give you some ideas of things to try in your company. Speeding up development is not without risk, however, and this chapter also addresses the impact to your company and your product's quality.

Development cycles are shorter than ever before

Over the last decade, the time allocated to develop and test a new product has been shrinking dramatically (Figure 13.1). This is happening in all industries, even those that have development times that are measured in years rather than months. Products, such as software, that were developed in two years during the 1990s now can (and must) be developed in six months. Products, such as microprocessor chips, that previously took five years to develop are now completed in three years or less. Development cycles have become shorter in response to competitive pressures, more efficient technical processes, and technology tools that enhance collaboration among developers or that automate time-consuming development tasks such as testing and documentation.

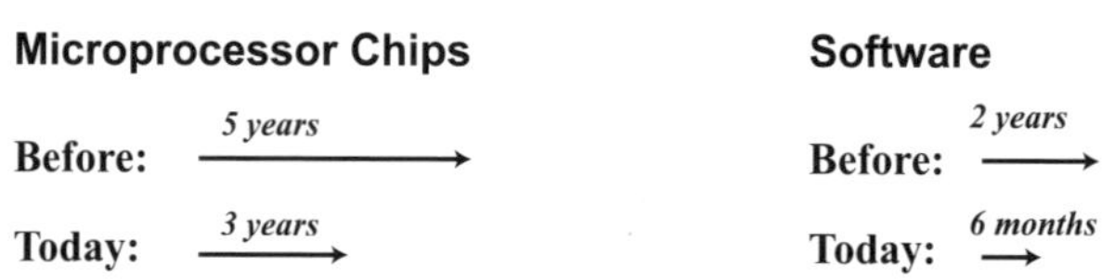

Figure 13.1: The Shrinking Development Cycle

Product life cycles are also shrinking. This is partly due to the pace of new technology developments that enable faster performance, improved ease of use, packaging, or delivery. Products may be built to last a long time, but customers often want newer or enhanced versions that utilize more current technologies, effectively decreasing the product's life. Fred Nikolac, General Manager of a business unit at Acuson, has observed tremendous changes in the life cycle of medical ultrasound equipment. *"Just five years ago, our primary ultrasound product had a useful life of up to 17 years. Now, the average life is just 5 years, and it's decreasing even further. The product life is not being reduced due to lower product quality. Rather, this reduction in life cycle is due to customer demands for features and functionality. To be competitive, it's necessary to develop products that have those features. That also means that we must get them to market sooner, which translates to a shorter development cycle."*

Investors are interested in shorter development cycles so that they can realize return on investment sooner. "*This is particularly true in startup companies that are funded by venture capital. There is more scrutiny during the development cycle by the investors to make sure that it proceeds according to schedule. There is a significant quality risk, however, especially if test cycles are shortened,*" according to Ciree Loftus, Software Development Manager at Luminate, an e-business software company. Today, the length of the estimated development time is often used as a criterion for investment in a startup company by potential investors. Leading-edge technology products that may take several years to research and develop may be outside of the scope of investors' portfolio requirements. Prior to the dot-com phase, investors were seeking investments that would provide returns within five to eight years. Today, three years or less is a more common requirement.

Even established public companies put pressure on the development cycle to speed it up. Until recently, the economic boom was a significant reason for increased development efficiency; being first to market was a way to compete or even survive. In times of economic slowdown, companies are more focused on the bottom line, which means getting revenue faster from new products, as well as spending less money on development (Figure 13.2). Regardless of the state of the economy, faster development cycles are here to stay.

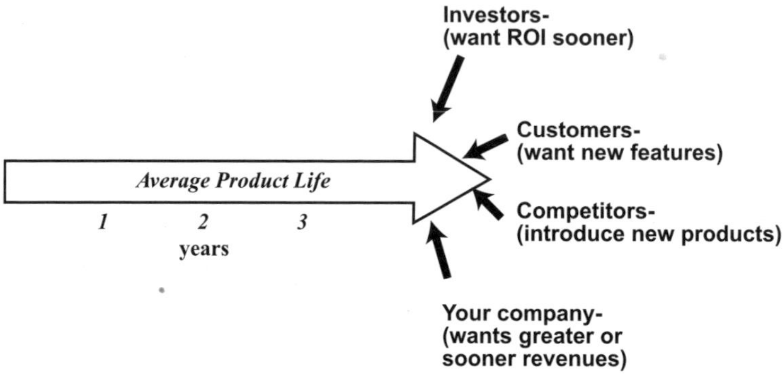

Figure 13.2: Pressure on the Product Life Cycle

Customer involvement is critical for speeding up development

A major trend in the development process today is an increase in direct involvement of the target customer. In every industry, companies are finding ways to get the target customer to participate in development. Sometimes a customer advisory board is assembled to provide feedback and guidance before and during the development phase. Even companies that still use a "product push" strategy (company develops product first and finds a customer) rather than a "market pull" strategy (customer need drives the product), tend to bring in the customer earlier in the process to obtain feedback on product features, functions, and applications. The result? Faster, less expensive development cycles, and a customer that is prepared to buy the product when it is launched.

Sometimes a new product may be similar enough to the existing products in the company that there is enough collective knowledge to develop it quickly. If the new product will be sold to a new or unfamiliar customer, the new customer still needs to be involved early in order to establish the marketing requirements at the beginning. Once the requirements are established or validated, efficiencies can be gained during actual development because the product is similar to existing products. However, if the company is developing a new, unfamiliar product for a new and unfamiliar customer, this is a high-risk situation. In these circumstances, it will be much more difficult to speed up the development cycle, and it may take longer in the beginning to fully define the customer requirements.

Karen Mackey has been involved in software development for 20 years in companies such as AT&T Bell Labs, TRW, IBM-Lotus, Lockheed Martin, and Cisco, and she teaches software development at the university level. *"In the companies where I have managed development, the new products that were developed in response to a customer need were the most successful,"* says Karen Mackey. *"If a company has the discipline and philosophy to get all employees involved in listening to the customer and addressing their needs, and then make new product decisions based on those needs, the risk is greatly reduced in a new product-new market scenario. If the market is very new with unfamiliar customers, then more time should be spent developing the new customer requirements before money is allocated for development. A significant assist to requirements gathering can be through a prototype, especially a user interface prototype. This prototype can concurrently help push the development effort along, especially if it is designed to be evolved. Thereafter, the new customers need to be involved throughout the subsequent evolutions of the product. This approach has additional benefits, too; involving the customer can help build that customer relationship into one that lasts well into the future. With careful attention to managing customer expectations, it's a win-win situation."*

Steven Puthuff has taken his knowledge from large-company environments and applied it successfully to eight different startups. He is currently Chairman and Founder of Sybersay Communications Corporation, a company that develops next-generation voice/wireless mobile communications projects. He has seen a tremendous shift in the last few years in how companies manage the product development process. *"As recently as two years ago, companies would follow the same two-year development process whereby alpha tests would be conducted internally, beta versions would be tested with a friendly customer, then the product would be completed, released, and launched, all without significant customer input. Today, the target customer (who may not be so friendly) is involved from the beginning, helping to establish pre-development requirements and providing validation during prototyping and beta. On top of that, the whole development is completed in six to eight months instead of two years. Companies must open up their product development processes to include the customer. That's the only way to be competitive today."* Some may argue that involving the customers throughout the cycle takes more time away from development. However, there will be a better fit between the product and the customer who is destined to buy it, eliminating features or functionality that the customer doesn't want or need. There is also likely to be less redesign or rework if the customer is involved, because of the

Table 13.1: Roles that Customers Play during Development

-Customer advisory boards
-Establish product requirements and specifications
-Validation of product functionality
-Feedback on product features
-Beta testing

closer fit. Essentially, the product is developed in response to the customers at each step of the way, and that saves time. When should the customer be involved in development; before it starts, in the middle, or near the end during final beta tests? Companies use a variety of approaches. Most often, the customer is consulted before development starts, when the market requirements of the product are defined. These requirements are captured in a document sometimes called a "Marketing Requirements Document", or "MRD". The other most popular time to involve customers is near the end of the development phase, when formal or informal beta testing is conducted, usually on the customer's premises. Some companies even bring the customer into the middle of the development process, to make sure that the requirements guiding the development are still valid, or to help prioritize product features.

Fred Nikolac believes that customers need to be involved during the entire development cycle to the extent possible, especially if the development cycle is long. *"We get customers involved at many stages of development. At the beginning, we will work with customers to help identify the desired functionality of a product. Later on in the development, we find the customers who will break the products for us. That enables us to make the design more robust and we can build in reliability; most of our products are used daily for several years. The people who must rely on our products to do their jobs are the people who should be guiding our development process."*

Whether you involve your customers at the beginning, middle, or end of the development cycle, or throughout the entirety of it, you will benefit from this interaction. Table 13.1 lists some of the roles that customers play in the cycle. Not only will it help with the development cycle, but this interaction will help in understanding the overall needs of your customers, so that future products can be developed with them in mind. It will also help build and strengthen customer relationships that will last through the entire length of the product life cycle.

Involving customers earlier can save time and money

Companies that involve the customer early in the development process have a better chance of producing a product that the target customer will buy and use. Products that are designed and developed by a technical person who makes assumptions about what a customer wants or needs might succeed, but there is a much greater cost and risk associated with that approach. Four seasoned veterans of product development believe that the earlier the customer is involved, the better. Here are some of their observations:

According to Karen Mackey, it's never too early to involve the customer. *"A company needs to use all the possible venues they can to get the customer involved in new product development – as early as the idea stage. Company-sponsored user group conferences, focus groups, field studies, and surveys can be used to help define the products that customers want and need, and then later customers can help refine the requirements that will be used to design and develop the product."*

"At Luminate, we normally do a market requirements study, and all of our major product features are based on product marketing and customer feedback. If we don't do this step early in the development process, we have learned the hard way that neither the customer's expectations nor the company's expectations are met. It's better to involve the customer earlier, and consistently – throughout the development cycle," according to Ciree Loftus.

"Every new product should be based on a customer need, and the whole product development cycle should be driven by customer in-

put. The first and earliest stage of development should be an initial review that serves to validate the customer need (market requirements). Thereafter, each time that development progress is evaluated, the market requirements should be re-validated. If the company begins the whole development process with customer involvement, the rest of the development will proceed more quickly, and the result will be the right product with the right functionality and features that customers will buy," according to Steven Puthuff.

David Stoner is a Principal Consultant with DNV, a firm that provides training in ISO 9000 processes. He is a veteran of many years of product development experience in several large companies. *"Sometimes a customer doesn't know exactly what they want, even in the beginning of the cycle when requirements are being defined. It may require several iterations of a product concept to come up with a product that will meet the customer's need. That's why it's necessary to get customers involved as early as possible in the cycle."*

It's clear that customers need to be involved to help clarify the specific requirements for the product. These requirements include basic functionality, product features, the problems the product will solve, what the customer might be willing to pay, how they want it delivered, and how they want it packaged. These are the things that must be known at the beginning of any development phase, so it makes sense to include the customer in shaping the products that they will be buying from your company.

Customers' role in beta testing

Beta testing refers to a stage of the development cycle when a working version of the product is given to, or tested by, one or more target customers. This often happens late in the development phase, when most of the product functionality and product features have been completed. Beta testing is a way to gauge how the customer will use the product, along with the quality and performance levels of the product. Feedback from beta testing may require that the product be redesigned, fixed, or changed in some way before it is ready for launch to the general marketplace. Beta testing is the most common type of testing done by companies today. The timing is critical, however; the earlier that beta tests are done, the better – especially if product features need to be modified or changed. Making these changes earlier saves money because development steps won't have to be repeated, which also saves time in the long run.

Waiting until the beta phase to get the customer involved is risky. There is a possibility that the product may have to be changed significantly in order to meet the customer's need, adding even more time to the development cycle. According to Ciree Loftus, beta testing should occur after the features of a product are developed and almost finalized. *"Before the beta testing, there should be some sort of a functionality test. At Luminate, we called this 'early adopter' testing, whereby the customer has an opportunity to evaluate the entire product functionality. This must occur early enough to incorporate changes during the remainder of the development process. It's too late to change functionality after beta test, and it will delay the development cycle significantly."*

Beta testing can help to refine products' features and how products are delivered. Even companies who sell services rather than products can benefit from beta testing. *"At DNV, we select clients to participate in a tuition-free version of our courses to provide feedback that helps us validate that our course meets the market requirements,"* says David Stoner. *"At first, we only invited our most enthusiastic customers, but then we realized that we needed to get feedback from customers that represented more of an average cross-section of our target market. Now we do this for all of our service offerings, and it helps us get to market more quickly."*

Techniques for speeding up the development phase

Today's development cycles have to be shorter in order for companies to compete effectively or even survive. Everyone is interested in speeding up the development phase. Where to start? You could hire more people, develop prototypes, overlap development efforts, reuse designs or components, manage developers more efficiently, and refrain from over-engineering. These are some of the ways that companies have gained some efficiencies and decreased the development time overall, and are summarized in Figure 13.3.

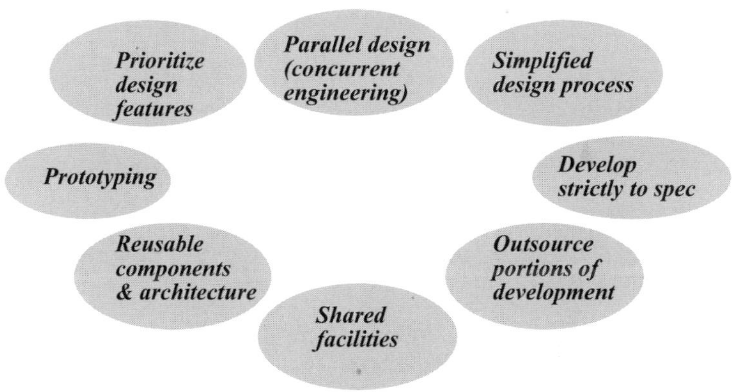

Figure 13.3: Ways to Speed Up the Development Phase

Shortening the cycle may require simplification of the whole development process. Years ago, it was common for product concepts to pass through several stages during development. These stages included initial design, development, alpha, beta, and final tests, along with several design or development reviews before each stage. Companies don't have that luxury any more and must eliminate some of these stages or find other ways to streamline the process. A lot of companies have eliminated alpha testing and conduct a more detailed beta test instead. To save time, many companies have also eliminated or cut back on formal reviews, choosing to do them online or less frequently.

Prototypes can help solidify product specifications, features, and functions

Prototyping is the creation of a preliminary version of a product in the form of a mockup or demo that can be used or tested. Some products are appropriate for prototyping, and if so, this is a great way to validate and prioritize the product functionality and features that customers will really use in the finished version of the product. Prototypes can also be used to test out new technology concepts, as well as new ways to package or deliver products. Prototypes are usually built at the very beginning of the development cycle.

"If the new product is based on very new or complex technology, it's even more critical to do a prototype," advises Karen Mackey. *"Prototyping can help prove the feasibility of applying the underlying technology to the product concept, as well as determine its usability in the customer's work setting. The prototype can also be used to assess the product's appeal and the best way to package and promote it for the marketplace."* Prototyping can answer two key questions: can your company apply the technology to the problem, and does this solution solve the problem from the customer's perspective?

Ciree Loftus is also a firm believer in prototyping. *"With new technologies, it's advisable to develop a prototype to determine whether the technology solution is consistent with the company's product roadmap and technical capabilities before a lot of money is spent on the development cycle."* In some situations, a company may find through prototyping that the proposed new product leads them away from their core competencies or core business, and as a result, they don't have the resources to provide an effective solution that meets the market requirements. It's better to know that before beginning an expensive development cycle.

Prototyping can also help the company determine the price range for the product. *"At Acuson, we begin the development phase by building a prototype that we show to selected customers. These customers provide us with feedback on how they would use the product, the desired functionality, and what they would be willing to pay for that functionality. That enables us to design in the functionality that we know we can sell, before we spend money on a long development cycle. By having an idea of the price range early on, we can also estimate the relative profitability for the new product,"* says Fred Nikolac.

Prototyping during the early stage of the development cycle can save time and money, and can help your company validate the technical fit of the new product with your strategic objectives.

Parallel development

Parallel development is the practice of implementing technical tasks in parallel, rather than a serial fashion where one task doesn't begin until a preceding task finishes. Depending on the nature of the product and its complexity, overlapping these development efforts can save time. *"At Sybersay, we often use a parallel design approach, whereby the detailed design or development stage overlaps the initial phase. This can create a cost risk when the design is not consistent with market requirements. However, if the design is validated with customer specs, parallel efforts can speed up the process and reduce time to market,"* says Steven Puthuff.

Managing and organizing resources

Another way to manage development resources more effectively is to use a team approach. Steven Puthuff has implemented a matrix organization within Sybersay for new product development. *"The matrix organization means that technical and research specialists are assigned to product teams during development. The technical experts work side-by-side with the people who will manage and market the product. A project manager who comes from either a marketing or technical background, and has good people management skills manages these efforts. This matrix approach is very effective because more knowledge transfer takes place, and the process is faster because more work can be done in parallel. I highly recommend a matrix approach for startup environments because of this synergy."*

Improving communication and collaboration

Managing communication and collaboration is another way to make the development process move more quickly. *"Use a 'light-weight' or bare-bones development process and develop some consistent vocabulary and project habits,"* advises Karen Mackey. *"Keeping the development process architecture simple eliminates the need for constant reinvention of development process, reorientation, and retraining of development staff – although the details may vary from project to project. Using email to communicate information such as spec changes or review-meeting minutes keeps everyone up to speed more quickly. It's also important to archive documents, specs and minutes and make them available on a dedicated server with access to the entire development team. Using and reusing templates for documentation and testing and making them available online also helps collaboration efforts and speeds things along."* There are many information technology tools that a company may already have that can help with communication and collaboration. Common databases, email, and design collaboration software are some of the tools that can also simplify the process for the development team. Today, company intranets can provide a way for the members of the design and development team to communicate and collaborate with each other online, which also saves time.

Reusing components and code

If a product such as software or hardware is normally developed from components (such as software code or hardware parts), then it may be possible to gain efficiencies by re-using components. Sometimes the reusable component is architecture. *"For all of our product lines, we use a common base architecture. Our software developers have an understanding of this architecture and how it is used as a foundation for developing new products. That can reduce development time significantly because it's not necessary to reinvent the wheel every time a new product concept comes along. It's also good to have a consistent architecture for all of our products because it's better for our customers and easier to support,"* says Ciree Loftus. Reusing product architectures means that the architectures must be scalable, however.

It's advisable to create databases of components and designed that can be reused, and many companies do that to speed development. *"At Sybersay, we use a modular design approach. We have created a huge design database with all of the customer and technical specifications. This database is accessible to the development teams who work on new products or enhancements. Each basic design yields at least five or six new products,"* says Steven Puthuff.

Resisting over-engineering

By their nature, engineers and product developers love to design things and be creative about a product's features. However great the temptation, products can be "over-engineered", meaning that extra features are added to the product that are not needed by the customer and have no added value. Customers may not be willing to pay for these extra features. Very often, customers are willing to make do with less, especially if it means that they can have the product sooner or pay a lower price. *"One of the most effective ways to speed up the time to market is to cut back on product features,"* says Karen Mackey. *"The company must decide what is truly important to meet the customer's value proposition. If there is doubt about features, it's best to ask the target customer, and make the decision based on their response."*

Facility solutions

Managing development teams becomes more of a challenge when there is pressure to speed up development. Some companies use co-location (team members' offices are located in one building) or shared development facilities to gain efficiency. According to Ciree Loftus, *"All of our product lines use a core development area. Communications are enhanced, and technology resources are readily available in one location. This allows us to reduce our development time from 9 months to 4 months, on the average."* David Stoner has also witnessed the effectiveness of co-location when he was Operations Manager at Schlumberger. *"We co-located design engineers with the operations team on the factory floor. This was not popular with the engineers at first, but this led to many interesting interactions. The engineers learned how to design for manufacturability. The operations team had an advance look at the new products being developed, and could more effectively plan the production phase. Overall, this resulted in much shorter cycle times as well as higher quality products."*

Can outsourcing help speed the development phase?

Outsourcing certain tasks to outside vendors or partners is one possible way to conduct some of the development tasks in parallel, reducing the overall development cycle. Depending on the type of product, there are tasks that can be outsourced, such as testing, quality assurance, parts of the design, or packaging the product.

A lot depends on the vendors and partners you already have in place. *"Outsourcing to established companies who are part of your company's 'ecosystem' can be a great way to speed up development, especially if those companies have been involved with similar products, or will be involved in delivering or packaging the new product after it is complete, or providing training to customers who will use the product,"* says Karen Mackey.

Companies should be careful about which tasks they outsource and which ones remain inside the company, because sometimes the benefit of the learning can be lost. David Stoner has seen this happen in his experience of working with large companies. *"It is possible to outsource too much of the development to partners or suppliers. The partner gets the benefit of the learning, and when the next new product comes along, the company may be faced with relying on the outsourcing partner again. However, if the skill or learning is not present within the company anyway and the partner has the right skills, then it's a lot faster to have a partner do those tasks. We even do this at DNV for some of our service offerings. It makes sense if it gets you to market faster."*

As with any outsourcing decision, there are tradeoffs that must be made. When outsourcing development tasks, you must consider the cost of the efficiency you will gain, not only for the current product, but also for other new products in the future.

The risk of lower quality with faster development cycles

If processes are streamlined by removing testing stages or formal reviews, there may be a risk of lower quality in the finished product. Quality must be defined from the customer's point of view. Does the product meet the requirements of the customer? Will they receive your finished product when they need it?

"It's important to design in quality for every new product," says Steven Puthoff. *"That means you must design a product for a worst-case scenario; if it works, you have already achieved a level of quality that hopefully fits your customer specifications. Designing in quality should automatically be a part of every development process, regardless of whether or not the development cycle is speeded up. It's a way of doing business, not just another step of the process."*

How the development cycle is managed can have an impact on quality as well. *"If you remove too many steps from the development process, just to speed it up, that can result in lower quality. It's all about how development is managed, and the 'whole product' concept must be taken into account. That means that the new product must meet customer requirements, must be packaged and delivered the way the customer wants it, and most importantly, when the customer wants it. If you take too long to develop a product, the customer may not want it, and you have fallen short of the customer's 'whole product' requirements. All of these requirements must be met; that's the definition of quality,"* says David Stoner.

Speed up development or increase quality – which is more important? Companies must do both in order to succeed in today's environment. The important thing to remember is that quality should be measured from the customer's perspective of the whole product.

14

Streamlined Business and Marketing Plans

There have been dozens of books written on how to write a business plan or marketing plan. Why are there so many? People in business just do a lot of planning. Sometimes planning has a specific purpose, and sometimes it is an entire waste of time. If someone tells you to write a plan, your first question should be: Why? The response should be one of the following: To obtain investment for our company, to make a major decision, or to figure out what we are going to do. The other important question to ask is: Who is going to use the plan? The response to that question will dictate the content that needs to go into the plan.

I have found that planning is useful because it makes you think through all of the issues. The very act of answering the questions and filling in the blanks of a business or marketing plan outline enables the creator and users of the plan to understand the whole picture. No business or venture is too small to benefit from the planning process. If you're an entrepreneur, you may not have an entire team who can gather information for the plan or write it. Your plans may be shorter in length and may have less detail in certain sections. As your company grows, you will have more information and complexity to add to your plan. Large, established companies can have the opposite problem: too much information is often added to the plan, resulting in confusion or lack of focus. Regardless of the plan content, business and marketing plans should be simple, concise, realistic, and written in such a way that they are easily understood by any individual who may need to refer to them.

The difference between a business plan and a marketing plan is a matter of scope and focus. A business plan contains information about an entire company or suite of products and includes financial, technical, marketing, operational, and organizational information. A marketing plan contains information about the marketing activities of an entire company or product and includes technical, marketing, and budgetary information. A product plan is another type of plan that is modeled after a business plan and contains similar information, but is focused on just one product.

Who needs business plans? Investors need them in order to evaluate a venture for return on investment and make an investment decision. Corporate executives need them to make important decisions and to allocate budgets. Product teams need them in order to have a baseline to guide their development efforts. Who needs marketing plans? Corporate executives need them to assess fit with corporate-level objectives and to allocate budgets. Product marketing and launch teams need them in order to have a baseline to guide their launch efforts.

Today, business plans and marketing plans need to be simple and meaningful. To keep up with today's new product cycles, plans need to be done quickly and thoroughly because the decision-makers are under time pressures. Products must begin the development cycle faster and must be launched faster. The business plans and marketing plans that are the basis for new product decisions should not hold up the process. This chapter focuses on how to streamline and simplify business and marketing plans, as well as how to target them for the intended audience.

Plans are meant to be thinking tools

A plan should be written for the purposes of thinking through what must be done; it is not meant to be a work of art that will sit on a shelf, unused. The outline and format of the plan should be constructed in such a way as to stimulate thinking. Sometimes one person creates the plan, and sometimes it is a team of people who brainstorm and collaborate to think "collectively." To facilitate this process, the outline of the plan must be thorough and cover all of the issues that need to be addressed. However, the writing in the plan needs to be extremely concise and simple to understand. The plan itself is evidence that the entire business concept has been thought through. The work of creating a business or marketing plan is in the thinking, not in the writing.

Templates for a business plan and marketing plan are included in Appendix B and on the CD accompanying this book. The templates are set up as a series of questions to think through and answer. The answers to the questions will drive the content that goes into the plan, and the answers may be in the form of written text, illustrations, or charts that go into the final version of the plan.

Who should write the plans?

The best rule of thumb about who should write a business or marketing plan is to find someone who can be objective about the product. If the writer is too caught up in the product development or the marketing programs that he or she wants to do, the content will be biased. Whoever writes the plan should also have a big picture view of the product and should understand the importance of the product in the context of the company and the overall marketplace.

Keeping it simple

The people who will be reading and referring to your business and marketing plans don't have a lot of time to weed through a long plan in order to grasp the key points and backup data. An executive summary at the beginning of the plan is a good way to present an overview, using a list of bullet points or a few short paragraphs. However, it is also a good idea to keep the body of the plan simple and easy to read. Use illustrations, charts and bullet points. If some of the content requires detailed explanation or justification, you can always create an appendix and place it at the back of the plan. That way, if the reader needs to refer to the detailed information, it will be there.

Who is the audience for the plan?

Just as customers have different needs and uses for your new product, readers of your business and marketing plans have different needs and uses for the information in the plan. Before you set out to develop and write a plan, think about whom the audience for your plan will be, and put yourself in their position. What would you want to know about the new product, and how would you want the information presented? Figure 14.1 is a list of considerations for targeting the reader.

Investors who read business plans are interested in the potential for the new product venture to yield a very good return on their investment of capital. Because they won't make money on the product venture for several years, they are evaluating the business potential over a period of time. They want to see realistic forecasts of market demand over several years and how that market will change in the future. Investors look closely at the customer value proposition to see whether the product is solving a legitimate problem and serving a critical need, because that is what will generate sales. They also need to feel confident that the people who will be developing the product and managing the business will be effective in generating profit.

-Who will read the plan?
-Why will they read it?
-What information do they need?
-What will they do with the information?
-Is there some information they don't need?
-How do they want the information presented?

Figure 14.1: Targeting the Reader of the Plan

Corporate executives and managers use business and marketing plans to make many different types of decisions. They are concerned with the reliability of the information used to forecast market demand and sales. These managers want to be sure that the plans are realistic in terms of the strategic objectives of the company, and that the business model fits the core competency and capability of the company. In the case of marketing plans, those managers may be allocating the marketing budget, so they will need to have ROI justification for all marketing programs.

Product team members and launch team members use business and marketing plans as a reference when they are implementing product development and launch. Sometimes these plans are used to resolve a conflict or to allocate resources. Such plans are also quite useful as new people join the teams, because they can get a better sense of how the product fits into the big picture and the role that they will be playing in the whole effort.

The framework and timing of the business plan

A business plan should be written toward the beginning of the new product cycle, before the product enters the development cycle. In fact, a business plan is most often used by startup companies to obtain capital from outside investors to develop and launch the product. Established companies not seeking outside investment for a new product may also develop a similar plan but may call it a "product plan". Such companies may also have five-year strategic plans that describe the overall product roadmap or direction but don't have the same level of detail as a business plan or product plan.

After the initial phase of the new product cycle, the idea validation work will have been completed. Figure 14.2 illustrates the major content pieces used in compiling the business plan. Any and all market research should be complete and analyzed. Characterizations of the customer, market environment, and competition should be complete. The business model should be developed, along with the strategy for getting to market (or "go to market" strategy). If key partners are involved, there should be a partnering analysis or plan that identifies partner candidates. There also should be a product development plan in place. All of these pieces will be used to compile the business plan.

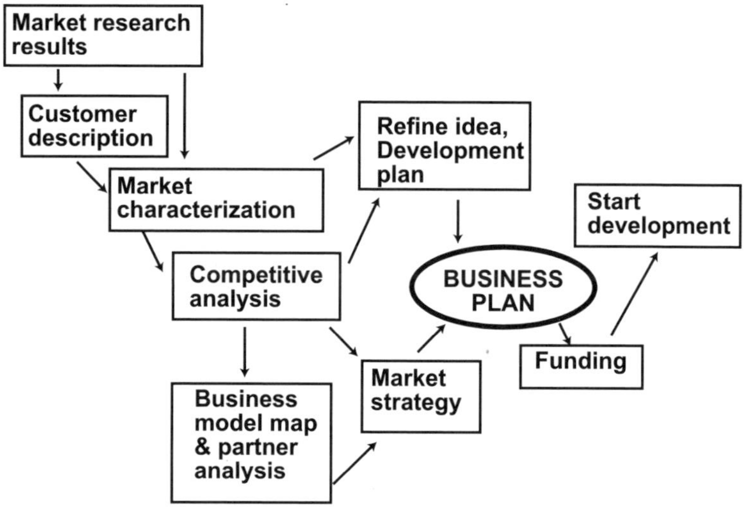

Figure 14.2: Compiling the Business Plan

The following outline describes the content of a typical business plan, section by section. You may choose to use a slightly different outline or template, or your investors may want to see the information arranged in a different order. That's easy to do, once you have thought through the entire plan and summarized the results in a concise outline, like the one below. Once you have this outline completed, you can easily cut and paste from it and use the pieces in different plans and documents.

BUSINESS PLAN OUTLINE

Executive Summary

At the beginning of the business plan should be a two to three page summary of the highlights. It is usually written after the business plan is complete. Its purpose is to give the reader a quick overview of the main points of the plan. There should be a paragraph or brief section on each of the following topics: product, customer problem and need, business model, market size and trends, competitive advantage, operations and support, management team, and financial information (investment required, revenue projection, expected return on investment).

1. Product Description

This is the section of the business plan where people tend to go overboard, especially entrepreneurs who are excited about their product concept. It is much more fun to describe the brilliant product breakthrough than it is to describe the business operations behind the concept. Whoever writes this section needs to be very brief and should use pictures and diagrams, wherever possible, to capture the product concept. The product description should be no more than two pages, including any illustrations. The information in this section should include the functionality of the product, the primary features that make it new or different, the relationship between the new product and existing product lines, how the target customer will use the product, and the benefits the customer will derive from it. Describe the product's overall life cycle, and whether product enhancements or product line extensions might be needed to extend product life. Also describe the level of intellectual property protection that applies to the product, such as patents or trademarks. Refrain from using acronyms and technical jargon; many people reading these plans are not highly technical, so you need to explain the product in layman's terms.

2. Fit With Strategic Objectives

This brief section needs to focus on how the product relates to the company's strategic direction, core business, and core competencies. This section should include a description of the company's core business and competency and how they form a basis for developing the new product and taking it to market. There also needs to be a description of business goals (such as growth, entering new markets, increased profitability, etc.), and how the new product will help to attain those goals. For startups and new companies, you must also explain how this first new product will set the future direction of the new venture.

3. Business Model

Using the guidelines in Chapter 10 of this book, a business model map needs to be constructed that identifies all of the entities that will be involved in getting your product to your customer. The business model map should include the cash flow to demonstrate how the product will return money to the company. All entities that will be participating in the business model should be identified by name. If these entities are yet to be identified, you should describe the type of company that you will be seeking. You also need to describe what role these entities will play in the business model, as well as the nature of the business relationship between your company and each entity.

4. Business Problem That Product Solves

This is one of the key sections of the business plan. You must demonstrate how the product will solve a problem for the customer. The problem should be real, and one that exists for the customer now (at the time the plan is written). The other information that should be included is the compelling reason for your customer to buy the product, and their typical buying behavior. If you have endorsements from potential customers, or feedback from a current customer survey, it's a good idea to include that in this section.

5. Customer Characteristics

Compared to the previous section of the business plan, this one includes more detail about your customer and their profile. The most basic information to include is simply a description of who your customer is: what do they do? What is their job title? What do they do in a given day? Are they a decision-maker? If not, who is, and how is the decision influenced? The other information to include is your company's knowledge of this target customer, and how you will go about finding beta customers and early customers when you are ready to sell your product. The customer's value proposition also should be described, referring back to the previous section that described the customer's problem. What is the value of solving their problem, and what are they willing to pay for it?

6. Market Characteristics

Depending on your target market, this can be a large section of the business plan. The information that you found when the market research was conducted should be summarized here. This section should describe the overall dynamics of your target market – how does it change over time, and what are the factors that cause changes? The other major portion of this section should estimate the market size. There are many ways to measure and estimate the market size – total available market, served available market, or market share. Regardless of the measure used, it is important to define the measure, and then present the numbers. For market size estimates, include a chart or graph that shows how the market size is likely to change over time. If you have published or purchased reports that you used to research the market, always cite the source of the information, as well as the date of the information.

7. Competitive Analysis

Entrepreneurs often claim that there are no existing competitors for their product concept. However, it's not advisable to state that in a business plan. There will always be competitors looming out there in the market, no matter what the product is. Sometimes it is difficult to find information on potential competitors, but it is important to address this issue in the business plan. One way to do this is to develop a 'profile' of a type of competitor who could enter your target market segment, and then discuss how you might defend your product in the marketplace.

For known competitors, it's easier to compile the information for the business plan. You will need to have completed the competitive analysis for each company, including company-level and product-level comparisons. (Refer also to Chapter 5 of this book, and my previous book, *High Tech Product Launch*, for more information on how to do competitive analysis.) The key factors to examine are strength and weaknesses of their company, comparison of product features, stage of development of their technology or product lines, and pricing information, if available. Once this information is gathered, you should also identify your key differentiators. All of this information can be represented on a matrix that should be added to this section of the plan. Within the matrix, highlight your key differentiators, so that the reader can easily see them. If you have a lot of competitors, and the matrix is very large, you can place it in an appendix to the business plan and just include the highlights in this section.

8. Product Distribution Strategy

In the business model section of the plan, you may have identified one or more participants who will distribute or resell your product to your customer. You may also choose to sell directly to your customers, along with these channel partners. In this section, you need to describe how the sales channels will get the product to your customer. If you plan to use more than one sales channel, estimate the percentage of sales from each channel. You should also describe how you will avoid channel conflict if it arises.

9. Marketing And Sales Strategy

This is an important section of the business plan and may be very large. For this section, you need to think through the entire marketing and sales process, especially when the first sale will occur and how sales will ramp up over time. Be as specific as possible, and identify the customers for the first, second, and third sales. There is a tendency to be over-optimistic in forecasting the rate of sales ramp-up, usually because the sales cycle often takes longer for a new product than people think. Be realistic, and err on the side of conservatism. That way, you won't be setting unreasonable expectations for revenue and return on investment.

Another part of this section should focus on how the marketing programs will help increase awareness, promote the new product, and support the sales process. Don't include the level of detail that would be in the marketing plan (see later part of this chapter). Rather, a simple list of the number and type of marketing programs and a description of the role they play are sufficient. You can always add an appendix to the business plan that describes the marketing plan in more detail, if people are interested.

10. Support Plan

For many new products and ventures, the product and customer support plan has not been thought through. However, customer support is critical for sales and the ultimate success of the product and venture. Building a customer support infrastructure, especially for a new company or startup, can be a daunting and expensive effort. In this section of the plan, you need to identify who will support the product, the infrastructure that is in place or needs to be in place to support it, and how the function will be managed in the greater context of the company or venture. Any product documentation should also be described, along with training that will be provided to the customer. Warranties and maintenance agreements should also be described, if applicable.

11. Product Development Plan

This section of the business plan is the one that often receives the greatest scrutiny and generates the most controversy. Because the product development phase is the longest part of the new product cycle, it requires the greatest investment. All of the stakeholders want to maximize their return on their investment, which often means shortening the development time to get to market sooner and spending less on resources to increase the profits. This section of the plan needs to describe the schedule and budget for the development cycle, along with a description of the expected technical challenges and risks that may be encountered.

12. Operational Plan

Basic business operations for the new product and/or venture are often left out of a business plan. Once again, this is part of the thinking process that must go on before a new product is launched. In this section, you need to describe such basic issues as where the new product/venture will be located and the facilities needed to support the day-to-day operations. Describe other business relationships that need to be a part of routine operations, such as those with vendors, suppliers, and strategic partners. The company's internal infrastructure should also be described, including such areas as internal and external network operations and telecommunications, accounting, and human resources.

13. Management And Organizational Plan

This section of the plan is often scrutinized very closely, especially by investors. For each key management position required for the new product or venture, there should be a brief biography of the person and a description of his or her specific responsibilities. An organizational chart should be included that shows how the different positions report in to management, and how they communicate with each other. Dotted-line relationships with strategic partners and board members should also be added to the chart. If there are key positions that have not yet been filled, then those positions should be described, along with a plan of how and when the position will be filled. For all remaining staff, there should be a description of the new hires that are planned, and a spreadsheet that shows the hiring plan by category for the first three years of operation.

14. Financial Forecast

This is the number-crunching section of the plan. If you will be submitting this plan to investors, there will be standardized financial spreadsheets to prepare. These financial statements include balance sheets, income statements, and cash flow statements. These statements are pro forma and are usually projected out at least three and sometimes five years. In addition to the spreadsheets, there should be a written narrative that discusses the highlights of the statements. The narrative should characterize the amount of investment required, when the product/venture will be cash-flow-positive, profitability, and return on investment. Exit strategies for investors should also be described. For company-internal business plans, the financial statements may be slightly different, as there may be specific financial ratios or calculations that need to be done. Figure 14.3 is a checklist of what business plan readers are looking for in each section of a business plan.

Section	Investors	Corporate execs	Product team
Product description	Easily understood, feasible to develop in short-term	Have competency to develop and produce	Functionality, features, how customers will use
Strategic objectives	Product consistent with long-term direction	Will help meet near- and long-term objectives	Priority of this product for the company
Business model	A profit-making one	Business model experience, partners easily added	Handoff points with suppliers, vendors, distributors
Business problem solved	Real customer problem with no current solution	Likelihood that customer will buy it	How customer will use it, features needed
Customer	Customer need exists now	Known customer, beta customers identified	Number and type of customer interfaces required
Market	Growing, big enough to be profitable	Relative profitability of product	
Competition	Few, strategy in place for each, barriers to entry	Number of competitors, what's known about each	Knowledge of competitors' products
Distribution strategy	Distribution partners and intrastructure in place	Partners, infrastructure that needs development	Strategy for working with partners
Marketing/sales strategy	Realistic for market size, customer and sales cycle	Market share targets, new strategies needed	Timing of beta and final versions of product
Support	Support plan in place	New support needs	Interface points for technical support
Product development	Short but realistic development cycle	Budget and resources required, hiring plan	Development team and budget
Operations plan	All business operations thought through	Adequacy of existing infrastructure	
Management plan	Experienced, proven team	Resources required	Development team
Financials	Cash flow positive point, rate of return and timing	Impact on financial forecast, budgets, growth plans	Preliminary forecasts

Figure 14.3: What Readers Look for in the Business Plan

The framework and timing of a marketing plan

The marketing plan may be started during the development phase, so that when it comes time to begin the launch phase, the sections can be updated quickly. Chapter 15 discusses the changes that can take place while the product is in development, and the information that needs to be updated before you launch your product. In this chapter, the content of the marketing plan is described. The following description is for a single product marketing plan, not a high-level marketing plan for the whole company. High-level corporate marketing plans are more general and are not within the focus of this book.

The marketing plan is a key document and planning tool for the launch phase. The purpose of the plan is to characterize the market environment into which you will be launching the new product, along with the strategy, the partners, and the programs that you will employ to get to market. It summarizes the who, what, where, and when for getting the new product to the market, and it guides the launch efforts.

When you develop the marketing plan, you will already have some of the information, such as market research data and your business model and strategy. Figure 14.4 illustrates the content that is used to compile the plan and the order in which it should be compiled. The market characterization, competitive analysis, product description, and strategic objectives are all used to compile the positioning statements. The resulting positioning statements, along with the customer description, are used to create the messages that will in turn be used in the marketing programs. All of your market characterization, your customer description, and your channel partners will be used to help identify the marketing programs that you will implement during launch. Those programs then become launch deliverables.

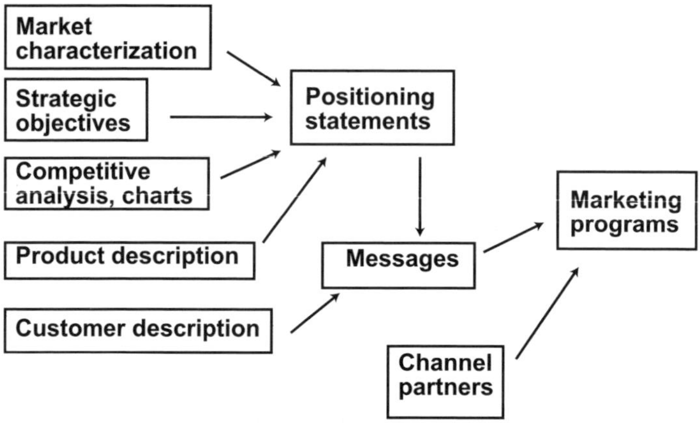

Each element is also included as a section in the marketing plan

Figure 14.4: Compiling the Elements of the Marketing Plan

MARKETING PLAN OUTLINE

Executive Summary

This summary should include brief descriptions of the following topics: product description, target customer and target market segment, competitive differentiators, business model, market strategy, and key marketing programs.

1. Strategic Business Objectives

The new product needs to be described in terms of how it fits into the greater context of the company. The new product might be the first product, part of a series, one that will help capture a new market segment, or one that will help the company's bottom line. Examining the fit with strategic objectives will help prioritize the product that is being launched and will clarify what the company hopes to achieve.

2. Product or Service Description

There should be a very brief description of the product in this section, along with any pictures or diagrams. The key functionality of the product should be described, along with a list of important features. The new product should be described in terms of its relationship to the overall product roadmap for the company.

3. Target Customer Description

Everything about the customer goes in this section. The detailed customer profile should identify a typical customer, their level of buying authority, and the customer problem that the product will solve. The detailed value proposition should be included, along with any feedback from customer surveys, beta tests, or customer feedback of any kind.

4. Market Trends

The market trends that were identified during market research should be noted here, along with the source of the information. The impact of these trends on the new product should be discussed, especially in terms of the timing of launch.

5. Market Size and Segmentation

The estimate of the market size for your new product is the focus of this section. This information may have come from industry publications, analyst projections, or your own market surveys. Forecasting market size is always an educated guess, and there are no guarantees as to whether the numbers will be accurate. The best way to approach this exercise is to use reliable sources of information and then revise the data based on your own company's experience. Once you have some numbers, you can use a TAM-SAM-SOM (total available market, served available market, share of market) graph or chart to show your market projections. The projections should go out five years, if possible.

The other information in this section relates to market segmentation. You need to identify how you will divide up the market and how the customers may be different in each segment. It's also important to identify which sales channels can be used to reach the customers in each segment, and how the sales must ramp up in order to produce the targeted market share in each segment.

6. Competition

This is the section for all of the detailed competitive analysis. You should include all known competitors and potential competitors, along with alternatives and substitutes that could 'compete' with your new product. The competitors should be described by name, competing products, price position, and marketing and selling strategy. A competitive matrix should be included that characterizes the product, feature by feature, relative to the competition, and it should also include the attributes of the competitor as a company. The narrative in this section should identify the top two or three competitors and the strategy for defending your market position against each one.

7. Market Strategy

In this section, describe the go-to-market strategy that you will use for your new product. There are several strategies presented in Chapter 9 of this book. For your chosen strategy, you need to describe how the strategy will help the company attain and maintain competitive advantage. You should also describe how this strategy fits with the chosen business model for the product.

8. Pricing

The prices for new products are often dictated by the development department or by senior management. However the pricing structure was determined, it needs to be explained in this section of the plan. Include information on price sensitivity of the customer, pricing strategy and how prices compare with competitors' products.

9. Positioning

The upper left section of Figure 14.4 shows several sources that should be used to develop the positioning strategy for your new product. In this section, you need to describe the overall positioning, in terms of differentiators. You can include a chart that shows features, advantages, and benefits, as described in *High Tech Product Launch* and Appendix B of this book. You should also include the list of positioning statements that capture that strategy.

10. Business Model

The business model section from the business plan should be repeated here in the marketing plan. In addition, you need to identify which of the participants will be involved in marketing the new product, and describe the role that they will play.

11. Distribution Channels

Your business model may include channel partners who will sell your new product. You may also have a direct sales force who will sell your product, instead of, or in addition to, these channel partners. In this section of the plan, you need to identify who will sell the product and in which segments. You also need to include a list of the marketing materials that they will need.

12. Strategic Partners

Your company may have other strategic partners who will be involved in the marketing process. If so, they should be identified in this section, and their role in the new product marketing or sales process should be described.

13. Messaging

Using the positioning statements and the customer description, you will need to develop a list of marketing messages that can be used in the marketing programs. Those messages should be listed in this section and organized into a 'hierarchy of messages', starting at the company level all the way through the product level. It's also a good idea to list the "proof points", or information that proves or justifies each message. These proof points might be facts about the product or customer testimonials.

14. Marketing Programs

This is usually the longest section of the marketing plan, because all of the promotional programs, marketing materials, and launch deliverables are included here. For each item that is planned, you need to describe its purpose, the intended audience, the budget, and the timing. These programs should be grouped according to this format:

- -External Marketing (direct mail, web, seminars, trade shows, events)
  - -Collateral (data sheets, brochures, white papers, multimedia, presentations, application notes, suc cess stories, web versions)
  - -Public Relations and Advertising
- -Internal Marketing (sales communications, guides, tools, training, intranet)

15. Customer Service and Support Plan

This section describes how the product will be supported after it is sold. This may not seem like an important part of the marketing plan, but this information is critical to the customer. This information may need to be included in marketing materials that are developed. The marketing team may also need to develop special materials to help train the customer support team on the new product that is being launched.

16. Sales and Channel Training Plan

During the launch phase, the marketing group must develop materials to help prepare the sales channels to sell the new product. Sometimes, there is a dedicated group within the company that has this charter. Whatever the situation, it is important to describe the extent of training needed, when it is needed, and what needs to be developed by the marketing team.

17. Risk Analysis and Mitigation

This last section is about risk and what do to if unforeseen events occur. Product launches are always risky, and many things can go wrong. In this section of the plan, some likely risks should be described, along with a contingency plan for handling these situations. Examples of these events are: slip in date of product release, competitor announcing a new product, and sudden reduction in marketing budget.

How the marketing plan is used

Decision-makers and product team members use a marketing plan differently. Figure 14.5 shows the uses of the marketing plan by these constituencies. It is important to keep this in mind when writing the plan, in order to allow for the appropriate amount of detail to suit everyone.

Corporate decision-makers

-How much budget do I need to allocate to this product
-How important is this product to the company?
-Are the programs appropriate, given the market size/trends?
-Will the market strategy maximize competitive advantage?
-Which partners need to be on board and when?
-What will the sales force need to know to sell this new product?
-What publicity is needed and what is the fit with corporate PR plans?
-What do our employees need to know about this new product?
-What are the key messages?
-What are the risks and how can we mitigate them?

Product/launch team

-What is the product we are marketing?
-How important is this product to the company?
-How difficult will it be to create and sustain our competitive advantage?
-Do we know this customer, and do we know these competitors?
-Will we need to work with any new partners during the launch?
-What key messages need to be used in all programs?
-Which programs are we going to implement during launch, and when?

Figure 14.5: How Different Constituencies Use the Marketing Plan

How to use business plans and marketing plans effectively

One of the things that you will notice is that there is overlap between the business plan and marketing plan. The business model, product description, strategic objectives, and partnering sections should be consistent between the two plans. For the marketing sections, there will be much more detail in the marketing plan; only the high-level market information should appear in the business plan. If a company is using a working business plan to guide the new product through the entire cycle, and a marketing plan to plan and implement the launch, the plans need to be consistent and not have conflicting information in them. They should be current and up to date, and 'version-control' should be in place, whereby the copies are date-stamped so that users are assured of having the latest versions.

Distribution of the plans should be controlled, as well. In the case of business plans (especially those targeted for investors), a record should be kept as to the date, version number, and recipient of the plan. For marketing plans, distribution control can be less formal; however, all plans that are distributed inside the company should be marked "company confidential". A marketing plan is not the type of document that you'd want to end up in your competitor's hands.

Business and marketing plans need to be kept simple and current. They are meant to be read by people who need information to make decisions. If the plans are not serving their purpose, then they need to be revised or updated accordingly. In some cases, a company may decide that it isn't really following or using the business plan, especially if the new product has reached a certain stage in the new product cycle. If people don't need the plan, then it should not be created or updated. In the end, plans only have value if people will use them.

15

What to Update When You're Ready to Launch

Between the time you did idea selection and validation, and the time the development is complete, the market conditions may have changed drastically. You need to revisit the six validation criteria as you are preparing to launch your new product, in order to update all of the information regarding the customer, the market environment, your company, and profitability goals.

Figure 15.1 is a diagram of the information that you gathered during the idea validation phase. You very likely conducted market research in order to assess the market potential, to characterize the customer and market, and to analyze competitors. If the results of that research are available in archived files, then it may be worthwhile to find any pertinent files. They can be used as a starting point for updating the information, as well as to provide a checklist for the sources used to conduct the market research. Sometimes the information used for idea validation is summarized in a market requirements document (MRD). MRDs are often used as a reference during the product development cycle to help guide developers in designing the product to meet customer requirements. If the MRD for the product still exists, then it also can be used as a starting point for the update. If your company doesn't retain documents for long periods of time, or if you can't locate old files, then you may need to meet with the development team and the initial new product decision-makers, in order to learn more about the market environment and specifications used as a basis for development.

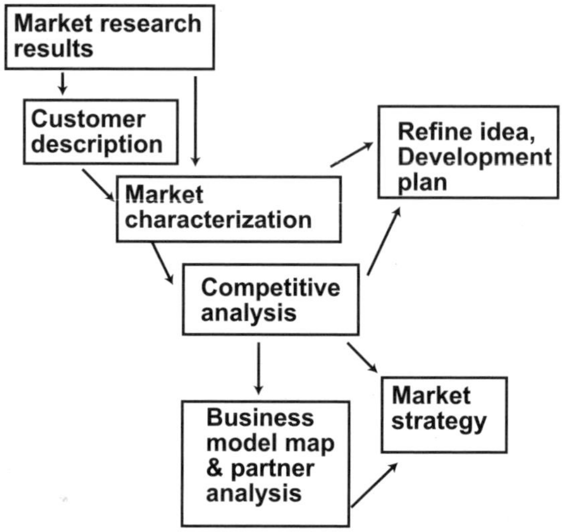

Figure 15.1: Flow Chart of Pre-development Information

During the development cycle, the business model and market strategy for your new product should have been formulated. Depending on the length of your product development cycle, the business model and strategy should also be revisited before you launch the product, to make sure that they will still work in the current market environment.

Changes that occur during the development cycle

Wouldn't it be great to only have to assess the market once, develop the product, and then launch it? If product development cycles were only a couple of weeks in length, it might be possible to get away with that. However, in the real world, most products take at least a few months, and usually many months or even years, before they are ready to launch. That means that there will be changes in the economy, in technology, and in the market environment for your new product (Figure 15.2).

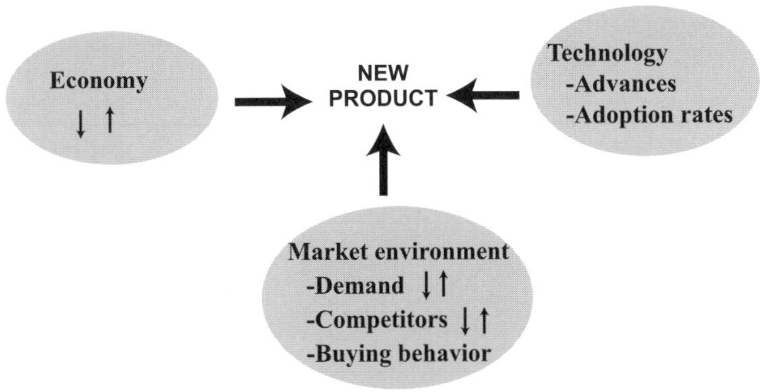

Figure 15.2: The Dynamic External World

The global economy is fluctuating at a faster rate than ever before. Global stock market fluctuations, exchange rates, lending rates, price indexes, and investment trends all have a huge impact on customers' buying behavior for your product, price sensitivity, availability of capital to launch and support the product, and shareholders' or investors' expectations of returns. This is true whether you are in the business-to-business sector or the business-to-consumer sector.

Technology advances and the rate of adoption also change rapidly, especially with the widespread use of the Internet and related technologies. You may think your new product has all of the latest features available, but at launch time, your customer's expectations may have increased, and it is possible that your new product could be viewed as not up-to-date, especially if you are late to market. When that happens, it becomes more difficult to position your product in the marketplace. Technology changes can also make a difference in terms of which venues you will use to launch your product. For example, if your customers are using the web more than they were at the time your product started its development cycle, then you may want to use your company's website as the primary marketing venue when you launch the product.

The area of greatest change is in the market environment. New competitors can enter your target market in a matter of weeks, especially in environments where there are few barriers to entry. Companies that were considered competitors at the beginning of your new product cycle may have been acquired or may have folded and are no longer a threat. Market demand for your new product will have fluctuated considerably; it may be greater or less than your initial projection, so you must be prepared to address that during launch by stepping up your marketing efforts or focusing them on a smaller number of customers.

Regardless of where and how the changes have occurred that affect your new product, it is important to keep an open mind and be objective – don't just assume that you know the environment without looking at the trends and the facts. The external world will always be dynamic, and you must focus on a moving target; that is the nature of marketing.

The Strategic Fit: What has changed?

During the development phase, your company may have shifted its strategic direction several times. Compared to the beginning of the product cycle, your company may have grown or shrunk, acquired partners or divested operations, or perhaps changed its brand or image. It is necessary to gather the latest company vision and mission statements and compare them to those used to screen and select the product idea at the beginning. There are several questions to ask, listed here (Figure 15.3):

-Does the product still fit the strategic direction of the company?
-What are the changes in the company's size during the development cycle?
-How has the product raodmap for the company changed, and where does the new product fit?
-For any new strategic partners, what is their relationship to the product being launched?
-How has the company's reputation or image changed since the begining of cycle; will this new product impact that image?
-Have there been any changes in core competencies or core technologies during the development cycle?

Figure 15.3: Changes in Strategic Fit

Once you have answered this set of questions, you will have an updated characterization of the product's fit with the company's strategic objectives. If the fit has changed, then you may need to make changes in market strategy, positioning, and messages. That is key knowledge for planning and implementing the product launch. For more specific information on the impact of strategic objectives on the launch, consult my book *High Tech Product Launch*, which has a chapter devoted to that subject.

The customer problem: Is it the same?

Customers and their buying behavior change rapidly and unpredictably. Assuming that the product was designed and developed to solve a specific customer problem, it is necessary to check back with target customers to make sure their need is still the same. This can easily be done near the end of the development phase with a beta customer who has been most recently involved with the team. Sometimes during development or even beta test, changes are made to more closely fit the customer's needs and specifications. It's necessary to find out all the changes that were made during the entire development phase, in order to develop all of the marketing materials with accuracy. Here is the list of questions to ask about your customer (Figure 15.4):

> *-How has the target customer profile changed?*
> *-How will the customer use our product today?*
> *-Does our new product solve the same customer problem as originally intended?*
> *-What is the updated customer value proposition?*
> *-Is the new product's price acceptable to the target customer?*
> *-What changes were made to the product as a result of customer beta test? What additional value will these changes provide?*
> *-Will the customer buy the product as it is currently developed?*

Figure 15.4: Customer Change Assessment

The customer description is probably the most critical area to update prior to launch. In chapter 4, I discussed which customer attributes to assess to validate the market, especially the customer's value proposition. If your product's value has changed from the customer's point of view, it impacts everything that you do during launch: messages, pricing, which programs to implement, and preparing the sales force to sell the product.

The Competition: What new competing products have evolved since you validated the market?

Another area of constant change is the competitive landscape for your new product. Hopefully, you have been vigilant about monitoring the competition during the development phase and have identified any new competitors that have appeared. It's also very important to do an update on the old competitors and assess their most current strengths and weaknesses. Figure 15.5 is a checklist of what factors need to be updated for the competitive analysis.

-Which competitors from the pre-development phase are still threats?
-What changes have taken place in the comp--etitors' companies and their product lines?
-Are the new product differentiators still valid?
-Are there new differentiators due to changes made to the product during development?
-What are the new competitive threats in the marketplace (including companies that sell different products to your market and who sell similar products to different markets)?
-How are competitors marketing their competing products now? Which programs do they use to sell their products?

Figure 15.5: Updating the Competitive Analysis

Competitors can change their strategy and promotional tactics very quickly. Once you update the competitive analysis prior to launch, you will want to make sure that someone keeps a close watch on competitors constantly until launch day.

The Market: Which new trends will affect your market size estimate or strategy?

The size of any target market fluctuates frequently, driven by demand, the economy, and customer buying behavior. It's necessary to research the latest market trends at the time of launch and reassess your target market size and market share.

After you have updated and verified your target customer description and value proposition (along with the customer's willingness to buy your new product), you should do some market research to find out what has been happening in the marketplace. Even if your customer's need is still valid, other factors, such as an economic downturn or upturn, can affect your market size estimate and sales forecast. Your updated competitive analysis will also help you fine-tune your market share estimate, based on how many competitors are entering or leaving your target market space. The competitive analysis update will also help verify whether the market strategy you crafted during the product development phase is still valid. Here are the questions to ask regarding the overall market (Figure 15.6):

-Who else is in our market space now?
-Does our proposed market strategy still make sense for the current environment?
-What does the media and trade press say about our target market? Is it growing, shirinking, or stable?
-What is the economic climate for the next 6 to 12 months, and how might this impact our customers' buying decisions?
-What adjustments need to be made to the available market size and target market share?
-How will the updated market size and market share affect our sales forecast?
-What does the sales force need to know about these trends and changes?

Figure 15.6: Market Environment Update

During the launch phase, you will be developing information for the sales force about your new product and the marketing programs you will be using to promote it. Don't assume that your salespeople are aware of all the changes going on in the greater marketplace. It's always a good idea to summarize the most recent changes in the marketplace, to add that to the marketing plan, and to make sure that the salespeople get a copy of it. These changes also need to be reflected in the sales training materials. The sales force needs this information in order to be able to develop a sales strategy and to close sales.

The Resources: Are people in place to implement the launch phase?

At the beginning of the new product cycle, it was necessary to assess the people and technology resources available to design and build the product. When you are preparing to launch the product, you need to assess the resource requirements available to manage and implement the launch. Some of the individuals who worked on the development of the product may be needed during the launch as well, to assist in developing demos or other marketing programs. Before the technical staff members are reassigned to other projects, it's a good idea to identify the staff that you will need to support the launch activities. This should be done at least three months before launch date.

Profitability: Are there changes in pricing or costs that will impact the launch?

The economy, in general, and your company's financial conditions, specifically, can impact both your marketing budget for the launch and the price of the new product being launched. Depending on the forecasted profit for the new product, and the updated market and economic trends, there may be additional pressure to generate revenues by changing the price, reducing marketing expenses, or conducting more targeted marketing campaigns. Here are the questions to ask (Figure 15.7):

-What is the change in the sales forecast based on current market demand?
-What are the changes in product pricing, based on customer price sensitivity and internal financial metrics (COGS, etc.)?
-What is the current expected return on investment for this new product?
-Are there any across-the-board cost reduction measures in place for the company?
-Has the competitive landscape changed such that additional marketing programs will be needed to effect sales?

Figure 15.7: Profitability Issues for the Launch

Evaluating profitability for the new product means looking at the changes in the external market and economic environment, as well as in the company-internal financial goals and metrics. Each product that is launched needs to be evaluated in this context before launch activities begin.

The marketing plan will be developed in more detail in preparation for launch

As discussed in chapter 14, the marketing plan must be completed prior to launch. By revisiting the initial six validation criteria and assessing the changes that have taken place, it should be relatively quick and easy to update the appropriate sections of the marketing plan.

From the previous sections of this chapter, it is clear that many things can change prior to launch, and these changes will affect the launch process and plan. Figure 15.8 is a sampling of the changes and the possible impact on the launch process.

Type of Change	Impact on Launch Process and Launch Plan
New product has lower (or higher) priority in company's strategic plan	Fewer (or more) marketing programs needed, marketing budget reduced (increased)
Customer's value proposition is different	Positioning and marketing messages need to be modified, marketing program mix changes
Customer less likely to buy than a year ago	More direct marketing programs needed, increased sales efforts (due to longer sales cycle)
Additional features/functions added to product during beta phase	Add differentiators, postioning statements, marketing messages
Price of product will be lower than originally intended	Change messages to reflect lower price (if differentiator), marketing budget may be reduced
New competitors in target market	Develop differentiators, change positioning and messages accordingly
Market size decreases (increases)	Implement more targeted, direct marketing programs (broader, and more marketing programs)
Company cost reduction measures in place	Implement less expensive marketing programs, leverage the web

Figure 15.8: Effect of Changes on the Launch Plan

Once you have reviewed these external and company-internal factors, you will have a much better idea of the market environment into which you will launch your new product. Assessing the impact of these potential changes and doing the necessary updates to the marketing plan will make the rest of the launch planning process proceed more smoothly.

16

Choosing the Best Marketing Programs for the Internet Era

Marketing programs include all the materials or events that are implemented during the launch of a new product or service. The purpose of marketing programs is to inform the target market about the product or service, in an effort to get market influencers to recommend it, and customers to buy it. Marketing programs are usually directed externally, from the company to the target market; however, internal marketing programs that are directed to the employees and strategic partners of the company also need to be implemented to support the launch of a new product or service.

In general, launching a new product requires more marketing programs than for an enhanced version of an existing product. This is because the marketing programs need to create awareness of the new product among the target audience; for existing products, the audience already knows about the product or product line. The audience that marketing programs need to reach includes prospects, customers, industry analysts, investors, trade press, channel partners, and strategic partners. Spreading the message to all of these constituencies translates to many marketing programs.

If a new, unfamiliar market is being targeted for the new product, then the marketing programs may be more complex and expensive, because you also need to create awareness of your company along with the new product. Because more programs and costs are required for marketing new products, it is more challenging to achieve profitability. Companies must find more cost-effective ways to deliver marketing programs, including use of Internet technologies and choosing programs that yield the greatest return on investment in terms of sales. Along with cost-effectiveness, the marketing effectiveness of various marketing programs needs to be measured. Companies need to establish these metrics and use them for every product launch and each set of marketing programs that are implemented.

In addition, in the Internet Era, a speedy time to market is essential for survival and competitive advantage. The marketing programs that are fast to implement and most effective in building awareness and moving customers through the entire buying cycle are the best ones to use today. Figure 16.1 illustrates the buying cycle and the various programs that can be used to support each of its stages. Building awareness requires that the right promotional message be delivered to the right customer at the right time. Marketing programs must be targeted and must deliver messages consistent with the customers' value proposition - down to the level of the individual customer. Other constituencies who influence the buying cycle must also receive a consistent message, which means that the appropriate venues must be used to deliver the messages.

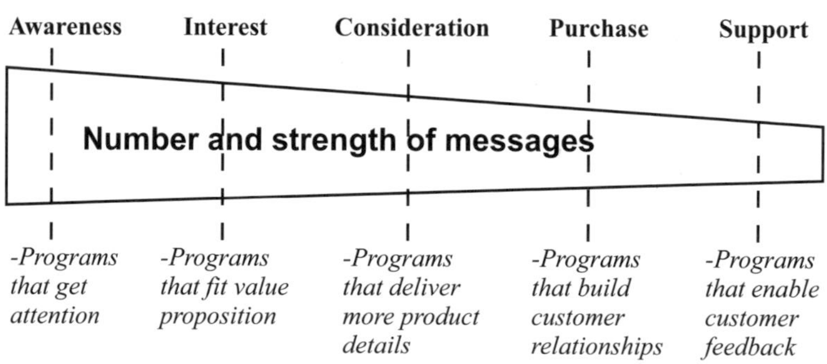

Figure 16.1: Customer Buying Cycle and Marketing Programs

Profitability now drives marketing programs

The chief lesson from the dot-com boom and bust was the need to focus on profitability, especially when planning marketing programs. Spending millions of venture capital dollars on expensive ads, with no solid business model in place to make money, just does not work in today's economic environment.

Each marketing program must be examined in terms of its cost to implement, its effectiveness in reaching the target customer, and the likelihood that it will result in revenues. One way to start the evaluation is to review the marketing effectiveness of previous marketing programs for similar products. If a program doesn't get the right message to the right audience, it's not going to generate revenues, or ultimately, profit. Randy Shattuck is the founder and CEO of the Shattuck Group, an integrated marketing consulting company in San Jose, California. *"Our clients are more cost-sensitive today than they were a year ago, and everyone is seeking a solid return on their investment. However, all of our clients also know that they cannot afford to stop promoting their products and services. Many of them are using multimedia marketing campaigns that will more effectively differentiate their companies. They are basing their decisions on cost, but also on effectiveness,"* says Randy. Solid business basics still apply when choosing marketing programs, and profitability should be the highest priority. With marketing programs, the cost must be weighed against the potential for revenue.

More programs are needed for new products

It can be a daunting task to develop and manage a set of marketing programs for a new product. All programs must carry consistent messages, and often the most important message to get across is: what is it about the product that is "new" or different? The timing must be orchestrated so that awareness precedes the selling cycle. The right media must be used to reach the customers, so that they can receive the messages and the information they need to purchase the product.

Contrast this situation with that of an existing product that is being enhanced by adding some new features, as shown in Figure 16.2. In that case, one or two pieces of printed collateral, a press release, and a website update are all that are needed for the product enhancement. With a new product, you may need an extensive public relations and/or marketing campaign, brochures, data sheets or white papers, product demos, new web pages for the product, sales training materials, and channel marketing materials. It may take longer to develop the content of marketing programs for a new product, to make sure that the information is accurate, factual, and consistent with the market strategy. Because it takes longer, the programs for a new product will cost more to implement. Careful planning, prioritization, and management will be required as the programs are implemented, if profitability ultimately is to be achieved.

Company launch/ new product launch	**Routine product launch or enhancement**
-Press release, press/ analyst tour -Brochure -Datasheet -White paper -Demo, if appropriate -Selected advertising -Big website splash -Events (trade shows, user conferences) -Sales training materials, collateral kit -Sales tools -Channel programs	-Press releases -Datasheet -White paper -Demo, if appropriate -Website update -Sales training materials -Customer presentation -Events (depending on timing -Channel program update

Figure 16.2: Marketing Programs for New Products versus Existing Products

The race to market: at Internet speed

With a new product, you need to build awareness, and you must get to market quickly to establish and maintain your competitive advantage. That means that the programs that you implement need to build awareness quickly and convince the customers to buy. Target customers must be able to instantly understand what your company does, what the new product is and does, and whether it fits their value proposition. The attention span of customers is shrinking constantly. People just don't have enough time to receive and process the information that is constantly thrown at them via phone, email, Internet, and in person. As Randy Shattuck observes, *"It's interesting to me that customers don't want to waste precious time hearing about stuff they'll never need or buy, yet they spend hours or days evaluating products they do want. This makes it more complicated for companies to develop an effective messaging strategy. I think the best approach is to put your most enticing and unique features first, then back it up with more detailed and thorough information about your product or service, on a website or in a brochure. Most importantly, whatever messages and information you deliver have to be in bite-sized pieces."*

If you are implementing online programs such as web banner ads, the attention span can be even shorter. Jose Geronimo is the Banner Ad Program Manager in the Internet Marketing Operations group at Cisco Systems *"When we developed our ad server technology, we had to measure how quickly the ad appeared on the page during a download. If the text appeared before the graphics, or was too slow, the user will have clicked over to another page. As Internet bandwidth increases, customers expect faster downloads and the attention span gets even shorter,"* says Jose. Getting your product to market quickly means that the programs that you choose need to quickly deliver the key messages and information to the customer.

Achieving a balanced program portfolio

The Internet and related technologies have added a new dimension to marketing. The dot-com boom showed marketers how to use the Internet for marketing programs, and examples of these Internet uses are included in Chapter 17. It's tempting to focus all the marketing resources on Internet marketing alone, and to forget the more conventional programs that marketers have been using for years, such as printed brochures or direct mail. Each time that a new product is launched, it pays to revisit the marketing programs that have been most effective for your company in the past. The ideal approach is to combine the old and conventional with the new types of programs, to create a balanced portfolio of programs that maximize speed and profitability (Figure 16.3).

Randy Shattuck advises his client companies to do just that. "*Effective marketing in the Internet era is as much about the business strategy you develop to promote your company as it is about the tactics you deploy to promote your company. Today we have richer and more effective marketing programs than ever before. However, they can only be effective if each program has a specific purpose and a measurable goal in mind. Our clients today are embracing electronic media for their programs where the content will change or be updated frequently, but may also continue to print conventional high-end brochures with content that will have relevance six months into the future.*"

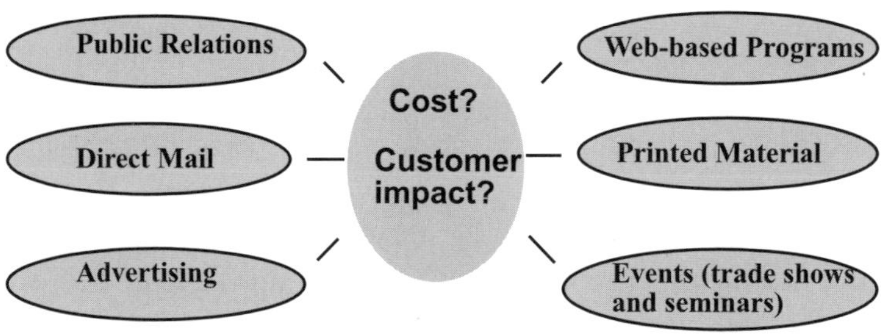

The cost of the program needs to balance with the impact the program will have on the customer

Figure 16.3: The Balanced Program Portfolio

The venues used to reach the target customer must be appropriate for what the customers will use. Cynthia Holladay is an expert in strategic marketing, and a former marketing executive in several high-tech companies. She was also a former analyst and is a board advisor to startups. *"Ultimately you need programs other than the Internet to reinforce your marketing messages. Customers might welcome a change from an overloaded email in-box and enjoy looking at a piece of printed collateral. Another consideration with Internet-related marketing programs is the privacy issue. Not everyone wants to give out his or her email address today because of spamming. The best approach is to have a mix of programs and venues that fit your customer's need for information,"* advises Cynthia.

It's a good idea to take a look at similar products to see what has worked for your company in the past, especially in terms of generating sales. Using newer Internet-related technologies as a way to augment the proven marketing programs is the ultimate objective. You can also use more conventional programs to refer people to online venues. An example of this would be to mail postcards that direct customers to the company website for more information. All of the marketing programs for a new product must work together as a portfolio to achieve profitability and fast time to market.

Advertising ups and downs

For decades, corporations have used advertising in varying degrees to help sell their products and services. Until the dot-com expansion phase, only established or growing companies with significant cash reserves could afford to do advertising. During the dot-com boom, many newly funded startups immediately jumped into the advertising arena, spending the bulk of their venture capital dollars for prime time, high-end ads. The advertising industry had never seen anything like this in their decades of history; this was definitely an up-tick in industry revenues. *"Dot-commers inflated the ad prices and in some cases they paid premium prices for the ads. Since the dot-com bust, ad prices are coming down again, and the rest of us can now benefit from more affordable advertising exposure,"* says Randy Shattuck.

Did this high-end advertising increase awareness of the dot-com companies and their products? David Platshon is the CEO of Fatbox, an award-winning multimedia production company whose clients include a variety of high-tech and services companies. David believes that the dot-coms missed the mark in terms of building awareness. *"Dot-com companies put all their eggs in one big expensive advertising basket that did not increase awareness of what the companies did, let alone what their products were. They pursued advertising at the expense of building a solid business infrastructure to support their companies' ability to develop and deliver the products and services. On top of that, some of the ads were just bad; the dot-coms didn't take to time to understand their target customers and develop the ads that might have worked. They were in too much of a hurry."*

If your company is a startup, you can't expect to advertise like a larger established company would, according to Cynthia Holladay. *"For ads to effectively build your brand over time, you must ensure that you can deliver on what you say. The company must have the infrastructure and sales channels in place in order to meet or exceed customers' expectations. A startup also needs to clearly define what the company does, before addressing detailed messages about their products and services. That was a problem with a lot of the dot-com fever advertising; it was difficult to figure out what business the companies were in, and in some cases, who the companies were at all. If you're a startup, you need to advertise your value for specific target customers, and gradually establish the company's credibility over time. It's a better use of the marketing budget and more effective in building mind share."*

Established companies may have also changed their approach to using advertising. *"At Cisco, we have always limited our corporate-wide advertising budgets,"* says Jose Geronimo. *"It doesn't matter what type of advertising that you do, but it is important to use your budget wisely and only advertise when you have a reasonable assurance that you can get your ad in front of your customer who will make the buying decision."* Sometimes large companies will only do corporate high-level ads that promote the company as a whole or the brand, instead of doing advertising at the product level. The many considerations of the advertising issue are shown in Figure 16.4.

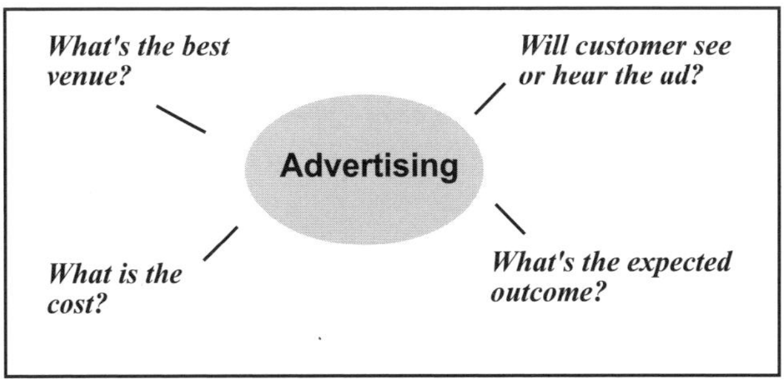

Figure 16.4: Key Questions about Advertising

Internet advertising in the form of banner ads is currently undergoing significant change. During the early years of the Internet, in the 1990s, banner ads were predicted to be the way of the future, even replacing conventional print advertising. However, the return on the significant investment in banner ads was not realized. Most people now believe that they just don't work. *"The primary problem with banner ads was that the promise of click-throughs did not materialize. Another problem with banner ads is that that they are on a site for a short time and then are gone or are changed significantly. Not so with printed ads in trade publications; those will be there at least in archive ten years from now,"* according to Randy Shattuck. Another issue with banner ads is the annoyance factor, according to Cynthia Holladay. *"Some of the banner ads are really annoying or distract-*

ing, especially if they create additional download time for a page. As web usage increases and users become more sophisticated, they have less patience with ads that waste their time or that don't interest them." Randy Shattuck further confirms this, based on focus groups The Shattuck Group has conducted: *"The constant feedback we have received about banner ads is to keep them out of the way."*

As with any marketing program, advertising should be done as part of a balanced portfolio of programs. Because advertising is expensive, it's important to know what you want to get out of the ad campaign, according to Randy Shattuck. *"Your objective might be to grow your company's brand, to sell specific products, to build awareness by educating your target market, or to create competitive advantage. The key thing to do, regardless of your marketing objective, is to quantitatively measure the effectiveness of your ad campaigns as you go. That's the only way to estimate your return on investment."*

One of the reasons that new dot-coms spent so much on advertising was because they were convinced that they had to build a brand quickly and believed that advertising could help them achieve that. That didn't happen. Who can remember the name of the company with the "sock puppet" ads on TV? Few people remember the company's name, but do remember the puppet. To be effective, branding must be done gradually, over a period of time that is measured in months or years, not weeks. The objective of branding is to "shape the customer's experience" in their mind by associating an image, icon, logo, name, or product with your company. That does not happen in one or two 30-second ads.

Whether or not to advertise, and in which venue, should be a part of the portfolio approach to choosing marketing programs. Because advertising can be rather expensive, it should be done sparingly, in a targeted way, and only if the budget can support it. Otherwise, it will hamper your company's efforts to achieve profitability.

How to achieve profitability and speed: packaging and targeting

The most effective marketing programs to use during the Internet Era are those that achieve speed through technology and targeting, and that are profitable because they are focused on the customer and use the right venues. It's also a matter of keeping the customer in mind when developing the style, quantity, and complexity of the content.

The content that is packaged in marketing programs varies considerably and may include product and company information, messages, guidelines on how to use the product, product support, and comparisons with other products and companies. What is the best way to package the content, and how much do you need? Ask your customer. *"For some of our high-end products like enterprise routers, the customers are engineers. They want a lot of detailed and complex product information along with suggested applications. For the low-end consumer products, simplicity is what our customers like. It's important to understand what content the customers need before spending a lot of marketing dollars on materials they won't read or use,"* says Jose Geronimo. Regardless of the level of complexity, it helps to keep the content targeted and factual. *"As customers become more savvy, they are more skeptical and ignore marketing fluff,"* says Cynthia Holladay. *"The best thing to do is to create information that is clear, targeted, and contains just the facts. It's faster for customers to read and to understand what you are selling."*

It also helps to figure out where your customers go to get information. *"You can't just throw a lot of marketing information out to the mass market to see what sticks,"* says Cynthia Holladay. *"You need to understand the whole ecosystem of your customer: What are their issues and priorities? What do they read? What events do they attend? Do they use the Internet to learn about new products and services? Developing this understanding helps to prioritize the most effective marketing programs and helps you manage your budget as well."* Packaging of marketing content also makes a difference in terms of how well customers receive your messages. *"We have found that the takeaway is much higher when the message is delivered in an audio/video environment rather than in print,"* says David Platshon. *"People's attention span is now shorter than ever. You not only have to have the right medium, but you must deliver the message more quickly in that medium."* You must have a thorough understanding of your customer in order to package material appropriately, which means that you need to take the time and budget the necessary resources to develop that customer profile before spending money on implementing your marketing programs.

Targeting essentially means one-to-one marketing, down to the level of the individual customer. How do you reach an individual if you are selling your new product to a market that has thousands of customers? It requires effective messaging. *"Companies really need to get serious about segmenting and prioritizing target customers, creating a matrix that identifies each customer by industry, title, issues, values, and the benefits your product or service will bring to them. You must tailor your message appropriately for each target customer, and then deliver it in a way the message will appeal to and be heard by that individual person,"* advises Cynthia Holladay. Developing and using a matrix like this is an excellent way to build your customer profile and also provides a baseline that can be used to measure the marketing programs' effectiveness as they are implemented.

Effective one-to-one targeting requires the building of a customer relationship, including the most-important element of trust. According to Cynthia Holladay, *"It takes a solid understanding of your customer in order to begin to build the relationship. You must listen to them, respect them, and deliver what you promise. That's the only way to create trust."* Building that trust starts with one customer who buys one product that you effectively deliver as promised. As your company adds each additional customer, the relationships build, which helps establish your company's reputation in the target market segment and in the marketplace as a whole.

Best Marketing Programs for the Internet Era

This section addresses the advisability of using various marketing programs. For more detailed information on these programs, including definitions and examples, I highly recommend that you use *High Tech Product Launch* as a reference (see Appendix A – Recommended Reading). You company may be accustomed to implementing the same set of marketing programs for every new product, just because you've always done it that way. However, it's important to revisit the programs in terms of cost, speed, and effectiveness in achieving the marketing goals for the new product being launched. That is the best way to choose marketing programs in the Internet era.

<u>Public Relations.</u> How effective are public relations campaigns for today's environment? Companies still need to pursue them, but as one piece of an overall portfolio of programs, not the centerpiece. Randy Shattuck believes that companies need to keep this in perspective. *"Companies shouldn't try to replace advertising with public relations coverage. This is not advisable because the mediums are so different. More importantly, the company has no control over the final messages that make their way into PR coverage; the editors can choose which parts of your message to publish and which to omit, potentially altering your intended message substantially. With advertising, you maintain control over your message."* Every company, regardless of size, needs to have an element of PR in their program portfolio, in order to build credibility and create influence in the marketplace. However, it must be appropriate in terms of the budget and fit with other marketing programs.

Public relations activities are still an important part of marketing today. There are more venues than ever before for media coverage, and a growing number of analyst firms to target. With email and the Internet, the media cycles have speeded up, according to Cynthia Holladay, a former analyst. *"The 'time to information' is the interval from the time something happens in the company (such as a new product being announced) and the time that people expect to read about it in the media. This time interval is much shorter than it used to be. From the media or analyst's point of view, there is more pressure to find, filter and be the first to report the news. The sheer volume and time pressure can lead to unintentionally omitting information or not having enough time to validate all the facts. On the other hand, with so much information coming at them at once, reporters and analysts will understandably ignore announcements if they are not clear or newsworthy. Companies need to be more effective at presenting the facts and not issuing press releases until there is a newsworthy event. That will go a long way to build more effective relationships with the press and analysts."* Today, it's important to include public relations in your portfolio of programs for a new product. However, you need to use a targeted approach in choosing how much press information you generate and which media to approach.

Printed/Electronic brochures, datasheets and white papers. These types of marketing materials are still going to be used extensively by companies in the Internet era. However, in most cases, there will be less printing done of these materials and more use of the Internet and email to distribute these materials. It's much more cost-effective to post these materials on the company website than to print them, especially for datasheets and white papers, which tend to be updated every few months. *"In the companies where I've worked recently, we have decided to not professionally print any materials that could change in two months or less, such as datasheets. We post those materials on the company website instead, after carefully testing to ensure that the web pages are optimally produced on local printers using a variety of configurations. However, for more general materials used in the sales pro-*

cess, such as brochures, we do selective glossy prints. It's a good idea to make the print decisions based on the sales process – when do you need a professionally printed hard copy to hand to a customer? You also need to plan how all of the pieces will fit together in terms of messages, content and graphics and which materials need to contain detailed or general information," advises Cynthia Holladay. Appropriate venues, the cost of print versus electronic, and how these materials are used are important considerations for these programs today.

Demos. Today, the customer has more power than ever before, and at the same time, there are more products and services to choose from than ever before. It's incumbent upon companies to inform and educate the customer about new products and services (once they get the customer's attention!) According to Randy Shattuck, *"Our clients' greatest obstacle to overcome is not beating out the competition or adding new features; it's educating their customer on why they need their goods. On top of that, customers will not buy without a clear understanding of how they will achieve some economic benefit from the product or service. Consequently, customer education and demos have become extremely important. There are more demo labs in use today than we have ever seen before."*

This trend is further validated by David Platshon. *"Budgets of our clients are tighter than ever before, and requests for demos have doubled in the past year. There are more decision-makers involved in approving budgets for marketing programs. Presenting a demo to a potential customer is a two-way learning process. The customer wants to learn how they can derive some economic benefit from the product or service and how they can serve their own customers better. Your company learns more about their needs and concerns in the process; essentially, it's a form of market research."*

It's important to develop a demo from the customer's point of view, however. *"Customers need to grasp the value of your product or service to them. How will that product or service benefit them economically or make them look good in their company? Demos should be developed to highlight the business benefits quickly; they should not be designed like a product training tool. Today's economy is moving too quickly to substitute training tools for sales demos,"* according to Cynthia Holladay. In the Internet era, be prepared to develop and use more demos as part of your programs portfolio.

Web marketing. Web marketing includes using the corporate website to showcase and promote new products, links between websites, direct email campaigns, and referral or affiliate programs. These programs can be very effective, especially for targeting customers down to the level of the individual. *"We consistently use direct emails for several of our clients to help them promote new products to their installed base. The cost of doing this is roughly one-third of what it used to be with direct mail,"* says Randy Shattuck.

The use of the company website for marketing is increasing today. *"Web marketing has really taken off,"* says David Platshon. *"The web makes it easier for customers to get information about products and services. There aren't many customers out there who truly enjoy talking to salespeople, so the web enables them to evaluate products and services before the sales process begins. The web gives customers more convenience and more access."*

The development and maintenance of a corporate website can be quite expensive, but as long as this asset is in place, it's important to use it as much as possible for marketing programs. The web can be used as a venue for marketing seminars and for webcast product announcements. For many types of marketing programs, the corporate website and other web marketing tools will still be more cost-effective than using print media.

Sales training and tools. Chapter 17 of this book addresses ways to leverage the web during launch, and using web casting for training sales people about new products is one of the ways to cut costs and to keep your sales channels up to date on the latest products. The sales people should also be involved in making recommendations on the marketing materials that they think will be most effective for selling the new product. Sales people might suggest tools that will help them learn how to sell the new product, or various types of demos to use with customers. You may have several different media for sales training materials and tools, including print, CD or video, and web-based. Along with the content, the sales channels need to specify which media will be most effective for them to use in the selling process.

Channel programs. Many indirect channel partners have co-operative marketing programs or other marketing resources at their disposal. In order to control your costs more effectively, it's a good idea to revisit which programs are available from your channel partners. Creating separate marketing materials for your channel partners can be an expensive undertaking, so be objective in determining what is really needed to result in sales. If an existing channel partner will be selling the new product, then they may only need basic new product information. They might be able to utilize less expensive media, such as electronic formats, rather than printed materials. It's best to discuss this directly with channel partners before creating a lot of materials that they won't use or that won't help increase the rate of sales.

Figure 16.5 is a summary of the best marketing programs for the Internet era. Although the programs themselves are not new, the way they should be implemented or chosen is new.

Marketing programs for new products	How to implement in the Internet Era
Press release and press tour	Implement public relations activities that are appropriate for budget and marketing objectives
Brochure	Do electronic versions Print fewer of them and send only to select customers
Datasheet	Post on website to enable updating
White paper	Post on website to enable updating
Demo, if appropriate	Produce more demos; post simple versions at website and develop full demos for sales channels
Selected advertising	Budget should drive advertising
Big website splash	Maximize use of website to showcase new product
Sales training and collateral kit	Use web casting for more timely and less costly training programs
Sales tools	Produce only the tools that are effective from the salesperson's point of view
Channel programs as needed	Use resources available from channel partners to reduce expense Target materials for both channel and customer

Figure 16.5: Best New Product Marketing Programs for the Internet Era

Now that you know what to do, it's critical to plan out *when* these programs need to be implemented. With a new product, some of the programs will be used to help create awareness in your target market; those programs need to be implemented first. Other programs provide additional information about your company and product that the customer will need as they prepare to make a buying decision. Those programs can be implemented later. In between, you need to be preparing your sales channels (direct or indirect) for making the sales. All of this needs to be planned out and managed. Figure 16.6 is a timeline that illustrates when these programs need to be in place relative to launch date for your product.

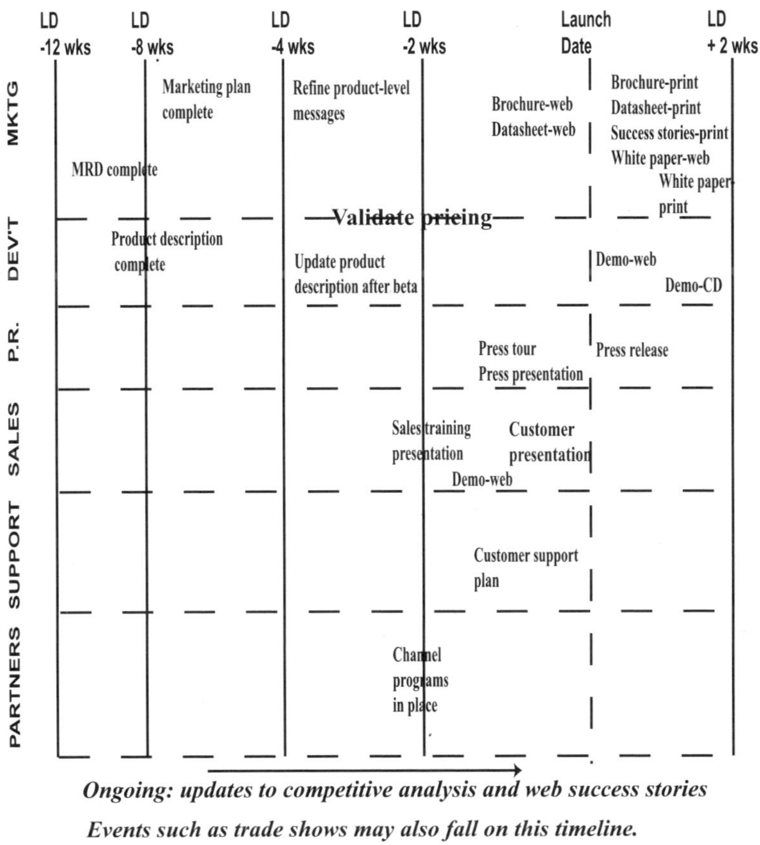

Figure 16.6: Marketing Programs Timeline

17

Leveraging the Web During Launch

Using the web as a marketing venue today is no longer an experiment, it's a requirement. Marketing programs that are deployed via the web are less expensive to produce and update, and web content can be deployed much more quickly than print media. That translates to faster time to market and greater profitability. That doesn't mean that you should abandon printed marketing materials, because they still serve important functions in the overall marketing program portfolio. However, the company website and intranet should be viewed as marketing assets of the company, and they should be leveraged extensively during the launch phase of a new product.

Marketing collateral for the new product that is intended for the external marketplace should be placed on the company website. This collateral may also be printed later, to be used by the sales force and given to customers. Printed collateral may also be made available at trade shows. The company website, however, is a great place to quickly post the new collateral to start the marketing process, while the printing is being done. Sometimes companies place the web versions on the company website first and then make final changes to the collateral, based on feedback from the web version. That can save printing costs in the long run.

If the company has e-commerce capability, sales and ordering information also must be added to the website, so that customers can order and purchase the new product. Press releases and other public relations material should also be posted on the website and sent out via online press and media networks. The company's intranet should be used before launch to help train sales people and channel partners about the new product. The launch manager and launch team can also use the intranet as a centralized workspace for all launch deliverables and monitoring of status.

Cost issues: web versus print media

In most cases, developing a web-based version of marketing collateral is less expensive than conventional printing of the collateral, especially if it is in color and contains lots of graphics. However, placing the material on the website isn't entirely free, either. Regardless of the ultimate venue, the material still needs to be developed, including the writing and editing of copy, and development of graphics and illustrations. The material also needs to be laid out for the proper venue. When the material is ready to 'publish', then the costs to be compared are those of printing versus converting the content to online format and having the webmaster or other authorized person place it on the website. For very large or complex websites, there may be two or three people involved in placing a marketing piece on the website, and it may take several days. In the case of printing, it is often outsourced to a printing vendor, who delivers the desired quantity of the printed piece within a few days or weeks. In most cases, companies must do both, because sales people need printed collateral. Having web versions of collateral, however, allows companies to print only the quantity needed to hand to customers, and no more, thus reducing overall printing costs.

Another cost issue is the 'reach' of a marketing piece. Placing the material on the website can reach virtually millions of people on the worldwide web, instantaneously. With printed material, you must print the quantity needed and then send them or hand carry them to customers. Each time you want to reach more customers, you must print additional copies.

Updating and changing the content of a marketing piece also has cost implications. For web-based content, it is very easy to update the content, both text and illustrations. The entire piece doesn't have to be recreated. However, with printed material, the printing master has to be redone. With digital printing, this isn't as much of an issue, but with printers who still use film masters, changing the master involves added time and cost. Either way, there will be an additional printing setup fee charged whenever the content changes.

To illustrate the tradeoff, here is an example of a comparison for a 4-color, 4-page product brochure. Assume you want to do an original printing of 1000 copies, and just to be conservative, let's say you have a potential of 1 million visitors to your website that you can reach. Mailing costs for the printing brochures have not been included here; assume that you will be handing them to customers directly. In-house staff, rather than an outside vendor, will do development of the brochure:

Task	Costs for 1000 copies of printed brochure	Costs for web-based brochure (reaches 1 million people)
Copy writing, illustrations, graphic design	$20,000	$20,000
Press setup fee	$1,000	0
Web conversion	0	$2,000
Printing	$10,000	0
Total: original brochure	**$32,000**	**$22,000**
"Reach" cost per person	**$32.00**	**$.02**
Time to produce (after design is complete)	*3 weeks*	*4 days*
Update of copy and illustrations	$4,000	$4,000
Re-layout for printing	$2,000	0
Make changes to web	0	$1,000
Press setup fee	$1,000	0
Printing another 1000	$10,000	0
Total: brochure update	**$17,000**	**$6,000**
"Reach" cost per person	**$17.00**	**$0.006**
Time to produce (after redesign is complete)	*3 weeks*	*1 day*

Table 17.1: Cost Comparison Print versus Web

Based on this chart, if you must decide whether to do a print or a web version of the brochure, and if you are concerned about total cost or "reach cost", it's better to do a web version. It's also much faster to do the web version. However, sometimes it is necessary to do both print and web versions of certain types of collateral. Sales people often need something to hand to a customer in person, and a printed piece still works better for that situation. Most companies try to limit the number of copies of marketing materials they print and only print enough for their highest-priority customers and sales leads.

Another possible approach is to place your brochure on the corporate website first, until you are sure that all the corrections that need to be made have been identified. Those corrections can then be made when you are ready to print. Some companies place new marketing material on their website first, in order to get feedback as to the effectiveness of the material from the customer's point of view. If the feedback is such that the piece is not effective for its intended purpose, then the company can save a lot of unnecessary printing costs by discovering that ahead of time.

Today, it's a good idea to place your key launch collateral on the company website on 'launch day' (the day that you announce the product to the outside world) and then do the printing of selected collateral pieces several weeks after launch, when the pieces are needed for other purposes. Because so many things need to be done in the few weeks or days before the launch date, time is at a premium, and focusing only on the web versions will save time that can be used for other critical activities.

Effective use of the web: low-cost, high-return programs

Using the web during launch allows your company to maximize the return on a relatively low investment. Think of the company website as a fixed asset; you own it, so use it. From a marketing standpoint, the web is like a direct mailing list of the whole global marketplace, and you don't even have to do mailings (Figure 17.1). There is no other marketing venue today that has greater reach. How can you best leverage the tremendous power of the web?

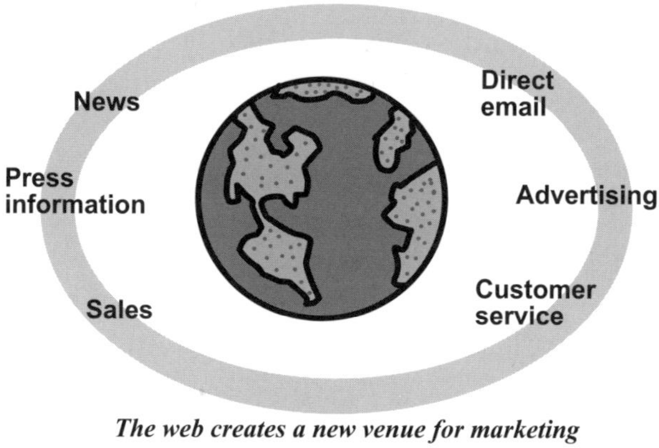

Figure 17.1: Leveraging the Web: a Global View

To reap the benefits of this low-cost, high-return marketing venue, you must give your site visitors and customers incentives to spend time at your site. You need to provide information, education, entertainment, and even free merchandise or discounts in exchange for their eyeball time. Just as with any marketing venue, the key is to find ways to get the customer's attention. The number of websites vying for that attention is in the millions and is increasing all the time. To be successful at using the web for marketing, your company's website must provide a better overall customer experience than that of your competitors.

Extending the marketing program portfolio with the web

Before the web came along, marketers seemed to produce the same old marketing pieces: brochures, maybe a white paper or two, a datasheet, a press release. They often looked so similar that the only way to distinguish between them was to look for the company logo on the front or back of the pieces. The web not only provided a whole new venue to deliver marketing information, but it also provided a way to facilitate creativity. Information can now be created in small pieces and then reassembled in many different places and formats. Graphics and charts can be interactive, engaging customers and even entertaining them. Audio and video can add whole new dimensions to content that can then be presented together with text and illustrations – in short, multimedia impact on a single online page. Today, the portfolio of marketing programs that marketers can use to launch new products is bigger than ever because of the web. Figure 17.2 lists some ideas for web-based marketing programs.

Company website:
- -brochures, datasheets, white papers
- -media relations (press releases, news, articles)
- -customer feedback
- -sales
- -customer technical support
- -special promotions
- -partner and channel programs
- -multimedia product demos

Email:
- -direct email marketing

Web seminars (or *webinars*)

Webcasts for sales training or product announcements

Figure 17.2: Web-based Marketing Programs Checklist

With this bigger portfolio comes difficult choices. The marketer's challenge now is to create a balanced portfolio of programs that will reach the greatest number of customers, at lightning speed, while staying within the marketing budget. How do you create such a balance? Begin with your customer. How do they use the web, and how can you leverage your company's website to reach new customers before your competitors do? If you have channel partners that will be selling the new product, can you use your website to help their sales performance?

The web can always help you when it comes to speed and staying within budget. However, with the expanded "portfolio" of marketing programs available today, it's tempting for marketers to do everything on the list. However, it is very important to implement only the programs that are likely to be most effective in reaching your customer. Jose Geronimo is Banner Ad Program Manager in the Internet Marketing Operations Department for Cisco Systems. *"At Cisco, we have learned to pay attention to which marketing materials our customers are really accessing on our website. The most popular and frequently consulted marketing materials are not always the ones that are fun and creative for marketers to produce. For example, our white papers and datasheets are used and accessed more than anything else. They are in black and white, with lots of specs and maybe a photo of the product, in other words, very dull. But, our customers (who are mostly engineers) just love them. So, that's what we will continue to emphasize and make available through our website,"* says Jose.

The web as an advertising and public relations platform

Whether you realize it or not, your company's website is your primary advertising face to the outside world. Does your website reflect your company's intended image in the marketplace, and does it send the right messages that will reinforce the company brand? Is this the face that you want your customers to see? So often, companies will engage web designers to develop a splashy, attention-getting website, but the resulting site is often one that does not fit the company's image or target customer. For example, a business services company whose customers are conservative, middle-aged CEOs of large corporations should not have a website picturing 20-year-olds collaborating in their garage 'startup'. Your customers must be able to identify with the graphics, images, and look and feel of your website. If customers think the company is selling products or services to a different demographic group, they will move on to another site. The 'creative license' of web designers and web developers needs to be managed carefully when your company's website is created and updated.

Advertising on the web and placing ads on other companies' websites, as discussed in chapter 16, are another way to leverage the web as an advertising platform. Although there have been mixed results from web advertising, if your company places ads on other websites to drive traffic to your own company's website, then you need to measure the effectiveness of those ads in obtaining more site visitors. Jose Geronimo is involved with developing and implementing to measure this effectiveness. *"Our 'ad server' technology enables us to track site visitors and identify how they reached our website. For each ad that we have at other websites, we can measure the ad's effectiveness in generating site traffic, and also track what that site visitor does once they reach our site. We can even track ads that have appeared in print media, by using special codes that the site visitor uses when they reach our site. It's a great way to effectively plan and allocate scarce advertising dollars."* The other important aspect of effective web advertising is that your website has to deliver on what is promised in the ads that send people to your site to begin with. If an ad is announcing a new product at a special introductory price, then that information needs to appear prominently at your site once the visitor clicks on the banner ad and reaches your site. This may seem obvious, but such inconsistencies do occur. Timing, consistency of message, and functional links are absolutely critical for effective web advertising. Figure 17.3 shows a screen shot of a banner ad, along with its destination page.

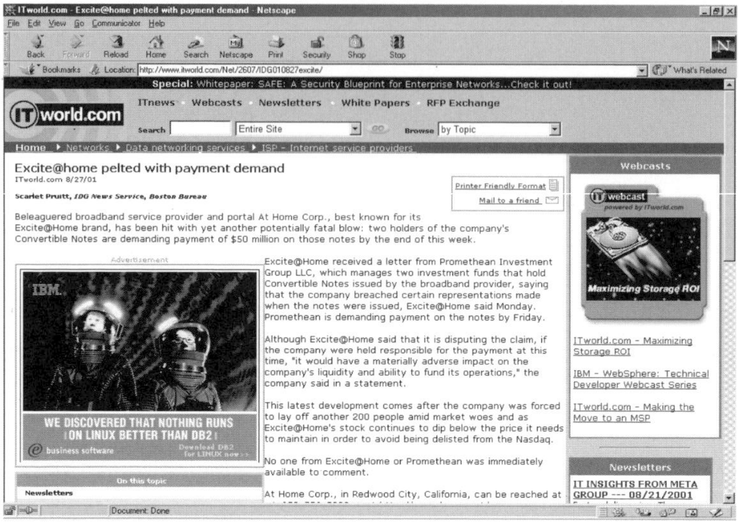

Ad in lower left of above web page goes to

this web page:

Figure 17.3: Screen Shot of Banner Ad, and Destination Web Page

Every company website needs to have a media or 'news' section that contains press releases, current and past, articles or links to articles that have appeared in media, and contact information for press representatives and analysts. This section of the website is your public relations (PR) platform for the market as a whole. For a new product that is about to be launched, this section will be one of the most important on your entire website. This PR section can be very creative; not only can you post traditional pieces such as press releases and published articles, but you can include demos, photos of the product, audio taped testimonials and success stories from customers, and links to other websites that help support the features, functionality, and value of your new product. With most of these materials, you have control over the messages that are presented, and you are not at the may write about your product (which sometimes may not be so favorable). In terms of traditional public relations activities such as conducting press tours, communicating with media representatives and analysts, and sending press releases to media, the PR section of your website should be used only as a supplement to those other tasks that are customarily done in person. You can refer press and analysts to your site if they need additional information, but in general, they still prefer to receive your company's news directly, in the format that they traditionally use. The content in the PR section of your website should be arranged and grouped in such a way that the media can easily go to one of the pages of the site and find everything that they'd see in a press kit, including company background information, management biographies, photos, and major company news and press releases. The easier you can make things for the media, the more cooperation you are likely to receive. Figure 17.4 shows an example of an integrated PR section of a company website.

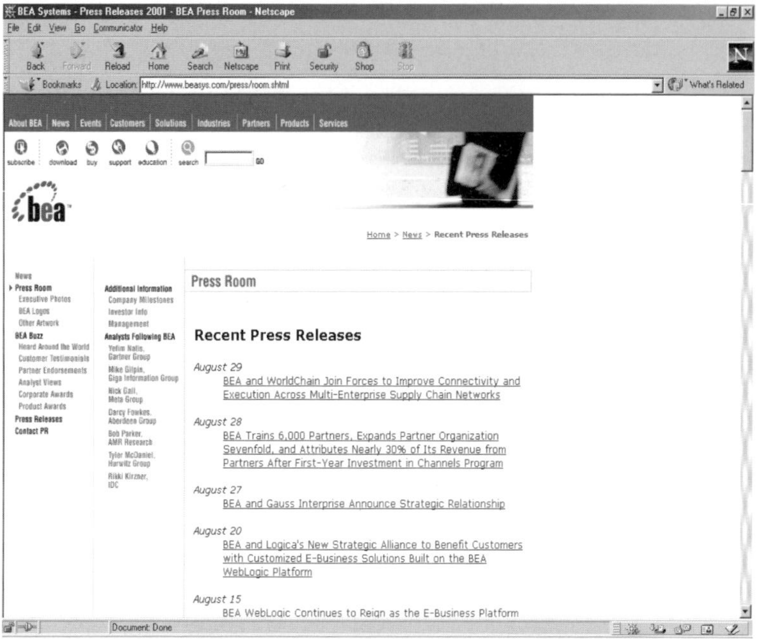

Figure 17.4: Screen Shot of PR section of a Website

The web as a customer interaction medium

Today, customers expect company websites to be interactive. That includes having the email address for key departments, so that customers can submit questions and requests for informasupport. If your product requires technical support, providing it can be a major undertaking. For web-based technical support, customers now expect to find a database of previous questions and answers, documented fixes, and even downloadable software code. All of these varieties of customer support can be deployed via the company website. For your new product, you need to decide which levels of support you will be providing online, and then you must make sure that the information is there and ready to be used at the time of launch. It's also a good idea to set up a special log-in area that is password-protected for your customers to use for support and product updates.

Figures 17.5 and 17.6 are screen shots of a customer feedback form and a web-based tech support area.

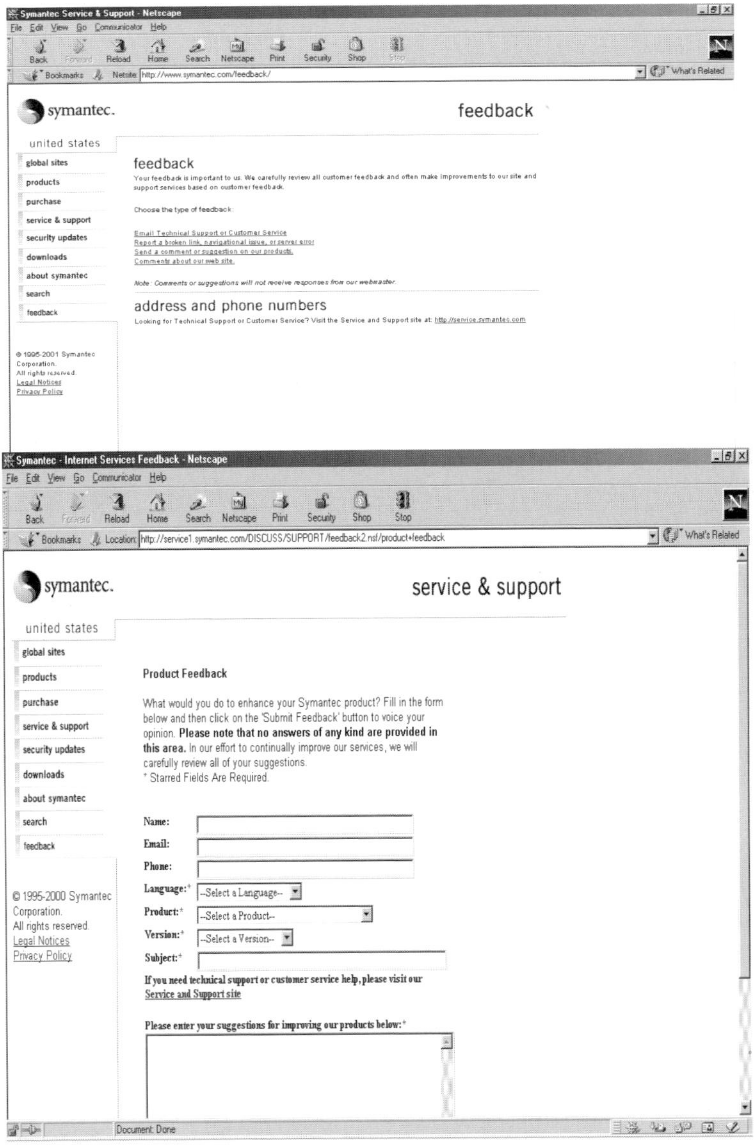

Figure 17.5: Screen Shot of a Customer Feedback Form

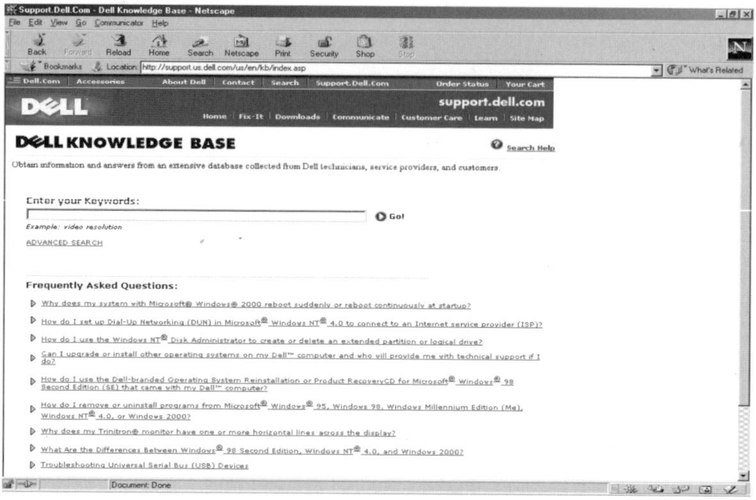

Figure 17.6: Screen Shot of Online Tech Support Area

The web as a sales channel

If your company has enabled your website for e-commerce, then the web is also a sales channel for you. Sometimes it is the primary sales channel for your company's products or services, and sometimes it is supplemental. Some companies have been very successful at using the web as their only sales channel. Pioneers like Dell and Amazon.com have such a widespread reputation, customers do not hesitate to conduct sales transactions online with them. However, some customers are still hesitant about engaging in credit card transactions with small or relatively unknown players in the online market. This hesitation is very common in the area of consumer goods or business-to-consumer markets but is also present in the business-to-business markets.

The extent to which your website serves as a sales channel will depend on your customer and the number of sales channels for your company. Even if the website will only be used for the occasional sale, it's still probably worth spending the programming dollars to set up an online ordering and credit card processing system. That way, it will be there when and if customers want to use it. Even a few sales will pay for the costs to set up and maintain the system. It just makes good business sense to leverage your website asset, however and whenever you can. Figure 17.7 is a screen shot of an online order form from the HPShopping website. If you plan to have the sales and order process in place when you launch your new product, make sure you allow enough lead time to get the programming and web work done and thoroughly tested. You don't want any glitches on launch day!

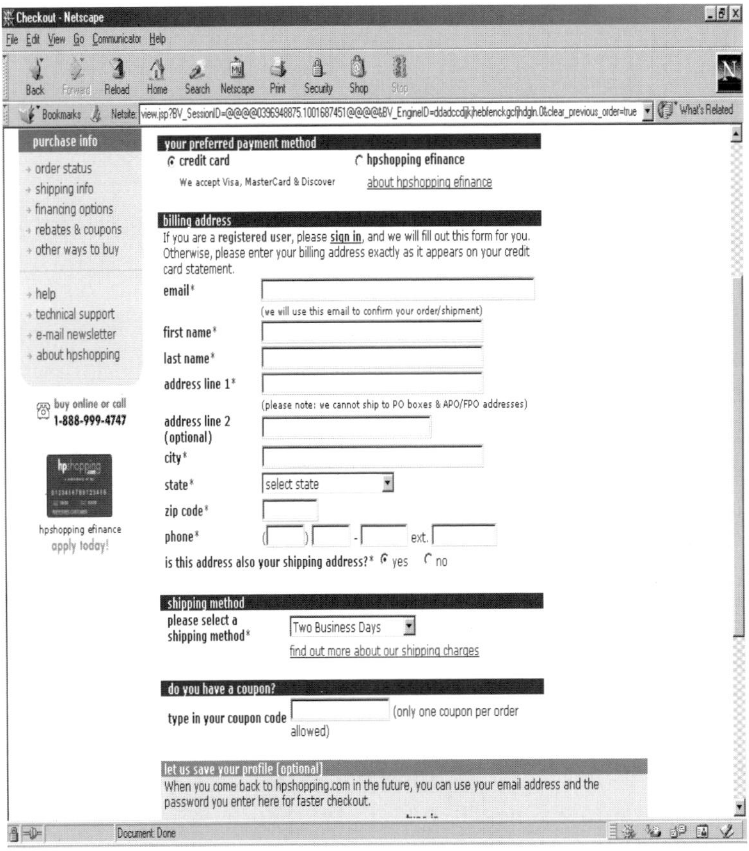

Figure 17.7: Screen Shot of an Online Ordering System on a Website

If you want to increase online sales through your website, then it's a good idea to offer premiums or special incentives to customers in order to get them to buy directly. When you are launching a new product, it's critical to link the new product's press release web page, along with other key marketing web pages, to the online order form. The easier that you can make it for customers to order your product, the more effective your website will be as a sales channel.

Multimedia over the web: tradeoffs

Advances in multimedia technology have resulted in an increase in multimedia content residing on company websites. Videos or audios of presentations or executive speeches, product demos, and animated graphics all provide variety and more depth of web content. However, you must keep the customer and web visitor in mind. The majority of Internet users are still accessing your website using a dial-up connection, and pages with heavy animation or multimedia content can take forever to download. Users often don't have the time to wait and instead move on to another site. You don't want that to happen with your company's website. With material that has lots of graphics, a good solution is to use PDF (Portable Document Format) files that almost anyone can access via Adobe Acrobat Reader, which can be downloaded for free.

Again, it is a question of balance and knowing your customer. It is possible to provide 'optional' multimedia content on web pages, by enabling users to click on a link to download or go to a secondary page on the web site that contains the multimedia content. If customers are interested, they can choose to download the information to obtain greater depth of understanding. It's also helpful to label multimedia content sections with an estimate of 'time to download' for common connection speeds such as 28.8 or 56k bps. Figure 17.8 is a summary of some of the multimedia considerations for the web.

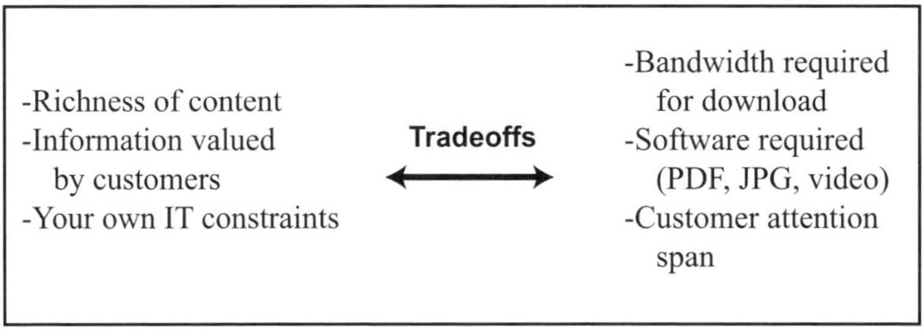

Figure 17.8: Multimedia Considerations

Integrating multimedia content into a website can be complicated. It's always best to give the information technology (IT) department as much lead time as possible, so that everything can be planned, implemented, and tested before the content goes live. In addition, the concepts that marketing people wish to implement can present huge challenges from an IT perspective. *"It's always a good idea for the marketing person to meet with the IT people or webmaster who will be converting and loading the content. The technical people know the limitations and tradeoffs involved regarding download times, site navigation, and integration of links, especially when it involves multimedia. It should be a combined effort between the marketing and technical departments to provide the content and experience that will best serve the customers and site users,"* advises Jose Geronimo. Sometimes, there needs to be a compromise between the marketing goals and the technology capabilities, in order to best serve the customer. That means that multimedia content may need to be provided to the customer using a different venue, such as mailing a videotape, instead of making it available at the website.

Leveraging the company intranet to support the launch

Today most companies of any size have their own private 'web' – the company intranet. Access to this internal network is usually restricted to employees, contractors, and sometimes, strategic partners and suppliers. During the chaotic time before a product launch, the company intranet can be used effectively to manage and track everything that needs to be done by launch date. It's a good idea to set up a dedicated product launch area on the intranet to enhance communications among the launch team members, employees, and the sales force.

The intranet is especially helpful for communicating with a sales force, because in most cases, salespeople are widely dispersed geographically. It's costly for sales people to travel to a centralized location every time they must be trained on a product that is about to be launched. *"At Cisco, we have a dedicated part of our intranet for our direct sales force called the 'Sales Dashboard',"* says Jose Geronimo. *"Each new product that is completing the development process and is about to be launched is summarized there in terms of target customer, applications, and specifications. Closer to launch, we also make available the basic collateral, such as datasheets and white papers, so that our sales people can download them and use them in the sales process. The Sales Dashboard continues to be an effective way for us to communicate with our worldwide sales force on new products, and the sales people find it indispensable for staying current with new products, and also for collaborating with other sales people on how to sell the new products."*

Some companies also maintain an area on the intranet to track competitor information and selling tips that are supplied by the field sales force. Training the sales people via the intranet is another way to leverage the intranet. This can also be done using 'webcasting' over the worldwide web, where a private link is set up and managed by a service provider during the training sessions.

Evolving Internet technologies will provide more options

The ideas mentioned in this chapter for leveraging the company website and intranet are based on current and proven technologies that are widely used. As additional network-related technologies evolve, there will likely be many other ways to leverage them for launch activities. Collaborative software and the wireless web will allow widely dispersed launch teams to communicate and work more efficiently to get information about products to the marketplace. There will be more ways for the customers to interact with your company, and there will be many opportunities to directly involve your customers earlier in the product cycle, so that they become partners in new product development. The key is to look for new opportunities to leverage these technologies and the willingness to experiment.

Note:
Permission to use screen shots from their websites generously granted by the following companies:

IBM
ITWorld
BEA
Symantec
Dell Computer
HP Shopping

18

A Repeatable, Streamlined Process

After a company has been through the new product cycle from beginning to end, it's time to document the process, so that the next new product team doesn't have to reinvent the wheel. Even if you're an entrepreneur, you will need to start thinking about your second product before your first one is ready for market. This chapter provides a framework for developing your own repeatable process for your company. In order to serve the needs of all sizes of companies, the process outlined in this chapter contains enough detail for a large company accustomed to using formalized processes. If you are an entrepreneur, or if you are in a start-up company, you will need to scale back the process to serve the needs of your organization. Regardless of size of company, the important thing is to keep the process as simple as possible. There is no reason to include five decision points in your process if only one is needed.

As soon as the new product is launched into the market, it's time to examine the whole process that was followed from idea to launch. This is often referred to as a "post mortem" or lessons learned review session. The important things to study are the mistakes that were made along the way and how they were remedied; that represents the real learning in the new product process. Look at how the idea was first identified, refined, presented, and validated. When the new product entered the development phase, what happened in terms of efficiency and customer feedback? Also look critically at the business model used, as well as the market strategy for launching the product. Evaluate what worked and what didn't – and why. To build a repeatable new product process, you must capture and document the knowledge and then train people to implement the process consistently.

Capture lessons learned as you are going through the process

In order to evaluate the process at the end of the cycle, it is obviously necessary to document what is done while you are in the midst of carrying it out. Even if you are reading this somewhere in the middle of a new product cycle, start the process of capturing what is happening as soon as you can. To reconstruct what happened all the way back to the beginning, you may need to track down some people who were involved with the new product during the idea phase. You should try to locate the decision-makers and inquire as to how and why key decisions were made. This will be worth your time, because it's difficult to fix a process if there's no information on what was done in the first place – what worked, and what didn't. You also need to find out how long it took to complete each phase of the product cycle, because all of it now has to be done at Internet speed.

There are other benefits of documenting the lessons learned in the new product process. If you are able to find ways to speed up decision-making, shorten time to market, or discover other efficiencies by examining the new product process, the rest of the company can learn from this and can apply similar approaches to other business processes. That happened at TRW-ESL. After two years of implementing the new product process, we found ways to streamline our more traditional core business, such as realigning our business units to better serve customer needs.

Knowledge to capture:

-Descriptions of ideas submitted
-Decisions made
-Basis for decisions
-Selection criteria and modifications
-How criteria are applied
-Identity of decision-makers throughout process
-Duration of each step of the process
-Handoff points among process participants
-Suggestions made for improvement

Building a business process for new products

There are several elements required to build a business process for new products. You need decision points, decision or selection criteria, the length of time between the decision points, names of decision-makers, possible outcomes, and links or dependencies with other business processes. You also need to clarify who in the company can submit ideas for consideration. In putting the elements together, you also need to build in flexibility and a way to easily modify the process as you go along.

Elements of the new product process:
-Where do ideas start and who can submit them?
-Decision points
-Idea screening and other decision criteria for entire process
-Decision-makers and their areas of responsibility
-Organizational responsibility for each phase of the process
-Duration of each phase of the process
-Key tasks completed during each phase of the process
-Possible decision outcomes and impact on remainder of the company
-Mode of communication among process participants to transfer knowledge
-Links to other business processes in the company

When we were faced with building a new product process at TRW-ESL, we used some of the recommendations from one of the ongoing quality action teams in the company that were part of our total quality management (TQM) efforts. The Product quality action team recommended that a product review board be assembled with cross-functional representation and that there be two decision points: one to screen the initial idea and fund a viability study, and the second to allocate development resources. We began with that as a skeleton process, and based on advice from external consultants, we refined the process further. We added another decision point between the first two, in order to improve the likelihood for success before the commitment of major resources at Decision Point 2.

Step/Decision	Description
Idea Step (30 days)	Initial screening criteria applied to idea; presentation prepared for New Ventures Review Board (NVRB)
Decision 1.0	NVRB evaluates fit with 1.0 level criteria and decides whether to accept and fund viability study or reject idea
Viability study - Market validation (30 days)	Market analysis conducted to validate market, including customer value proposition, market trends and size, and competition
Decision 1.5	NVRB evaluates fit with 1.5 level criteria and whether to fund the business plan or reject idea
Viability study - Business plan (30-45 days)	Business plan is prepared using a venture capital model/outline. Business partners are sought. Technical demo or prototype is prepared.
Decision 2.0	President's Office evaluates business viability to spin out and seek investment, using 2.0 level criteria. If idea is accepted, it is spun out. If not, it is rejected or postponed.

Figure 18.1: The Steps and Decision Points of the TRW-ESL New Ventures Process

In Figure 18.1, note the durations of the steps of the process, especially the viability study. Developing a full business plan and identifying strategic partners in thirty days' time is very streamlined. When we started the process, these timeframes were a goal. In actuality, most of the new venture ideas were prepared and evaluated within these timeframes. As long as we kept it simple and managed the steps of the process, we found that it could be done in a streamlined fashion.

For your own company, you will likely need to add decision points to cover the development and launch phases. Our TRW-ESL process ended at Decision 2.0, because we were spinning out ventures. Once they were established, they would then begin the full development phase and then market launch. For the rest of the new product process, here are the additional steps and decision points:

Step/Decision	Description
Development phase	Technical development and production begins according to market specifications
Decision 3.0	Development check: review body determines whether development is on time, on budget, and is proceeding in accordance with specs
Business model development	Business and operational model is developed for new product; partner requirements are assessed and partner candidates identified
Decision 4.0	Review body reviews and approves business model and selects partners as required
Market strategy development	Market environment re-assessed to determine if changes are required in market strategy
Decision 5.0	Launch readiness; review body reviews market conditions, market strategy, and whether developed product is ready, sets launch date

Figure 18.2: Additional decision points for new product process

These are the basic building blocks of the new product process. At this point you can customize it for your company and add in optional checkpoints for further validation. Figure 18.3 is an example of an end-to-end process, with some optional decision points.

1	2	3	4	5	6	7	8
Select ideas	**Screen ideas for validation**	**Validate ideas**	**Prepare business or product plan (seek investment & partners)**	**Begin development**	**Develop business model, select partners**	**Develop market strategy**	**Launch**
ongoing	*30 days*	*30 days*	*30-45 days*	*variable*	*30 days*	*15 days*	*12 weeks*

Figure 18.3: A Model New Product Process

Document the decisions made for each new product and why new product ideas were accepted or rejected

Each new product idea presented for consideration will be accepted, rejected, or postponed. No matter what the outcome, it's important to characterize the reasons for the decision. Not only can this information be used when a similar product is presented in the future, it can also be helpful in refining the selection criteria. If too many ideas are rejected and nothing makes its way into the development phase, then the criteria are too rigid. Conversely, if everything goes into development without close scrutiny, you run the risk of getting an unacceptably low return on a potentially large investment in development.

The first step in building a process is to identify the major decision points that are needed from beginning to end; how many will you need? The number of decision points is often driven by budgets and by how much your company wants to spend validating and developing new ideas. It also is driven by complexity. You have too many decision points if you are spending too much time, in too many meetings, with the tenth iteration of the same idea. (At the TRW-ESL incubator, the entrepreneurs became frustrated if they were asked to refine their idea and present it to the board again; they would refer to such meetings as Decision Point 1.75358. We took the hint.) You can also have too few decision points, such as a single idea review before writing that check to send the idea into development. At a minimum, you need two decision points; one at the very beginning, when ideas are being tossed around at a high level, and one more to consider the results of idea validation. Thereafter, you can add one or two more before development to get a better handle on the development and marketing costs for the new product, before making the final decision.

Once the idea is in development, it's important to have one or two status checks of progress, which can turn out to be decision points, especially if things aren't going according to plan. During development, the details of the business model and market strategy should be completed. If new strategic partners are involved, then another decision point should be added to evaluate and select partners; otherwise the intended business model can't be implemented. At the end of the development phase, there should also be a launch decision point to discuss launch readiness and to set a product launch date.

All together, five decision points should be adequate for a new product process – beginning to end. This will enable you to keep it simple and streamlined, so that you don't get bogged down in meetings, postponed decisions, and too much detail.

Document the selection criteria and changes made to them

The TRW-ESL new ventures process went through multiple iterations before we found a workable set of selection criteria. The highest levels of criteria were easy to identify, and everyone universally agreed on the high-priority issues such as market, costs, and strategic fit. However, when it came to deciding how to manage the next level of precision with regard to the criteria, our progress stalled. In a brainstorming session, we came up with so many detailed and secondary criteria (all seemingly critical) that we had to take the time to re-prioritize them and characterize how they related to the six high-level questions. We refined the list of detailed criteria and then assigned them to the different decision points of the process; at the earliest decision point we used the high-level criteria and for later decision points we added additional detailed criteria. If an idea passed all of the criteria at all of the levels, then it would "graduate" to the launch phase. Figure 18.4 shows an example of the nested criteria for the market category.

In customizing selection criteria for your company, begin with the six major criteria in part one of this book. Are there more detailed questions in each category that you would ask at different decision points? Very likely that will be the case, so for each major criterion, add clarifying questions and levels of detail as you develop the process. As you do this, make sure to obtain consensus among the decision-makers as to which criteria to add and how they will be applied. You will need the cross-functional perspectives of the decision-makers to make sure that the criteria address all of the business considerations of the company.

The MARKET criterion

Acceptance criteria for Decision 1.0:

-customers must be named
-customer must have an economic reason to buy
-product concept must satisfy customer need
-clear value proposition
-large and growing market
-market research that justifies market trends and size
-customer needs to solve problem NOW - in next 12 months

Additional criteria for Decision 1.5:

-feasible business model
-realistic market size estimate relative to competitors
-beta customer identification

Additional criteria for Decision 2.0:

-whole product must be in place
-technology expert must be in place
-market size must justify the development investment

Figure 18.4: Nested Selection Criteria

Document the process as to how the decisions are made and by whom

If you have a team of people or some sort of an approval body making new product decisions, then each member will evaluate a new idea from a different perspective – either formally or informally. In documenting the decision-making process, you may want to describe these different points of view. For instance, if there is a representative on the board from engineering or development, they may be evaluating the challenges involved in technology resources and costs to develop the product. Similarly, each member may in fact be assigned to evaluate the new idea from the point of view of a single criterion, to make sure that the person who is most knowledgeable is also the key decision-maker for that criterion.

At TRW-ESL, once we settled on the criteria, we discussed how they would be applied. At the beginning, we tried a checklist with weighting factors. That took too long to fill in during our one-hour presentation and meeting. Next, we experimented with a subjective score of the six major criteria and voted on each one. That was better, except not everyone applied the criteria the same way. We spent a few weeks having a threaded email discussion about how to uniformly apply the criteria until everyone on the board had a common understanding of it. Finally, we settled on a system whereby the more detailed criteria were handed out to board members before the presentation. Then, after the presentation, each voting member of the board discussed how they applied each of the criteria and how they came up with their final yes-or-no vote. That seemed to work best for us, as well as for the entrepreneurs, because they had a chance to hear the decision-making in action and had a better understanding as to the reason behind the decision.

Documenting the decisions:

- -Record decision for each product idea
- -Describe each decision-maker's area of responsibility
- -Document individual decision-makers' votes
- -Identify which criteria were most useful in facilitating the final decision

Keep it simple: use simple checklists, charts, matrices and diagrams

The new product process moves pretty quickly, especially during the idea and validation phases. At the same time, it's important to document the decisions made. The best way to accomplish this, given the time constraint, is to use simplified forms, checklists and guidelines. Keeping it simple does not mean eliminating vital information; rather, it means focusing on the highest-priority issues and criteria.

The CD that accompanies this book (Appendix B) contains several tools and checklists that you may want to experiment with in your efforts to simplify the process. You can customize and print these out for your own use. Figure 18.5 is a portion of an idea evaluation checklist that we tried at TRW-ESL.

Rating 1-10 (10 is highest)	Criterion
	Large and growing market
	Difficult to copy technology
	Eager strategic partner
	Fit with core competency
	Compelling customer need
	High return on investment
	Strong management team
	Competitive environment
	Investment required

Figure 18.5: Idea Evaluation Checklist

It had many of the key criteria, but it was too lengthy to fill out during a one-hour review session. It was also difficult for each board member to assess all of the criteria because the board members were from different functional areas. One of the ways to solve this problem is to "assign" detailed criteria to each board member, so that each person has the responsibility to evaluate only those during the review session. At the end of the session, then the full board can tally the lists and reach a decision. Figure 18.6 is an example of how to allocate criteria to various decision-makers.

Title	Focus	Decision Criteria
VP of Marketing	Market strategy, launch implementation	Customer value proposition, market size, competitive analysis
Director of Engineering	Technology solutions, research and development	Development costs and schedule, difficulty in copying technology
CFO or VP of Finance	Profitability	Investment requirements, ROI, all costs
VP of Operations	Operational models, business infrastructure	Fit with core competency, business model, partnering

Figure 18.6: Board Members' Selection Criteria Assignments

Another approach is to list all screening and selection criteria and assign weighting factors for each one ahead of time, using a consensus from all reviewers. Once that is established, each reviewer evaluates the criteria assigned to them, and when the results are tallied, the weighting factors can then be used to develop an overall score for the idea. This approach also can be used to break ties in voting and move the decision process along. For weighting factors to work, however, they need to be updated as business conditions and company priorities change.

Within your company, there may be an organization or team of individuals who develop the new product ideas for the whole company. Another alternative is to open up the opportunity to submit ideas to any employee of the company, as we did at TRW-ESL. Regardless of the source of the idea, it's helpful to develop a consistent format for presenting ideas to the decision makers. At TRW-ESL, our entrepreneurs were required to follow a ten-slide guideline for the Decision 1.0 presentation, shown as Figure 18.7. We limited them to a maximum of ten slides, and to these specific topics. If we hadn't, every presentation would have contained 27 slides on the technical concept, and one slide on the market, customer, and financial projections, and each review board meeting would have lasted hours.

Slide #	Content
1	Strategic fit with company
2	The technical product concept
3	Customer value proposition, market size
4	Pricing information
5	Development costs
6	Resources required
7	Investment required
8	Exit strategy
9	Venture development schedule
10	Revenue and ROI forecast

Figure 18.7: The Ten-Slide New Idea Presentation

For the later decision points such as 2.0, we added more slides on the market trends, competition, market strategy, venture management team, and business model. The content for these additional slides was derived from the business plan that had to be completed before the Decision 2.0 presentation.

Streamlining the new product process:

- -Reduce bureaucracy and simplify paperwork
- -Use simple checklists, templates and manuals for fast implementation
- -Provide organization-wide training so people can quickly come up to speed
- -Use only the criteria that are meaningful and no more

Appoint a keeper of the process so that all modifications are captured

A person should be appointed to oversee the new product process in the company. Even in a startup company, someone should have this responsibility. It may not be a full-time job for someone, but as a company continues to develop new products, it can become a full-time effort and one that is important for long-term growth. With the frequent shuffling of people between departments these days, if a single individual can't provide the necessary continuity, then there should be a department that has the permanent charter to do this. The new products person in charge should be responsible for documenting the new product process and key new product decisions, tracking all modifications to the process, and communicating new product information to the appropriate managers and executives.

Product evaluation sessions and presentations are very fast-paced meetings. It really helps to have someone capture minutes of the meeting, especially questions asked, recommended actions, and decisions made. Once the minutes are captured, they can be compiled and distributed to management, or kept on file by the person who oversees the new product process.

As you refine the process, it will be necessary for the process owner to identify ways to make improvements, such as clarifying or modifying selection criteria. All constituents of the process, the idea presenters as well as the decision-makers, should be consulted as to suggestions for improvement. At TRW-ESL, we held separate feedback sessions with entrepreneurs and with the review board, in order to identify the best ways to improve the process so that it would work for everyone.

Create training materials so that people can learn the process

When a new entrepreneur entered the TRW-ESL incubator, we had a mandatory training "course" on video that they were required to go through – at their own pace. This course included marketing principles, financial forecasting, and development of a business plan, all at a very basic level but with practical examples. We had brought in specialized consultants to develop and teach these courses live, and we videotaped them for later use. These were tremendous tools for the entrepreneurs and enabled them to more quickly grasp the business fundamentals they would need for starting a new venture.

In your own company, you may have internal experts who can put together training materials or lead informal sessions on key topics. There are also many online training courses, videos, and cooperative programs between companies and local universities to provide such training. If you do seek outside resources, you will want to make sure that they are consistent with your internal new product process, and that they don't confuse people with conflicting concepts. I also recommend that you put together a training course or video focused on the new product process itself that can be delivered by one of the decision-makers involved in the process.

Create a handbook or manual for people who will be involved in new products

We created a complete handbook for the TRW-ESL new ventures incubator, so that incoming entrepreneurs would have a complete picture of the entire process – their responsibilities, the available resources, and how the decisions would be made. The table of contents is shown in Figure 18.8.

Incubator Handbook
Table of Contents

-Getting Started
-Expectations
-New Venture Process Description
-Business Plan Outline
-Selection Criteria
-Terms and Conditions
-New Ventures Review Board Members
-Incubator Staff and Resources
-Customer/market Research Techniques
-Partnering Guidelines
-Intellectual Property Guidelines
-Glossary

Figure 18.8: Incubator Handbook Content

This 35-page guide was assembled fairly quickly with the help of the new ventures staff. A simple guide like this might be something to consider doing in your company. It's a great learning tool for people who are new to the process, and who must quickly come up to speed. It can be used by the people who are submitting ideas for consideration, as well as by the decision-makers.

Here is an excerpt from the TRW-ESL handbook that describes what happens in the viability phase of the new ventures process:
"*Phase 1.0-1.5 Business Viability: Upon approval of the New Ventures Review Board, you will now officially enter the incubator. At this stage you will begin to seriously validate whether or not there is a market for your idea. Again your focus will be on the customer. What is the customer's compelling reason to buy your product? You will focus on: product definition, the competition, pricing and, identification of beta sites.*"

This handbook was written for the entrepreneurs who were submitting ideas for consideration. However, these handbooks can be targeted for anyone in the company who will be involved in new products. In your own company, there may be a wide variety of people who will submit ideas for consideration, such as representatives from marketing, sales, or development.

Maintain a portfolio analysis of new products and their actual profitability

One of my job responsibilities as Director of New Ventures at TRW-ESL was to brief the executive staff weekly as to the current status of our new ventures "portfolio". I created a one-page status sheet that gave everyone a quick snapshot of where each venture was in the process. Figure 18.9 is an example of this status sheet.

Market Segment	IDEA PHASE	MARKET VIABILITY	BUSINESS PLAN	LAUNCHED
Wireless Communi-cations		Venture S1		Venture AR Venture OF
Information Technology	Venture ISC		Venture ID2	
Transportation		Venture LR		Venture AT
Terminated: Venture GT Venture E1 **In the freezer:** Venture EP				

Figure 18.9: The Venture Status Timeline

At any given time, we were tracking up to 30 ventures that were either in progress or had been through the process already. It was an effective way to look at the portfolio as a whole, so that we could obtain feedback as to which ventures were worthy of our investment. We also knew that we couldn't spin out every idea that made its way through the entire process. This portfolio status helped us prioritize which of the new ventures would be pursued, and in what order. I put together another chart that listed timing and financial information for the ventures that were in the launch phase. A sample of this chart is shown below as Figure 18.10.

Venture	*1st customer sale*	*Year 1 revenues*	*Year 4 revenues*	*Cash Flow Positive Date*
Venture AR	June '02	$20M	$85M	2003
Venture IDV	April '03	$2M	$14M	2003
Venture ISC	September '03	$1.5M	$21M	2005
Venture DC	December '03	$2.5M	$10M	2003

Figure 18.10: Portfolio Analysis – Launched Ventures

With this chart, the main discussion was short-term versus long-term revenues and how to create a balanced portfolio that would help us reach our goals. Other factors were the date that the venture would be cash flow positive, which had an impact on the investment requirements, and the first customer sale, which helped determine the order in which the ventures would be pursued.

This is a good way for any company to view its new products at various stages of progress: as an investment portfolio. Of course, it is also necessary to evaluate the factors and financial measures that fit your strategic goals at the time. These other factors include investment required, anticipated product or venture life, market timing, and most importantly, profitability.

And some final words....

New products are the lifeblood of companies and also of the greater economy. We must visualize the whole new product cycle, from idea to launch, and then implement the process at Internet speed. Acting on the opportunities we encounter, with a constant eye on profitability, will ensure business survival and growth well into the future.

All of this doesn't happen magically overnight. It takes hard work, creativity, a strategic view, the willingness to make mistakes and learn from them, and consistent attention to the bottom line. We need to be smarter about how we find the initial ideas and develop them into products that customers really want. The cycle needs to move fast enough to get the products to market on time, with the right partners, while using the most efficient business models. Maintaining profitability throughout the process means being willing to make tough decisions during any part of the process when economic or market conditions change. We must return to the basics in order to prosper in the Internet Era.

I hope that the concepts presented in this book will serve to inspire, inform, and energize you and your entire organizations to build and strengthen our business future. I welcome your ideas and feedback, so that I can share them with other business professionals. Please visit my website at www.launchdoctor.com to share your views and submit issues for discussion.

APPENDIX A

Recommended Reading

APPENDIX A

RECOMMENDED READING

Launch

High Tech Product Launch, Catherine Kitcho, 1999, Pele Publications, (available at discount from: www.pelepubs.com).

Marketing

Crossing the Chasm, Geoffrey Moore, revised edition 1999, Harper Business.

Inside the Tornado, Geoffrey Moore, 1995, Harper Business.

Customer Relationship Management

Customers.com, Patricia Seybold, 1998, Times Business.

Real Time, Regis McKenna, 1997, Harvard Business School Press.

Market Strategy

Blown to Bits, Philip Evans and Thomas Wurster, 1999, Harvard Business School Press.

The Cluetrain Manifesto, Fredrick Levine et al, 2000, Perseus Books.

Business Models and Distribution Channels

Logistics and Supply Chain Management, Martin Christopher, 1999, Financial Times Prentice Hall.

Product Development

Setting the Pace in Product Development, Michael McGrath, 1996, Butterworth-Heinemann.

APPENDIX B

Tools and Templates

Appendix B
Tools and Templates

<u>Contents:</u>
In this section of the book are the printed versions of the tools and templates that you will find on the accompanying CD, along with suggestions for using them.

<u>Guidelines for Using the CD (IBM-PC or equivalent):</u>
The hardware and software requirements for using the CD are:
- CD ROM drive
- Windows 95 or later
- Microsoft Office '97 or later (Word, PowerPoint, Excel)

To access the CD, place it in your CD-ROM drive, double click on the drive. Select and click on the file you wish to open. You can use these tools as a basic framework, modify them for your purposes, and save them to different files on your own computer. Here are the file names, applications, and descriptions:

ReadMe (Notepad): list of files, suggestions for using the tools and templates.
1.Criteria Checklists (Word): Recommended criteria to include from chapters 3-8, along with reject/postpone guidelines (can customize your own version).

2.Idea Evaluations (Word): Evaluation forms for evaluating new product ideas.

3.Scoring Sheet (Excel): Spreadsheet for tabulating new idea evaluation criteria.

4.Business Model Map (PowerPoint): Basic business model framework to expand for the product.

5.Business Model Map – Channel Performance (PowerPoint): Business model map for comparing channel partners.

6.Business Plan Template (Word) – Business plan with questions to answer for each section of the plan.

7.Marketing Plan Template (Word) – Marketing plan with questions to answer for each section of the plan.

8.Launch Timeline (PowerPoint) – Chart of marketing deliverables relative to launch date.

9.Venture Timeline Diagrams (PowerPoint) – Chart for comparing progress of new products.

10.Portfolio Analysis (PowerPoint) – Spreadsheet for tabulating financial performance of new products.

11.New product process model (PowerPoint) – End to end decision process for new products.

Suggestions for Using the Tools and Templates:

<u>1.Criteria Checklists:</u>
This is a consolidated list of all of the recommended types of criteria to include from Chapters 3 through 8. For each category (such as Strategic Fit, Customer, etc.), there are also recommendations on rejecting or postponing ideas if they don't meet the criteria. Use this list as a baseline to construct the

detailed criteria you will use to screen your new product ideas, as well as how to make the decision to accept, reject or postpone your new product ideas. Delete those that don't make sense for your company. You can then take the criteria that remain and include them on your evaluation form, the next tool in this set.

2. Idea Evaluation Form:

Decision-makers who are screening new product ideas can use this form as a scoring sheet that they can fill in after they have heard a new product presentation. The middle section should be modified to fit your established set of criteria. Expand the table in the middle of the form to make room for additional criteria; place your cursor in the bottom right cell of the table and hit the tab key, and you can add rows to the table and fill it in.

3. Scoring Sheet:

This is a spreadsheet that can be used to tally the scores from multiple evaluators, and also to assign and apply weights to the screening criteria. Start by filling in the criteria you will use, along with the weight for each one expressed as a percentage (those in the template are just placeholders). If you have more than three evaluators, you will need to add additional columns. Once you have the right number of criteria and evaluators, then you will need to revise the formula in column G that calculates the average of columns D,E, and F accordingly. You will also need to revise the formula in column H that calculates the product of columns C and G. The last formula goes into the cell where your total score goes – at the bottom of column H; this will be the sum of all the values in column H.

4. Business Model Map:

This is a PowerPoint diagram that you can modify to fill in the entities in your business model. It has been developed in PowerPoint so that you can use it as part of a presentation. Fill in names of companies where the question marks are. You can add extra boxes and arrows by selecting them, and pressing (ctrl + D), which will generate duplicates. You can them move them around and place them where they need to go.

5. Business Model Map – Channel Performance:
You can use this map to do tradeoff analyses with different channel partners. Label the boxes marked "Channel A" with the name of a potential distributor. Where the "$$" are shown on the diagram, replace them with the revenue (in dollars) you will receive less the discount that goes to the channel partner. Once everything is labeled, then you will be able to make comparisons. You can also add additional channel partners to the diagram by duplicating boxes and arrows (see description of business model map above).

6. Business Plan Outline:
This is a template that is set up as a sequence of questions to be answered. The business plan can be filled in as you go. A good way to do this is to delete a question once it is answered. Continue to add material as you go until all of the questions are answered; this provides a guide for the content, as well as a checklist of progress for completing the plan.

7. Marketing Plan Outline:
This template should be used in the same way as the business plan template, except that this template is focused on detailed marketing content.

8. Launch Timeline:
This simple chart is a one-page view of all launch deliverables and schedule relative to launch date. To modify this diagram, put in a calendar date where it is labeled "Launch Date", and then put in calendar dates for the other time markers at the top as well. You can also add or delete marketing programs, along with their due dates. The functional responsibility for the deliverables is labeled at the left axis, and you can move the deliverables vertically around the page to reflect different responsibilities as appropriate. You can also generate multiple

versions of this chart to reflect the "planned" versus "actual" progress of deliverables as you move through the launch process.

9. New Product Status and Timeline:
For companies that must track multiple new product efforts, this chart can be used to monitor where each new product is relative to the new product cycle. The market segments are identified in the first column, and the product names are labeled in the first column. There is also a place toward the bottom to track rejected or postponed product ideas. This chart is developed in PowerPoint so that it can be used as part of a presentation if desired.

10. New Product Portfolio Analysis:
This is a high-level view of new products that might be useful for senior management to review. This chart analyzes the financial forecasts for multiple new products, along with key milestone dates. This chart is developed in PowerPoint so that it can be used as part of a presentation if desired.

11. New Product Process Model:
This is a map of a recommended new product process. You can use this as a basis to customize it for your own company as you build a repeatable new product process. The number of steps can be adjusted by adding or deleting boxes, and you can also adjust the timeframes for each one. This was created in PowerPoint.

Criteria Checklists with Reject/Postpone Recommendations

Strategic Fit

Categories to include:

-the business you're in and want to be in
-core competencies
-company culture
-fit with operational and business models
-new product/new market experience

REJECT the idea if:

-you have no core competencies to develop the product or service
-it would create an obstacle to meeting strategic goals
-major revamp of business operations would be required
-it would disrupt the internal corporate culture
-the new product would require a new company image campaign

POSTPONE the idea if:

-the idea is more than 12 months ahead of market
-the new product would require finding and developing new strategic partners

The Customer

Categories to include:

-value proposition from customer's point of view
-value propositions of your customer's customer and distribution channels
-detailed knowledge of customer and their buying behavior
-likelihood that customer will buy
-affordability of product by customer
-sales cycle issues
-Customer's Profit Value (CPV)

REJECT an idea if:
-ambiguous value proposition
-you can't deliver the value required – throughout the value chain
-product not affordable by customer
-you don't have a precise solution to the customer problem
-sales cycle too long given dynamics of marketplace
-Customer's Profit Value (CPV) is too low

POSTPONE an idea if:
-likelihood of customer purchase low but has potential
-evangelism is involved in sales cycle
-price is too high for customer now

The Competition
Categories to include:
-description of competitive environment
-alternative customer solutions
-names of competitors
-summary of new versus existing competitors
-analysis of competitors at a company level
-analysis of competitors at a product level
-additional factors specific to type of competitive environment

REJECT the idea if:
-the customer is happy with a competitor's existing solution
-the market is too mature to enter as a new player
-you don't have differentiators that relate directly to the customer value proposition
-creating competitive advantage means significant investment in new infrastructure

POSTPONE the idea if:
-a competitor is about to launch an identical product
-it's a new market but you don't have the resources to sustain a first-mover position
-it's a very fragmented market and you need more time to assess the competitive strategy

The Market

Categories to include:

-the trends you want to see in the target market
-the minimum acceptable market size
-measures you will use in evaluating the market (total available market, served available market, and/or share of market)
-reliable sources of market trend data and market size estimates

REJECT the idea if:

-the market demand is declining
-the market size is too small
-the market size is adequate, but the profit is too small

POSTPONE the idea if:

-the market trend is flat in an emerging market
-the market is too small now but is expected to grow within a year

Resources

Categories to include:

-human resource gaps and total resource requirement
- key skill gaps
-core technologies and existing collective knowledge
-intellectual property protection requirements
-feasibility of outsourcing

REJECT the idea if:

-you have less than half of the required resources in-house
-the missing skills would take more than 6 months to hire
-you don't know how to solve the technical or business problem
-there are no identifiable outsourcing options
-the idea is easily copied and you have no established brand identity

POSTPONE the idea if:
-internal resources would need significant training to facilitate product development
-the intellectual property protection would take more than 12 months to obtain
- new strategic partners would need to be located for the development phase

Profitability
Categories to include:
-price as determined by customer value proposition
-length of sales cycle
-market size target (demand)
-all possible costs associated with marketing, selling, developing and supporting the product
-company profit goals
-the profit metric and how it's calculated

REJECT the idea if:
-the estimated profit is less than the company's minimum acceptable target
-the product would cannibalize another product line and decrease overall company profit
POSTPONE the idea if:
-the sales cycle can't be shortened without acquiring new channel partners
-the demand is too low in the short-term to recoup costs soon enough
-the break-even point or profitability point occurs too late (due to long sales cycle)

Date: ______________

Evaluator name: ____________________

Product name: _____________________

Idea champion: ____________________

Rating system: 1-10 (with 10 = highest rating)

Criterion	Score
Strategic Fit - Core competency	
Strategic Fit - Known market	
Customer - Value proposition	
Customer - Likelihood customer will buy	
Competition - Competitive environment	
Competition - Our differentiators	
Market - Market size	
Market - Growth rate	
Resources - Skills required	
Resources - Technology required	
Profit - Costs to get to market	
Profit - Expected profit year 2	
Profit - ROI	
TOTAL:	

RECOMMENDATION:

ACCEPT ____

POSTPONE ____REASON ___________________________

REJECT ____REASON ______________________________

ACTIONS AND NEXT STEPS:

____

____

Scoring sheet for

Product Idea: ______________________

Category	Criterion	Weight	Evaluator 1 score	Evaluator 2 score	Evaluator 3 score	Average score	Weighted average
Strategic Fit	Core competency						
	Known market						
Customer	Value proposition						
	Likelihood customer will buy						
Competition	Competitive environment						
	Our differentiators						
Market	Market size						
	Growth rate						
Resources	Skills required						
	Technology required						
Profit	Costs to get to market						
	Expected profit year 2						
	ROI						
	TOTAL SCORE FOR PRODUCT						total score

Business model map

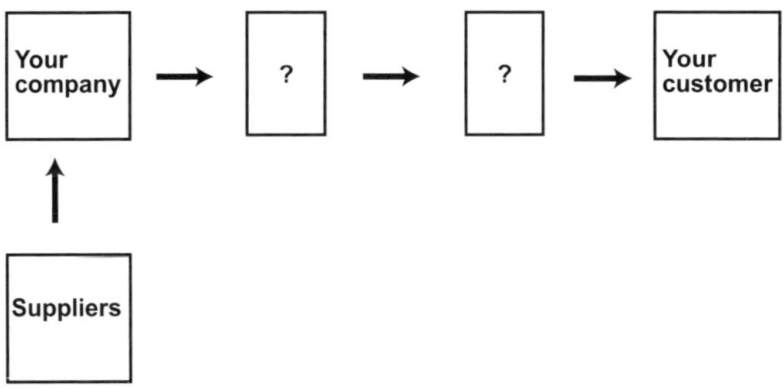

Business Model Map for Evaluating Channel Partners

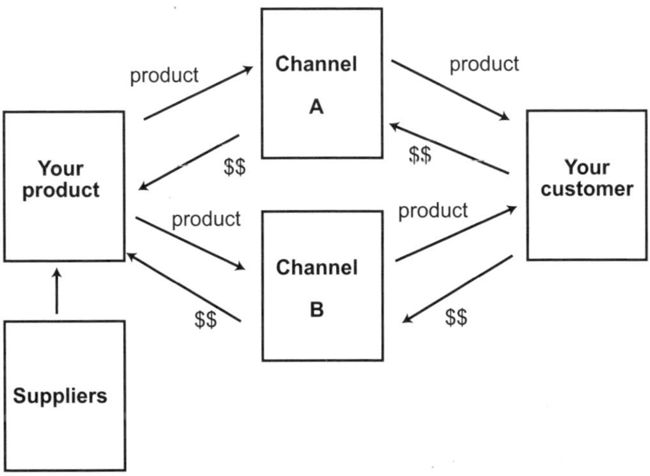

BUSINESS PLAN OUTLINE

Executive Summary

This should be written last, and should include the highlights of the product, customer, business model, market characteristics, competition, operations, management team, and financial information.

1. Product Description

What is the functionality of the product?
(Include a diagram of the product if possible)
Relationship to other product lines (why is the product new?)
What is the level of intellectual property protection for this product?

2. Fit With Strategic Objectives

What is the fit with the company's core business or technology?
What is the fit with the company's business goals and objectives?

3. Business Model

How will the venture get the product to the customer?
How will the venture make money?
What other entities are involved in the business model?
(Include a business model map)

4. Business Problem That Product Solves

What is the customer problem that is solved by the product?
Does the problem exist for the customer now?
What is a customer's economic or business reason to buy the product?
What is the customer feedback from surveys that validates the problem?

<u>5. Customer Characteristics</u>
Who is the customer (in as much detail as possible)?
Who makes the buying decision for the product, and who influences the decision?
What is the value proposition for this customer (how much are they willing to
pay for it)?
Why would they buy this product from us?
When would they buy this product from us?
Who is a likely candidate for a beta customer?

<u>6. Market Characteristics</u>
What is the target market?
How large is the market?
What are the dynamics of this market?
What is the target market share?
Does market size justify investment in a new product?

<u>7. Competitive Analysis</u>
What is the competitive environment?
Who are the competitors?
How many are there?
How do the competitors' products compare (feature/function)? (use matrix)
What are the competitors' strengths and weaknesses?
What are the primary differentiators?
How will the product be positioned against the competition?

<u>8. Product Distribution Strategy</u>
Distribution Channels – who are they and what role do they play?
What is the estimated percentage of sales from each distribution channel?
Strategic partners if any – who are they and what role do they play?

9. Marketing And Sales Strategy
What is the price for the product?
Who is the first customer or what is the first sales milestone?
Who/what is the second?
What is the sales plan for the first three years?
What is the high-level promotional plan for the product?
What are the major marketing programs that will be pursued?

10. Support Plan
Who will support the product after it's sold?
Is the infrastructure in place to support the product? Who will provide it?
What product documentation will be developed?
What warranties and maintenance agreements will be in place?

11. Product Development Plan
How much development is required for this product?
How long will it take?
Provide a simple project schedule for the development and test plan.
What are the technical challenges and risks anticipated during development?

12. Operational Plan
How will the company (or product group) operate on a day to day basis?
Who are the critical vendors and subcontractors?
Where will the company be located?
What are the facilities requirements?

13. Management And Organizational Plan

Who are the key managers for the venture and their responsibilities? (include
biographies or brief resumes)
(Include an organizational chart, showing reporting responsibilities and key positions)
What is the staffing plan for the venture? Which key positions will be filled and
when?

14. Financial Forecast

Develop a 3- or 5-year pro forma income statement, balance sheet, and cash flow
statement.
Are the margins consistent with the product and target market?
How much new investment is required?
What is the return on investment at the end of the 3 or 5 years?
When will the product venture be cash-flow positive?

MARKETING PLAN OUTLINE

Executive Summary
Summarizes the main points of the plan; usually one page in length. This is written last, after all of the other sections have been filled in. Include the product description, details about the customer, competition and differentiators, business model, market strategy, and key marketing programs.

1. Strategic Business Objectives
This section addresses the company's strategic objective for the product. What does the company want to achieve with this product? Enter a new market? Keep up with the competition, etc.?

2. Product or Service Description
What does the product do, or what is the service offering? What is the function and application of the product? Include a picture or diagram where possible, so that the reader can quickly grasp the concepts. List major features of the product or service. What role does product play in the overall product roadmap or strategy for the company?

3. Target Customer Description
Who is a typical customer for this product? What is their level of authority in the buying organization? What is the customer problem that the product or service will solve? Who are their customers? Articulate the customer's compelling reason to buy your product or service, and the value proposition for the customer. What are the results of focus groups or primary market research conducted with target customers?

4. Market Trends
What are the market trends that affect this product? Is the market dying, growing, or emerging?

5. Market Size and Segmentation

How large is the market for your product? A TAM-SAM-SOM analysis can be done in this section (total available market, served available market, share of market). The projections should go out five years, if possible. What is the company's targeted sales forecast for the product? What would the level of sales need to be in order to attain the desired percent of market share? What market segments are you targeting? How are the customers different in each segment? Do they work with different distribution channels to buy your product? Explain how each segment is different.

6. Competition

What is the competitive environment? Who are the competitors for the product? The competitors should be described by name, competing products, price position, and marketing and selling strategy. A competitive matrix should be included that characterizes the product, feature by feature relative to the competition, as well as company-level comparisons. What are your key differentiators at a company and product level?

7. Market Strategy

What is the high level strategy you will follow for this product? How does this strategy assure you competitive advantage? Under what circumstances might the overall strategy need to be changed? How does this market strategy fit your chosen business model?

8. Pricing

What is the pricing strategy for the product or service? What are the revenue projections for the product in terms of the overall corporate-level objectives? What is the pricing sensitivity of your customers?

9. Positioning

How does your price compare to your competitors' products? What are the differentiators at a product level and at a corporate level, compared to your competitors? Include a list of positioning statements in this section.

10. Business Model

How will you get your products to the customer? How will money flow through the value chain? Map the business model, showing the supply chain. Where are the gaps, and what other partners will you need to fill the gaps?

11. Distribution Channels

Will you only use the direct sales force, or will you usc cstablished or new indirect channels? Who are the existing channel partners, and will they sell your product? If new channel partners need to be developed, what is the plan for engaging them? What percent of forecasted sales will each channel be responsible for? What marketing materials or support will your channel partners need?

12. Strategic Partners

Other than channel partners, are there other external organizations involved in the process of getting your product to market? These can include marketing partners, OEMs, investment partners, or joint development partners. Who are they and what role will they play in the overall marketing plan?

13. Messaging

What are the corporate level and product level messages for the product? How will the messages be used in the various marketing programs that are planned? The hierarchy of messages belongs in this section.

14. Marketing Programs

What marketing programs will be used to get the messages to your target customer? For each of the following major categories, describe what deliverables are planned:

-External Marketing (direct mail, web, seminars, trade shows, events)

-Collateral (data sheets, brochures, white papers, multimedia, presentations, application notes, success stories, web versions)

-Public Relations and Advertising

-Internal Marketing (sales communications, guides, tools, training, intranet)

15. Customer Service and Support Plan

How will the product be supported? Who is the responsible group or channel partner? How will value-added service/support be sold and positioned? How is it priced and bundled with the product? Will the customer support organization be encouraged to help sell the new product?

16. Sales and Channel Training Plan

How will the sales force be educated about the product? Who will develop the course curriculum and deliver the training, and via what vehicle? What will be the training schedule? What sales events can be leveraged during product rollout? How will you educate your channel partners on the product? What vehicle will you use to train your partners? How will your indirect channel partners know when to sell your product instead of your competitor's?

17. Risk Analysis and Mitigation

What are the risks of executing the marketing plan, and how can these risks be mitigated? Possible risks are:

-slip in date of product release

-competitor announcing product before you do

-indirect channel doesn't sell product

-inadequate funding to do everything in the plan

Describe a contingency plan for the risks that are most likely in your particular company environment.

Launch Timeline

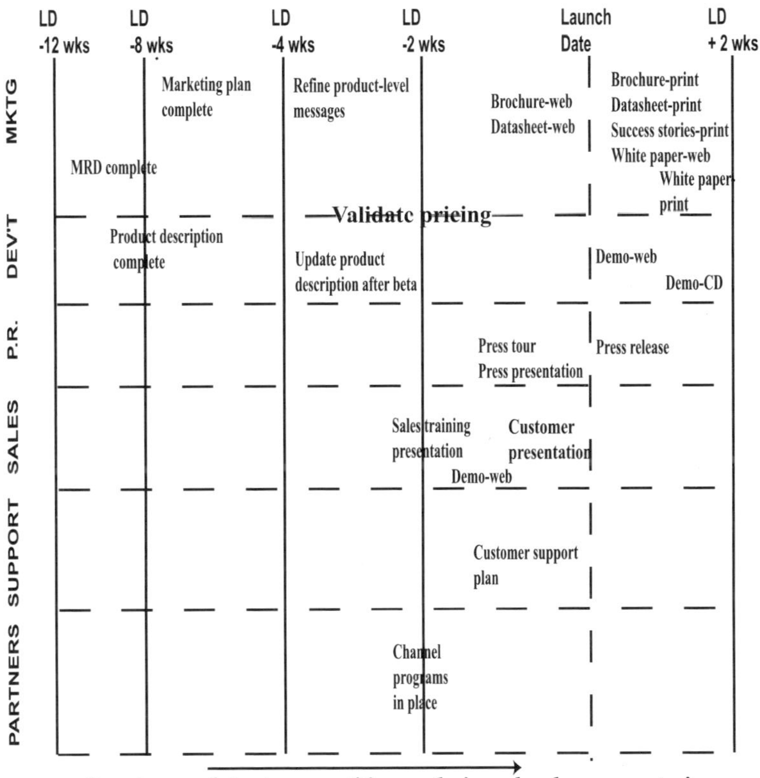

Ongoing: updates to competitive analysis and web success stories

Events such as trade shows may also fall on this timeline.

New Product Status and Timeline

Market Segment	***Idea Phase***	***Validation Phase***	***Business / Product Plan***	***Development***
Segment 1		Product A Product C		Product B
Segment 2	Product D			
Segment 3	Product G			
Rejected: Product xyz Product tuv				
Postponed: Product abc				

New Product Portfolio Analysis

Product or Venture	***1st sales milestone***	***Year 1 revenues***	***Year 4 revenues***	***Cash Flow Positive Date***
Product 1	June '02	$20M	$85M	2003
Product 2	April '03	$2M	$14M	2003
Product 3				
Product 4				

New Product Process Model

1	2	3	4	5	6	7	8
Select ideas	**Screen ideas for validation**	**Validate ideas**	**Prepare business or product plan (seek investment & partners)**	**Begin develop-ment**	**Develop business model, select partners**	**Develop market strategy**	**Launch**
ongoing	*30 days*	*30 days*	*30-45 days*	*variable*	*30 days*	*15 days*	*12 weeks*

Index

A

B

C

D

E

F

G

H

I

S

T